Praise for Angry Whit

'A book of unexpected brilliance. It is subtle, funny, stimulating and original – a rites-of-passage story, an exploration of an alien culture, and an inspiring work of philosophy'   Patrick French

'Brilliant . . . everyone should read it'

Tony Parsons, *Late Review*

'This is a splendidly written adventure, something sane at last on the craziness of the martial arts'   *Independent on Sunday*

'Communicates the existential purity of his elective regime with irrepressible passion . . . it also has the unmistakable stamp of authentic experience'   *Daily Telegraph*

'A rattling good yarn and very funny into the bargain'

Tim Hulse, *Independent on Sunday*

'Poetry in motion'   Sue Townsend, *Sunday Times*

'Wonderfully oddball . . . Here is a cult book all right, which could do for Japan and the martial arts what Hornby did for Highbury and the football terraces'   Frank Keating, *Guardian*

'His explanation of how to come to terms with intense pain should be read to every footballer who has writhed about in agony after a kick on the shin . . . It is a clever, enthralling book'   Ian Wooldridge, *Daily Mail*

'Twigger vividly captures the wince-inducing physical and emotional trials endured by those who would wear the black belt. But he also offers a rare insight in aikido's peculiarly Darwinian group dynamic and how it fits into modern Japanese society. After this marvellously insightful account I will snigger no more at Steven Seagal's po-faced chop-sockey'

Ben Farrington, *Literary Review*

Robert Twigger won the Newdigate prize for poetry in 1985. *Angry White Pyjamas* won the Somerset Maugham Award and the William Hill Sports Book of the Year Award; he is also the author of *Big Snake, The Extinction Club, Being a Man, Voyageur, Real Men Eat Pufferfish* and *Lost Oasis*. Robert Twigger lives in Oxford.

By Robert Twigger

Angry White Pyjamas
Big Snake
The Extinction Club
Being a Man
Voyageur
Lost Oasis
Real Men Eat Pufferfish

Angry White Pyjamas

Robert Twigger

PHOENIX

A PHOENIX PAPERBACK

First published in Great Britain in 1997
as an Indigo paperback original
This paperback edition published in 1999
by Phoenix,
an imprint of Orion Books Ltd,
Orion House, 5 Upper St Martin's Lane,
London WC2H 9EA

An Hachette UK company

19 20 18

Reissued 2007

A CIP catalogue record for this book
is available from the British Library.

ISBN 978-0-7538-0858-0

Printed and bound in Great Britain by
Clays Ltd, St Ives plc

The Orion Publishing Group's policy is to use papers that
are natural, renewable and recyclable products and
made from wood grown in sustainable forests. The logging
and manufacturing processes are expected to conform to
the environmental regulations of the country of origin.

www.orionbooks.co.uk

Every man thinks meanly of himself for not having been a soldier

Dr Johnson

for Ikusan

Contents

How Does a Man Prove Himself in the Age of
   Nintendo?   9

Beginner's Mind   23

Cannibal Talk   37

Foaming at the Mouth   57

Police Academy   77

Zen and the Art of Being Really, Really, Angry   93

Challenge   114

Good Cop, Bad Cop   134

The Hottest Summer Since 1963   144

Punch-Up at a Funeral   170

The Bad Guys Have Hairstyles   188

How to Commit the Perfect Murder   226

Survival   246

Natural Nazis   260

The Mount Fuji Test   274

Breaking the Mirror   283

An Honourable Exit   292

Unlikely Bodyguard   304

Glossary   309

How Does a Man Prove Himself
in the Age of Nintendo?

'In general ours is a civilization in which the very word "poetry" evokes a hostile snigger.'
George Orwell

'It is better to have some unhappiness when one is still young, for if a person does not experience some bitterness he will not settle down.'
From the seventeenth-century Samurai manual *Hagakure*

I was walking to work when I noticed a shiny ball bearing in the gutter. It was a pachinko ball, used in a kind of Japanese slot machine as a prize. At the end of a pachinko session you cash in the steel balls, which can number thousands for a jackpot, for prizes of either household goods or money. Usually the balls stay in the pachinko parlours, so I was surprised to see another, and a little way off another, and then another. Following this treasure trail, I picked them up, dusted them off, smiling to myself in the warm sunshine. The sun glinted off the steel and I chinked them together like a small boy picking up pebbles on a beach.

The trail led up to the main road, which I needed to cross to reach the train station. I was bending down to pick up yet another ball when I heard the screech of tyres skidding and saw timber spill on to the road from the back of a small truck. A red Mazda sports car faced the truck as other cars went into the opposite lane to avoid the incident. I wasn't sure what had happened but I stopped to watch, clinking the pachinko balls together in my hand.

The truck driver was a young man with a 'punch perm'

hairstyle, the style preferred by Japanese men with thuggish tendencies, taking its inspiration from the hairdos of the *yakuza*, organized crime, mainly involved in gambling rackets. He picked up a piece of fallen timber from the back of his truck and swooped on the driver of the sports car. In guttural, macho Japanese he yelled: 'What're you doing? Who do you think you are?', interspersed with repeated threats of, 'I'm gonna kill you!'

The car driver, I could see, was very frightened. He was also a young man and wore a suit. The truck driver banged his 2×4 piece of wood down on the car windscreen, making as if to smash the glass. The driver shielded his face in automatic anticipation. This show of fear made things worse. The enraged truck driver banged the glass a few more times and the Mazda driver repeatedly apologized: '*Sumimasen. Gomen nasai. Gomen. Gomen nasai.*' Then the truck driver reached in and grabbed the man in the Mazda by his tie. This is it, I thought, violence time. I ought to intervene – but how? There seemed no pause, no thoughtful gap, allowing me to interject a worthy comment, a restraining arm. I was frozen, immobile, fearful.

Bunching the tie into his fist and hauling on this makeshift rein, the truck man corralled the Mazda man, forcing him to drive to the side of the road. Then the truck man hit the Mazda on the hub caps and the driver, who was still apologizing, got out. He bowed to the truck driver, a 90 degree bow, a total apology. The truck driver ranted some more, bellowing, '*Buku-rossu*' ('I'm gonna kill you'), and beat the bumper and hub caps to emphasize his dissatisfaction.

Then it happened. Something so strange and out of place in modern Tokyo I could never have predicted it. As cars winged past on the highway, the truck driver pushed the Mazda man down on to his knees on the grass verge. The besuited salaryman looked pathetic kneeling on the grass in front of the enraged truck driver and his big piece of wood. I thought perhaps he might cry. Instead, the professional executed a full emperor bow, arms outstretched, prostrating himself face-first into the dusty grass. His corporate head rose and fell several times as he spoke in the politest Japanese I had ever heard, literally begging forgiveness from the truck driver.

The apology worked. The truck driver reloaded his truck and the salaryman drove hurriedly off to work. Somehow the childlike innocence of finding the pachinko balls had been lost. I tossed them back into the gutter. Could I have intervened if things had taken a nasty turn? Perhaps I could have lobbed a pachinko ball if things had got really heavy. But I was never much good at throwing. I coolly noted my reactions: fear, curiosity, and a sense of being excluded, on the outside. I had seen certain precise rules of violence at work in a place where I hardly expected to see violence at all.

Violence was not my thing. That's why living in Tokyo suited me – it was probably the safest capital city in the world. But, increasingly, I asked myself what I would do if I got mugged, attacked, picked on, targeted by blade-wielding mutants in a dark, dank alley; the dark, dank alley that reeks of piss and old burger wrappers, the urban softie's nightmare last stand – alone, defenceless, crouched in a foetal ball protecting his privates with a soggy newspaper. Frankly it made me uneasy. I became convinced that the uneasiness, which would not go away, was connected to my general lack of fitness. Decrepitude was creeping up on me and I was only thirty. Some kind of innate healthiness had kept me going throughout my twenties, but the minute I turned thirty I went into a major decline. I began to suspect I had ME or some other mysterious and debilitating illness. This decline was admittedly not helped by smoking, drinking lots of coffee and living off boil-in-the-bag curry rice. My room-mates suffered with me. Chris developed acne on his back. Fat Frank, an Iranian, was beset by permanent and terrible wind.

Chris was short, plump, bald and bespectacled. Beneath his impressive shining dome was a brain of immense power and complexity. In a former age he might have been a general, a

11

university professor, an adviser to courts and kings. In Thatcher's Britain he had been a tax consultant. Chris's massive mind invented tax avoidance schemes of such intricacy that 3-D diagrams on conference-table-sized pieces of paper were necessary for their description. Chris was the original whiz-kid, burnt out at twenty-seven after earning hundreds of thousands telling rich people how to save money. As a casualty of the money-mad eighties he had turned his back on conventional life in order to pursue his many interests. But, most importantly, he always put his friends first, helping them even when it put himself at risk. He had gone from being a tax guru to a multi-purpose guru, and whenever I had a problem my first stop was often to ask Chris his opinion. He knew everything, had been everywhere, had almost done it all; and if he hadn't, his near photographic memory spewed out a reading list of absolutely essential books on the subject in question.

As a full-time guru and a part-time English teacher, Chris considered the modern world to be unhealthily obsessed with cleanliness. He liked the dishcloths to be nicely grimy so that we wouldn't be cheated of a daily dose of microscopic fauna, necessary for keeping our immune systems in tip-top working order. Rather than exterminate the helpful bacteria in his odorous shirts he preferred to douse them with a peculiar smelling male perfume called Mandom, which was conveniently available at all Japanese 7-Elevens twenty-four hours a day.

Chris had teamed up with the genial Fat Frank in an ill-fated carpet venture in Dubai. They had come to Japan to try and sell Persian masterpieces to the Japanese, arriving just as the 'bubble economy' burst. They had stayed on, trapped by the easy money of English teaching, rewriting and doing voiceovers for business videos.

Before coming to Japan Fat Frank had been, variously, an amateur Iranian wrestler, a professional belly dancer and a medical student. He was Iranian, though educated in the UK, and he loved to construct arcane and pointless sentences just to practise a new word. 'Be that as it may,' was one of his favourite phrases.

Fat Frank had a big belly and hair all over his back. 'When the river is dry I rest,' he once said. 'And when the river is full I swim.' He was lying on his back perusing a Japanese textbook at the time. He paused and turned a page. 'Right now the river is dry.' When things got depressing Fat Frank would start snapping his fingers, singing and belly dancing in his underpants. He had a special Iranian way of snapping his fingers, using both hands, which was incredibly noisy. All his songs started with the word *guftam*. In the end I asked him what *guftam* meant. Fat Frank smiled. '"I said",' he replied. Chris hated the wailing Iranian songs, but I liked them.

Our apartment was in a dilapidated block called Fuji Heights, a place of peculiar odours, bad vibes, Chinese and Korean immigrants, a quartet of Soka Gakkai cultists who buttonholed newcomers and spouted conversion to their extreme and political Buddhist faith. A small boy who wore transparent air-filled sandals with a built-in squeak, a squeaky toy on each foot, he tramped relentlessly along the balconied walkway that passed above our front door, unaware perhaps that he was in possession of the most irritating invention known to mankind. Fuji Heights, a place neither high, nor in sight of Mount Fuji, was a thirty-year-old barracks for tired workers, slave ants of the Japanese wonder economy who'd all moved out to brand new mansion blocks with underground parking, leaving the old places to the paupers and foreigners who didn't mind having the washing machine plumbed in and standing outside the front door. The interior was dark, the windows overshadowed by enormous new blocks on either side. There were two rooms, each ten foot by twelve foot, or, by the Japanese way of measuring, they were both six mats in size.

A mat is a traditional room-size measure in Japan, about a metre wide by two metres long. Most rooms are laid out with mats woven from tatami, a slightly springy rice straw matting.

13

One of our rooms had six of these tatami mats and the other had scuffed lino. Compared to Tesshu, a nineteenth-century Samurai poet I admired, we were rich. He only owned three mats – one for meditation, one for guests and one for his wife and himself.

The tatami room was the sleeping room and the book-storage room. We had nearly a thousand books stacked up against the walls in neat piles by Chris, who was a compulsive book purchaser. Fat Frank preferred to borrow or 'find' his books. All of us considered reading as necessary as eating; Frank spent a great deal of time doing both, so the piles just got higher and higher. We had to be careful when we went to bed in case a pile toppled down on to us. Each night we unrolled futons and slept on the floor. Each morning we rolled them up and stored them in the corner.

The other room was a kitchen and dining room. The modular orange plastic bathroom was accessed from the kitchen. So was the temperamental lavatory. We had a lot of electronic appliances, which Fat Frank collected from other people's garbage. In Japan, the garbage pickings are very good because people don't have enough space to store old hi-fis and TVs when they replace them. So they often throw away things that still work. Fat Frank hated to see good consumer durables going to waste so he brought them home and stored them in his part of the room. After a few days of storage, gently acclimatizing us to a new reduction in space, he would release them for general use. We had two fax machines, both slightly damaged, one for sending and one for receiving. Two video recorders – one had a defective fast forward, the other a defective fast reverse. Two or three cassette players. Two computers. Two answering machines. We drew the line at getting a microwave. Chris felt it would only encourage us to eat even more Japanese junk food: one-minute noodles, friend instant *gyoza* (garlic-stuffed pastries) and re-heated *yakitori* (chicken on a skewer), from the mute *yakitori* man whose shop was only one block away.

Our only nod at physical exercise was shooting the slow-moving monster roaches that infested Fuji Heights with replica Luger BB handguns. Chris was generally disapproving: 'It'll do no good — a dying cockroach secretes a hormone that tells all the others to hide.'

I felt control of my life was slipping away, that I was fading fast, becoming a slothful blur with an existential value approaching zero. My other worries were tame enough: the fact that I was thirty and going nowhere and living with two other guys who were also thirty and going nowhere. The fact that I didn't have a steady job, a steady girlfriend, or even a very steady hand, what with all the caffeine and nicotine coursing through my veins. The fact that someone had recently stolen the lid off our washing machine, which, being outdoors, was particularly vulnerable to crime. A washing machine which ran off cold water and failed to get my shirt collars clean, forcing me to reflect that for a dirt-sensitive nation the Japanese manufacture very poor washing machines for the home market.

The only possible lifestyle in such cramped conditions was communal. We ate together, we slept in the same room, we went out together. If, on the rare occasion when it happened, someone's girlfriend came round, we had to arrange to be 'out' so that a few hours of privacy could be had. In the end we knew each other's thoughts, finished each other's sentences and read each other's mail. It was as if the cramped conditions had forced three personalities to become one as the only means of survival.

Our self-imposed suffering was logical. Partly it was because of the high cost of living in Tokyo and partly it was because Fat Frank was unemployable. There had been a backlash against Iranians in Japan and it was impossible, with his dodgy visa status, for him to find work. Previously, a generous visa agreement with Iran had allowed Japan to be flooded with over a million Iranians. They were needed initially to do low-status menial jobs. Now there were too many Iranians and the Japanese considered them a problem. There were periodic 'clean-up' campaigns when the police swooped on a certain station and arrested for deportation any Iranian without a valid alien registration card.

Chris, too, was going through a difficult patch. He had been approached by a publisher to write a risqué guide to learning Japanese, entitled *Sexpertise in Japanese in Seven Days*. With a true scholar's intensity Chris had attacked the subject so thoroughly that even a Japanese porno video director he grilled for vocabulary had been embarrassed by the unswerving obscenity of the glossary. Chris was fond of reminding the prudish that Arthur Koestler's first published work had been a sex encyclopaedia. Like a driven man Chris uncovered examples of dialogue and handy phrases for everything, from bargaining with an SM rubber fetishist to the fifteen synonyms for the Japanese pudendum. On a taste scale from A–Z, *Sexpertise* was about Z. The publisher eventually backed out, even after Chris had agreed to axe his section on bestiality. Chris had spent many unpaid hours researching *Sexpertise* and our resources were at their lowest ebb.

Despite the *Sexpertise* fiasco Chris maintained his leadership role at Fuji Heights by virtuoso displays of competence, which happened just regularly enough for us never to lose faith in him. During one lengthy argument after lights out, between Fat Frank and me about the impossibility of doing one-finger push-ups, Chris sighed, switched on the sidelight and did five, which stunned us into silence.

My own path to Japan had started with a desire to escape. Whilst at Oxford I had won a prestigious poetry prize, the Newdigate, whose previous winners included Oscar Wilde, John Ruskin and Matthew Arnold. It convinced me that I was either A POET or A WRITER, a vague ambition that succeeded only in carrying me through a series of dead-end jobs. Various business schemes of Balzacian complexity had further buggered up my chances of ever returning to the world of credit ratings and hire-purchase agreements. My only writing was either self published or journalistic and perfunctory, commissions gleaned from more successful and compassionate friends.

The solitary achievement of my mid-twenties was to walk alone the 700-kilometre length of the Pyrénées mountains from the Mediterranean to the Atlantic. On some stretches I walked for days in the high air without seeing a soul, and there, away from the city, I glimpsed the possibility of escape. But I couldn't exist on air, I needed to earn a living somehow.

After two years of prevaricating I bought a ticket to Japan, lured by the promise of high wages, new places to write about, exotic girlfriends and Tesshu. Yamaoka Tesshu was my great discovery. I had been recommended to read Basho, the Japanese haiku master, by the erudite English poet Peter Levi, who had been something of a mentor while I was at Oxford. From a commentary on Basho I read about Tesshu, a nineteenth-century Samurai poet who also wrote haiku. But Tesshu wasn't just a poet, he was a warrior, a Zen adept, an artist who penned more than a million pieces of calligraphy, drank half a gallon of *sake* every night, was bodyguard to the Emperor and started his own austere school of swordsmanship.

Tesshu was an extremist, undaunted by huge tasks. When he planned to copy out the entire Buddhist canon he was asked, 'Won't that be a great hardship?'

'Not at all,' replied Tesshu. 'I only copy one page at a time.'

There was a certain urgency about life in Japan. Living was expensive and stressful. Tokyo combined a feeling of artificial calm with cheap, tinny frenzy. Trains ran on time, gliding you in and out of neighbourhoods that all looked the same. Round each station were clustered pachinko parlours, neon-lit fun palaces full of slot machines. The incredible clatter of a million ball bearings spewing into plastic trays to be cashed for prizes is, for me, the noise of modern Japan.

I earned, and spent, more money in a year in Tokyo than I had in the preceding four in London. I felt the first peptic prickling of a nascent ulcer. I lost my job as a teacher, borrowed money to survive, watched the bubble economy burst, found the cheapest place to drink coffee and moved in with Chris and Fat Frank. I found part-time work and started to write again.

I put together another collection of poems and pondered the example of Tesshu. He was a poet *and* a warrior. He was incredibly productive and still had time left over to swing his sword, meditate for hours and imbibe the huge quantities of *sake*. What was stopping me? Television? A job? The necessity to travel everywhere by electric train? What did Tesshu have that I lacked? Discipline. He got up early and he went to bed late, and he trained every day. Discipline. I just didn't have it.

In fact I'd always lacked discipline. Bursts of enthusiasm had partially made up for not sticking at anything, but the pattern of brilliant starts and dismal finishes was beginning to bother me. I remember the banal moment when I decided things had to change. I was on the 'up' escalator in a shopping centre. It was so crowded that I had to stand without moving. I was packed in with all the other suit-wearing urban workers, all expressionless, all containing their irritation at being trapped and moving so slowly to their destination – or maybe they just didn't care. The 'down' escalator was just as full. It slowly passed in front of me like a tracking shot in a sci-fi movie – not a horror movie but one of those hopeless, nihilistic futuristic films where minds have been wiped and everyone is content. I stared at all the blank faces and realized *this is it, your life, you don't get another*. This was *it*. I was unfit, unphysical, an intellectual, a bookworm, a poet, a sensitive guy. It was time to change.

Perhaps Chris sensed the imminent collapse of Fuji Heights. It was he who most persistently suggested we should get physically fit again. But it was my suggestion that martial arts were the answer, though I had never practised fighting and barely knew my fist from my elbow. Ever since the school bully had punched me in the face with a stippled rubber cricket glove I'd wanted to do martial arts, but the Guardian-Angel, kung-fu-fighting freakishness of it put me off. For twenty years.

Because Chris gave the impression of knowing everything, I questioned him further about the way of the warrior. I knew he had studied kung fu to fend off his particular school bully, and 'karate-kid'-fashion had entered full-contact tournaments. It was one of Chris's main attractions that, as well as being a brain box, he could also deliver a devastating one-inch punch. 'After getting knocked out I used to be too sick to eat for three days,' he reminisced. I'd never been knocked out. I hadn't given it much thought until now, but it sounded extremely unpleasant.

'Is it essential to get knocked out to be any good at fighting?' I asked.

'If you can't take punches you won't be much good in a fight. But getting knocked out is a hazard rather than a necessity.'

Chris had very definite ideas on martial arts. Kung fu was badly taught, judo was now a sport, shotokan karate ruined the knees and tai chi was for housewives, unless you found an authentic teacher, when it then became the deadliest art. Shorinji kempo, Japanese kung fu, was a cult, ninjitsu too weird, kendo too expensive and kyokushinkai karate too much like kickboxing.

Jason, a blond-haired Australian I taught English with, actually practised kyokushinkai karate. He was a black belt and trained at the kyokushinkai dojo, or training hall, in west Tokyo. The first time I met him he had a smear of dried blood on the side of his face. 'Kick,' he explained. The next time he had a black eye. 'Elbow,' he said.

Getting beaten up on a regular basis wasn't exactly what I had in mind, but I was prepared to try anything to get myself fighting fit. Chris was definitely against kyokushinkai: 'It's brutal – which doesn't mean the practitioners are necessarily tougher than anyone else, but it does mean they're stupider.'

I met Jason once a week, as we both taught in the same high school. He told me about his latest exploits at the dojo. Then one week he appeared looking blankfaced, shocked, completely bemused. His brother, also a martial arts expert, had been fatally stabbed in a brawl outside a hotel he managed. He was murdered by a member of a Hell's Angels gang with a three-inch blade that punctured his liver. In half an hour he was dead.

I tried to console Jason. We talked about revenge, but Jason was a committed Christian and believed revenge was pointless. He showed me a photograph of his brother, who looked tougher and older than his twenty-one years. He had been the kickboxing champion of Northern Queensland.

In some ways it made me more determined. I wanted to find some art that not only dealt out punches but also trained you against knife attacks.

Being bookworms our stack of books now began to include martial arts magazines and books with such titles as *Secrets of the Dragon's Touch*, *Get Tough – A US Marine's Handbook*, or my favourite, the completely eccentric *Prison's Bloody Iron*, which was written and published by two odd-ball ex-convicts from Terre Haute Prison in America. I liked it for its bizarre mix of scholarship and prison yard experience, giving you the illusion you were an expert on knifefighting now that you knew such jargon as 'shank', and 'moves with the ice pick grip'.

But you can't learn to fight from a book. We agreed, or rather Chris decided and we agreed, that our terminal physical decline and lack of discipline could only be cured by seriously studying some martial art or another.

I found out about Tesshu's sword school. The school still existed and was called Muto Ryu. Unfortunately it only had thirteen practising students. In Tesshu's day there had been over four hundred. It seemed to me that Muto Ryu had lost its way since the great founder had died.

I wondered what Tesshu would study now if he was alive. 'Aikido, without a doubt,' said Chris. 'Aikido has a Zen element that has been lost in many sword styles.' It was true that one of the major commentators on Tesshu, Professor John Stevens of

Tohoku University, studied aikido. Tesshu himself could never have studied aikido as its techniques were largely secret in his day.

'Aikido, like judo, comes from jujitsu. In some styles it is soft and flowing, in others it is hard and fast, more like karate. All forms of aikido involve using joint controls to overbalance and throw people.' I realized Chris was already an expert on the subject.

Chris read various brochures and magazines and pronounced Yoshinkan aikido 'the best'. It was one of the hard styles and had a tough reputation. Every morning at 8.30 a.m. they taught a special lesson for foreigners. It was taught in English. Somehow that was comforting. When I'd learnt a few deft moves and punches, then I'd move on to the Japanese-only lessons. But English was just fine for a raw beginner like me.

Chris showed me a magazine produced by the Yoshinkan organization. In it there was an article about 'the Riot Police course'. The article said it was the toughest martial arts course in the world. The course, which was for the *Kidotai*, Japanese Riot Police, was held at the same establishment as the one we wanted to attend.

I had to face up to the fact that I wasn't a tough guy, nor would I ever be. Perhaps other men confronted this when they were twelve, but somehow I'd been able to put off facing the facts. For an example of physical toughness, I had always looked to my grandfather, Colonel H. Twigger. Even at eighty-seven he was less wimpy than me. He had boxed and shot for the army. He had a ridge of bone above his eyes that seemed precisely designed for headbutting someone.

Before leaving for Japan I went to see him and he demonstrated in slow motion how to use the fist and elbow in a blistering double-edged attack. He told me about the Nagas, headhunters on the Burmese-Indian border, he'd joined forces with during the turning-point battle of Kohima in 1944.

He didn't believe in seat belts, thought they were for invalids.

'And dangerous too!' He'd once driven off a cliff in a jeep with his pet Labrador tied by a leash to the dashboard. He, of course, was unbelted. 'I was thrown clear. Dog was killed. Proves seat belts are no bloody good.'

After India and then Malaya, Colonel H. lived in a freezing mansion deep in the Oxfordshire countryside. On the main stairs there was a huge Japanese shellcase filled with Naga spears. As a child visiting my grandfather I used to thrill myself by feeling the human hair that decorated the spear handles.

When Colonel H. had toothache he pulled out the tooth himself with a pair of rusty pliers.

In his forties he could still do handsprings on the lawn, even though he drank half a bottle of whisky and smoked sixty cigarettes a day.

In his eighties, now a non-smoking teetotaller, he gave up sitting down – 'Organs are all in the wrong place' – and he threw out all his chairs to pursue this novel course of therapy.

In one of his display cabinets was an aluminium cigarette case given to him by a friend and fellow army officer who had survived four years in Changi Gaol during the war. It was skilfully fashioned from an aluminium mess tin, with a securing clip made from a pen nib.

To me, because I never really knew him, Colonel H. symbolized a previous era, the tough age, when illness meant either death or a miraculous recovery, where pain was ignored, aspirins laughed at, all doctors thought of as quacks, all psychiatrists considered frauds. It was an age when people suffered and didn't complain. Now they took Prozac and still complained. I wasn't exempt. I took two Paracetamol the moment I got the slightest headache. Chris preferred Ibuprofen. The Colonel would have sneered mightily.

Beginner's Mind

'Everybody want to go Heaven, but nobody want to get dead.'
Screwface, in the Steven Seagal movie *Marked for Death*

'In the judgement of the elders, a Samurai's obstinacy should be excessive.'
From the seventeenth-century Samurai manual *Hagakure*

'I've been sacked,' Chris announced, 'for being bald.' He had just returned from his most lucrative part-time job, teaching at an exclusive language school run entirely by Japanese women in their fifties. He had done the job for a few months but business had not been as good as the boss wanted. Chris tried to put a brave face on it, but I could tell he was annoyed, even hurt, since he'd been getting on so well with some of the students. The boss had decided that the only way to increase revenue was to hire some fresh and sexy English teachers to attract the lucrative college-girl and office-lady market. Chris, being bald, was the first to go.

'The deputy boss suggested I got a wig. "Even Sean Connery wears a wig," she told me. I responded by saying that if they paid for a wig I'd wear it. Then, in the nicest possible way, they fired me.'

Chris needed cheering up. We got out *Enter the Dragon* on video. It was one of his favourite films, though I'd managed to get by without watching it before. As we watched, Chris took pleasure in quoting the famous Bruce Lee lines just before Lee spoke them. But it wasn't the words that stuck in my mind, it was the opening helicopter shot of Han's Island, where we see

23

row after row of white pyjama-clad men practising basic karate *kata*. All in time together they punched, one-two, one-two, the canvas of their sleeves snapping in the air, making an amazing thwacking sound. These were the footsoldiers of the martial arts, the grunts, the pikers, the squaddies, and I wanted to join them.

One night Chris reconstructed a technique from an aikido manual he'd bought. Frank and I stood opposite each other and Frank held my wrist. It seemed an odd sort of attack, but Chris explained that the wrist grab was common in feudal Japan — it was to stop someone reaching for their sword.

I was then propelled by Chris through some complicated hand and footwork which left me folding Frank's arm back over his shoulder. 'Is this right?' I asked Chris. He consulted the manual. 'Yes,' he said. 'And now you either throw him or take him down to the ground.'

'Leave that part out,' said Frank, as he flopped of his own accord back on to the inviting pile of mattresses. 'It's all pretty complicated, isn't it?'

It was time to get some real tuition. Getting up far earlier than we were used to, Chris, Fat Frank and I trudged to the station to make our way to the famed Yoshinkan training hall, the dojo. Chris advised us to 'keep our heads down' for the time being. He told us that etiquette was very important in the martial arts and doubly so in Japan. The dojo was on the third floor of a three-floor office building. We took the lift.

The double wooden door to the dojo was surrounded by cedarwood plaques carved with Japanese inscriptions, rather like an upmarket Japanese restaurant. Inside it was grey and functional, a dusty smell giving everything the feel of something official and neglected. It was dimly lit and portraits of the founder, Gozo Shioda, who was now seventy-seven, were everywhere, together with a series of photos of celebrities who had visited the dojo. There was a boxed-in glassed reception and a young Japanese live-in student sat behind the counter. Behind him, in the dojo office, the teachers stared out of the windows or smoked or puzzled over the screens of Japanese word processors. From the main training room, also known as the dojo, came intermittent shouts and thumping sounds.

I stared at the celebrity photographs. Robert Kennedy had visited the dojo shortly before his assassination in 1968. Mike Tyson had visited shortly before his less serious assassination in the twelfth round by Buster Douglas in 1989. The King of Norway had also dropped in, but then the King of Norway had visited my college bar in 1978 – as celebrities went, the King of Norway was a little too available to cut any serious ice.

We quietly took our shoes off and shuffled into the main hall. It was big and high-roofed and smelt of sweat and straw, the filling of the tatami mats on the floor. The fittings were wooden and tasteful. I noticed a rack of swords on the wall.

All the students knelt respectfully as the teacher, a middle-aged Japanese man with a crew cut, spoke in a soft voice. Frank, Chris and I sat down on some seats at the side, provided for watching.

Two students jumped up, one holding a knife and the other a sword. On a word of command they both charged the teacher like madmen possessed. The teacher looked bored, impassive. I felt I was watching nothing special, and then suddenly the one with the knife was flying through the air and the teacher was holding the sword and pinning an attacker to the ground with its tip. Hold on! Was this a magic trick? I leant forward to get a closer look. Now the teacher was demonstrating on an unarmed attacker how the throw was made. It looked a bit like a wrestling throw, except when the attacker was thrown he dived through the air and did a forward roll.

Now the students broke off into pairs and started throwing each other. I became hypnotized by their graceful diving and rolling. I'll never be able to do that, I thought.

The actual technique of throwing looked easier. Once you

had the secret knowledge of which joint to twist, and when to twist it, the attacker just flipped right over.

Suddenly I saw aikido as offering an arcane knowledge of the body's weak points. It was a living alchemy; immense, complex, a whole structure of thought and action I never knew existed. Just punching and kicking looked crude by comparison.

Now the students were practising on their own, sliding their feet along the floor and moving their hands up and down in front of them. It looked bizarre. On the other hand I definitely knew I could shuffle around like a drugged ballet dancer. This basic exercise gave me hope, even though I couldn't connect it to anything else I'd seen.

For the first time in my life I was seeing something I didn't understand and yet wanted to be a part of. I was fed up being excluded in Japan. I wanted to join something. The fact that it would take years to master didn't put me off. In fact it comforted me. It meant that aikido must be really complicated and serious and therefore worthy of my attention. This wasn't kickboxing with the lads, this was nearly religion.

The religious air continued as the students all bowed to each other. The early morning sun shone down through the dojo windows, high up near the ceiling, and illuminated the students' white pyjamas in a glowing bar of light. Then they stood up and performed a final exercise in pairs, shuffling and holding hands like couples practising a Highland reel. The atmosphere, the dedicated, light-filled atmosphere, and the heady seriousness of it all, along with the inexplicable nature of their movements, held me entranced.

We stumbled out of the dojo, adjusting our eyes to the darkened corridor. 'What do you think?' I asked Chris.

'That teacher, Chida Sensei, I believe he's called, is the third best in the world. He's obviously very good.'

Trust Chris to already know the form.

'It's a bit like judo,' said Fat Frank.

26

'No it isn't,' replied Chris. 'It isn't in the slightest bit like judo.'

'So are we going to join, or what?' I asked.

'I don't know about you two, but I'm definitely signing up,' said Chris, signalling to the disciple behind the glass for a pen.

'I think it's all staged,' said Frank. 'But it looks like a good way to lose weight. Did you see how high they flew when they were thrown?'

It was decided. We were all going to start aikido.

Out of the gloom appeared Paul, a British detective on leave from the London Metropolitan police force. He was cheery and tall and was part of the international teaching staff at the dojo. He told us he had survived the rigours of the Riot Police course the year before. Hustling us into a small room with drinks machines, he handed out forms to fill in.

'What we offer here is training,' said Paul. 'Nothing flashy, nothing instant, but if you keep at it, it works.'

He outlined the teaching on offer. There were regular classes, special study classes and senshusei classes. We signed up for regular classes, which were the cheapest and the only ones we were qualified to take.

'What are senshusei classes?' I asked.

'Riot Police,' said Paul.

There was a silence.

'Have you ever met Mike Tyson?' It was the only question I could think of, and Paul's function seemed to be to answer questions.

'No. But as you can see, he came here to watch Kancho Sensei.'

Paul used the honorific 'Kancho' whenever he spoke of Shioda, the founder. At the dojo Paul said he was respectfully known as Kancho Sensei. Later, Frank pointed out that *kancho* also meant 'enema' in Japanese. I made a mental note to learn the correct pronunciation for the founder's title.

Paul nosily scanned our entry forms. 'So you went to Oxford,

27

did you?' There was a hint of mockery in his voice and I instantly regretted divulging this information. Though he looked like a martial artist he was still a nosey British bobby at heart.

We bought uniforms, which came straight out of the storeroom wrapped in plastic. I handled mine lovingly. Suddenly it felt like the real thing. We had decided to take the next regular class for foreigners, which was half an hour later that morning.

After unpacking our uniforms we got changed in silence in a locker room full of dusty grey lockers. Fat Frank and Chris walked purposefully out towards the main dojo. I sneaked a look around the changing rooms. The few foreigners getting changed looked muscular and fit. I wasn't fat but I didn't have much muscle. My chest was almost entirely lacking pectoral development, and there wasn't much hair on it either. Fortunately we wouldn't have to train in the nude.

The dojo training room consisted of a big hall laid with traditional tatami mats, over two hundred in number, covered in rubberized canvas to facilitate the easy removal of sweat and blood. At the 'beginner's end' there was a huge mirror, ten metres long by five metres high. Every day it was polished spotless using newsprint and solvent glass cleaner.

I entered the main dojo trying to look at ease in my new dogi uniform. The dogi is the white top and bottom, the pyjamas worn for all Japanese martial arts. I was a little disappointed that mine were almost yellow in colour when everyone else wore pyjamas of beautiful white. Chris said that washing would make mine white too. I planned to wash mine as often as possible so that I wouldn't stand out as a raw beginner.

A Japanese high-school teacher who taught kendo at the school where I worked had told me that no Japanese wears underpants beneath their dogi when doing martial arts. I decided to keep mine on. I felt more secure that way.

Chris and Frank were warming up in the corner. There were about ten non-Japanese also warming up around the dojo. Two or three Japanese practised diving rolls in another corner – they

28

had attended an even earlier class, held in Japanese, at 7.00 a.m., and were still hanging around. I had some difficulty making out Frank and Chris, despite their both being overweight, definitely the two fattest guys in the dojo, because I wasn't wearing my glasses. Everything was a blur at any distance more than five metres. Chris too wasn't wearing his glasses, but his eyesight wasn't as bad as mine.

I squinted and recognized Chris and Fat Frank. I copied Chris's warm-up procedure, which was something he remembered from his teenage kung-fu days. I wasn't sure whether we were allowed to talk in the dojo or not, but I risked it. 'Chris,' I whispered. 'Why does everyone keep saying "oos!" to each other?'

Since entering the dojo I'd heard 'oos!' said, shouted and hissed back and forth at least fifty times. It seemed an all-purpose greeting, a bit like the cockney 'awright?'

'Mark of respect,' he snapped, and bent to touch his toes. Chris didn't approve of chatting in the dojo.

Someone called out *'seiza!'* and we all obediently knelt in a line facing the shrine. The dojo shrine was a high wooden shelf containing objects of Shinto religious significance such as vases, incense holders, plants, sprigs of greenery called *sasaki*, even fruit. We sat in *seiza* (the Japanese kneeling posture) for five minutes. I had never knelt down for so long before.

After five excruciating minutes a tall, blond-bearded and nearly bald man strode with vigour up to the shrine. His name was Robert Mustard and he was the top foreign teacher in Japan, and arguably one of the best foreign aikidoka in the world. At that stage, when aikido still seemed glamorous and remote, he struck me as powerful and exceedingly direct; someone to be feared even. The senior student barked out the command to bow and everyone bowed.

We then spread out and did callisthenic type warm-ups for about ten minutes. There were all done to a shouted count in Japanese: *'Ichi, ni,'* shouted the teacher. *'San, shi,'* we shouted back. *'Go, roku,'* he continued his shout. *'Shichi, hachi,'* we shouted back. I later discovered this warm-up routine had not changed in over fifty years, and was the same routine used by the pre-war armed forces.

After the warm-up the teacher called loudly for the beginners to go to the mirror. He took the rest, who all had black or brown belts, over to the other side.

I walked over to the mirror and Paul, who was also tall and blond, but not bald, shouted at me to run. It was a bit of a shock, but for some reason it was also pleasing. It was good to be in a place where people didn't pussyfoot around, weren't afraid to give orders.

The beginners, numbering about six or seven, lined up in front of the mirror and were drilled by Paul. He looked fit and tough with his close-cropped hair and strong, easy movements. We beginners, by contrast, lumbered and wheezed at the basic movements we were instructed to learn by rote.

Paul had been one of four foreigners to attend the previous year's Riot Police course. Robert Mustard, had also attended the course back in 1986. The police course had been running for over thirty years. A traditional dojo was still seen as the best place for training the *Kidotai*, Japanese Riot Police, who are an élite section of the national Japanese police force. Their duties vary from diplomatic policing and air-sea rescue to wearing their Kevlar 'Samurai' armour during street demonstrations in Japan.

From out of the corner of my eye I could see the black belts cartwheeling and diving and throwing each other all over the place. There were heavy smacks as they hit the mats to break their falls. It all looked far too difficult and acrobatic for an ordinary person to master. I tried to concentrate on the matter at hand, which was standing in the basic fighting stance, called *kamae*.

Robert Mustard left the black belts for a moment, came over, and in two swift moves bent me into the correct stance, which was leaning forward, as if holding a sword but with arms extended, fingers splayed. He smelt of cigarette smoke and had sure, powerful wrists; a combination which reminded me of my

30

father when I was a little boy. 'Everything starts with *kamae*,' said Mustard, 'and everything comes back to *kamae*.' He snapped into the fighting stance several times. His blue eyes bored into me. I was not able to judge whether Robert Mustard could do aikido or not, but he looked pretty frightening in his white pyjamas.

We practised other basic movements. These involved sliding the feet along the mat instead of stepping. This was a way of learning to smoothly shift the body's weight. We practised pivoting on one foot, the other sweeping around behind you. This taught you how to move the whole body as a unit, which is vastly more powerful than moving each part separately, or *barabara* as the Japanese say.

The movements are exaggerated so that important principles, such as putting the full weight of the hips behind a punch, which may be lost in natural movement, can be highlighted, practised and developed. This is a key to the Yoshinkan system and why it is successful at getting students to a high level of aikido relatively quickly. If only natural movements are practised people can go for years without unearthing some basic principle which is the real heart of a technique.

When the lesson finished we again knelt in a line and bowed to the teacher, the shrine and the assistant teachers. Then everyone bowed to everyone they had worked with, muttering a hurried '*Domo arigato gozaimashita*' ('thank you very much') before moving on. It looked like an awful lot of bowing to me. Fat Frank derived his own pleasure by intoning '*harrigata guzzimashita*', which if said fast sounds all right, but is actually a double obscenity in bastardized Japanese and Persian meaning 'the dildo that brings forth smelly farts'.

After the lesson I learned the story of Tyson's visit from one of the disciples. It was important to all of us beginners that Tyson, symbolically the greatest fighter in the world, had deigned to visit the same dojo as us. It meant that what we were about

31

to study wasn't a load of useless posturing, that it counted in the hard world of fists and knockouts.

Don King and Tyson had asked to see 'the real thing', a real martial arts magician, just like in the comics and movies back home, a tiny old man who could take out three or four people of Tyson's size at the same time.

Kancho had provided his usual amazing display. He threw people halfway across the dojo with effortless ease. When five teachers came at him wielding knives and swords he evaded the attack, ducking and chopping his attackers in the neck as they fell like skittles around him.

King agreed it was, indeed, the real thing. Tyson remarked, 'It's all in the knees, isn't it?' Which was remarkably perspicacious for a first time view of aikido.

Kancho, just as much of a showman as Don King, offered to put a *nikajo* lock on Tyson. Here was a tiny old guy asking to put a wrist lock on the greatest heavyweight boxer in the world. But Tyson backed down: 'These [he indicated his arms] are insured for thirty million dollars. I can't afford to let you mess with them.'

The disciple explained that that was the difference between sport and *budo*, fighting arts. In *budo* you never spare yourself.

We returned to Fuji Heights full of our newfound aikido knowledge. The washing machine was loaded with dogis, which we hung on the lines about the front door of the apartment. Neighbours who usually chose to avoid the noisy foreigners asked politely, '*Judo desu ka?*' No, aikido, we were able to proudly reply. Our white belts we neither washed nor displayed. Not that we were embarrassed about being beginners, it was just more enjoyable to let people assume we were already experts. I had convinced myself about the correctness of the superstition that the belt is a repository of '*ki*', or life energy, and to wash it was to dissipate such energy. This is the origin of the black belt, which shows simply how long the person has been training.

With the introduction of tests for black belt they are now ready-made black. By an odd paradox the really long-term aikidoka have black belts that are almost white with age. Naturally those with impatience try to scuff up and degrade their black belts as fast as possible.

We still had a roach problem. When we got up early and turned on the lights hordes of them would scurry away. These were a new super-breed of cockroach, genetic mutants that moved at lightning speed and lived inside electronic consumer durables. They were extremely small and very cunning. How can you put poison or a roach trap inside an answering machine, a computer printer or a CD player? Executing the monster roaches had disturbed the kitchen ecosystem and given rise to this new infestation. It looked as if we had to accept them as permanent co-residents.

In the evenings when there wasn't something gripping like a gameshow on TV, we'd run through the technique we had learnt that morning. We couldn't practise throwing each other but there was just enough room for one of us to take the other down to the ground. Chris would provide a continuous critique as Fat Frank attacked me with a standard forearm smash to the face or grabbed my wrist in his meaty hand. I would then evade the attack and apply a wrist or arm lock, making Frank lose his balance. At this point he was supposed to be taken smoothly to the ground but sometimes it went wrong. Usually he resisted and refused to have his head pushed into a pile of books. We weren't good enough to make the technique work if there was real resistance, so the practice session would break up amidst recriminations and accusations of poor sportsmanship.

Frank and Chris seemed to enjoy aikido more than I did. I liked it when I was there, and I liked the long sessions in the coffee shop after training, but when I thought about aikido it was never very often with fond anticipation of the next class. But if I missed a class I felt bad, and this, initially, was enough to keep me going.

Then there was the idea of aikido, which was another thing altogether. This was what really interested me. I wanted to master the secret techniques, *ogi*, that made aikido teachers so formidable. Of course, first I had to master the basic techniques, but to an outsider even these have something magical about them.

Chris's favourite technique involved attacking a pressure point on the wrist just above the thumb. He enjoyed torturing Frank and me by pressing the point and controlling our movement through pain. We, of course, had to pretend we didn't feel a thing.

I was quickly getting the picture that learning martial arts, or aikido at least, involved pain and humiliation. When we practised throwing each other at the dojo we would line up in a corner and one student would throw everyone in turn. I never liked being the thrower because then all eyes were upon you. Every mistake was glaringly obvious. Some days I got into a humiliating tangle and then all the throwees would come out of their neat line and cluster round giving contradictory advice.

One day I got it almost right. Fat Frank lunged to grab my wrist and, with lucky timing, I turned, feeling his huge bulk accelerate as he tried to hang on. It felt like swinging a bag of shopping around your head. When I let go it wasn't a *great* throw, but that didn't matter. I'd felt the sheer beauty of moving and controlling someone in a circle. The beauty and the power. Now I understood what all the fuss was about.

With his nose for information Chris was soon a repository of all the dojo gossip. We made new friends at the dojo – Will, a wry American, and Paul the policeman, who we discovered was into New Age healing and modern poetry. He also let slip that he'd once been in the Boy Scouts.

I started going to the dojo three mornings a week. Fat Frank and Chris, with more time on their hands, went every day. Quite soon they were beginning to outpace me despite their physical handicaps of weight and bulk. Fuji Heights had gone from being

34

a rudderless vessel with an apathetic crew to a tight ship with dawn rises and sensible bed times.

Pride forced me to try and keep pace with Chris and Fat Frank, who were now learning more and more techniques. I tried to catch up by going to the Japanese-taught classes in the evening. These were more regimented than the foreigners' classes, slower paced and better organized.

It was there I made an enemy, or so I thought. I was training with a nervous young man, who was even more uncertain and clumsy than I was. We were interrupted by the senior teacher of that lesson, Oyamada, who came strolling over to have a cursory look at the beginners. Oyamada had thinning hair. He also had an incredibly long body and short legs, which is the ideal aikido physique. He indicated that I should grab his wrist. I did so, and he moved to one side and lifted my arm so that my grab was broken and he now had my wrist in his paws. He then jerked down on my locked wrist with what felt like his full body weight. I collapsed to my knees, a shooting pain going right up my arm. I actually thought something might have been broken. Then I was incredibly angry.

I shook myself clear of him, which I already knew to be very bad etiquette in a dojo. Oyamada just gave me a blank look and walked off. I couldn't understand what had happened. It seemed like a pointless act of brutality. The pain went away and nothing was damaged permanently. But it was inexplicable. Had he picked on me because I was a foreigner? Or was his style the real aikido, and what we had been practising a pansyish imitation? Nothing I'd felt from the other teachers was anything like the force I'd felt from him, or the pain.

I went home and complained to Chris and Fat Frank. Chris already knew all about Oyamada. He was trying to establish his reputation in the dojo and didn't water his technique down for anyone, especially foreigners. What I'd felt was the pain I could expect from 'full-on' aikido. It was then that I realized my attitude to pain would have to change. I'd have to recognize that

35

there were guys out there who wanted to train as Tesshu did: taking pain as a matter of course, and dishing it out as a matter of course too.

When I attended the morning class I increasingly took notice of a small group of foreigners who trained on the far side of the dojo. This group, who all stood at attention when not executing a technique, all wore white belts and sweat-soaked, blood-spattered pyjamas. I noticed one young man, tall and athletically built, who had six-inch red 'suns' on each knee. He seemed to ignore the fact that he was bleeding profusely as he performed a series of moves that required him to walk on these same bleeding knees. From their end came shouts, screams, grunts and yells. The teachers verbally and physically abused them. Sometimes it was disturbing, as if the teacher was going too far.

Chris told me in the tea room after the lesson that they were doing 'The Course'. They were the foreigners who were doing the Japanese Riot Police course. 'They're the crazy ones,' muttered Chris. I immediately wanted to join them while at the same time realizing that it was probably physically impossible. They seemed to be on another planet, there was something completely professional about them which made our own efforts seem tame and ineffective. At an irrational level the idea had taken hold: if you want to do the real thing you have to do the Riot Police course.

Cannibal Talk

'It is good to carry powdered rouge. It may happen that when sobering up or waking from sleep a Samurai's complexion may be poor. At such a time apply rouge.'

From the seventeenth-century Samurai handbook
Hagakure

Mr Wada offered me a Virginia Slim cigarette. For a man who liked to project a tough image, it was something of a weak accessory. Hemingway, for example, wouldn't have been seen dead near a Virginia Slim. I took one.

'*Ki* is very important,' he said, coating his lips with an even layer of saliva. 'I think *ki* is the soul of the universe.'

'Um, yes,' I said. I wanted to agree, but I couldn't agree too strongly for fear of intruding into Mr Wada's personal vision. We were both very careful not to tread on each other's toes. And though I always seemed to be on the brink of becoming Mr Wada's friend, it never quite seemed to happen.

Mr Wada was the head of the English department at the girls' high school I taught at on Mondays. I had been lucky to find a job that allowed me to work only one day a week. If I ever did the police course, I could just about support myself by working all day Monday, which was the one day of the week the dojo was shut. For the time being it was just one of a clutch of part-time teaching jobs that kept Fuji Heights afloat.

Mr Wada was a fourth-degree black belt at kendo, Japanese fencing, and taught English and kendo at the school. He was good looking and very popular with the girls. With the girls he made jokes but with me he was always deadly serious. You could tell he really liked his students and felt at ease with them.

But he did have wet lips. It was probably a nervous habit.

We were sitting in the staffroom drinking green tea and talking about *ki*.

School staffrooms in Japan are not the havens they are in the West. In Japan they are like open-plan offices – rows of grey metal desks, one for each teacher, and open access for the schoolkids to bother you.

Because Mr Wada was so popular our conversation was often interrupted by lovestruck fifteen-year-old girls asking him to translate the unprintable lyrics of American rap bands. Sometimes, out of generosity, he handed such assignments over to me, and I would hunch over the tape recorder wondering how to translate 'motherfucker' or 'cocksucker'.

'*Ki* is in our bodies,' continued Mr Wada. 'And it is in the universe. It is a very difficult thing.'

'Can you increase your *ki*?' I asked.

'We Japanese,' Mr Wada began – it was one of his favourite openers and was a direct translation from the Japanese. It always set my teeth on edge – 'We Japanese believe that *ki* is variable. A man in poor health has low *ki*.'

'Is *ki* another word for physical health?'

'I think *ki* has a connection to healthiness. But *ki* is very hard to understand.'

'Yes,' I said, but *ki* didn't seem so hard to understand to me. I could see that what Wada had in mind was a kind of vitalism, *ki* being the basic energy of the universe. *Ki* gave humans their energy and also animated the universe. When the flow of *ki* was blocked the energy was wasted and dissipated – this was what happened during illness. Aikido aimed to facilitate a perfect flow of *ki* energy, though if you asked Chida Sensei about *ki* he would pick up a locker-key and say, 'This is *ki*! Here, have some *ki*!'

'How is your *ki*?' I asked Mr Wada.

'My *ki* is very good, thank you,' he replied.

We lapsed into silence and I hoped he would offer me another menthol cigarette.

'Americans do not understand *ki*,' he said, after a while.

'No, they don't.' I always agreed strongly with his condemnations of American culture. I think he wanted to criticize the whole of the West, but out of politeness he stuck to America.

'If they understood *ki* they would not have such a problem of drugs and crime.'

'Um, yes.'

'They do not see that *ki* requires discipline. The United States has no discipline.'

'You're right,' I said.

'How about your country?' he said.

'Oh, we don't have much either,' I said cheerfully. For some reason Mr Wada brought out my desire to humour him.

'But in aikido you learn discipline,' he said, re-wetting his lips.

'Yes, in aikido we learn discipline.'

Then I remembered Wada had told one teacher my shirts were not always spotless. Somehow it sat uncomfortably with assertions about discipline.

'But it's more than just discipline,' I said. 'It's more than that.'

Kancho Sensei, the founder, rarely spoke about *ki*. He talked about *kokyu* power instead – breath power.

As I was walking home from the dojo one day Paul, the policeman, offered to show me a local landmark which had some connection to Kancho's *kokyu* power.

'That's the lamppost,' said Paul. We were standing next to a lamppost down the hill from the dojo. 'The one that Kancho Sensei crashed his bike into.'

I looked at the pole with increased interest. There were no dents or scratch marks to suggest its collision with the greatest living practitioner of aikido. Though it did look like it had recently been repainted the light pastel green favoured by the Tokyo public works department.

'It was a long time ago, some time in the early seventies,' he added.

Paul had an ironic twinkle in his eye, a combination of fractionally raised eyebrow and barely detectable smile, which Westerners adopted when retelling the miracle stories of Kancho Sensei. Not that a bike crash was much of a miracle.

'Well, apparently,' said Paul, 'Kancho had such amazing hip power that at the instant the bike hit the pole he sent a full body thrust back through the bike and bounced off completely unharmed.'

I was prepared to admit the theoretical possibility of such an action. After all, I'd seen Chida Sensei 'bounce' people off him through a concentrated exertion of hip power delivered through the shoulders and back – why not, then, through a bike saddle and handlebars? Though I imagined most Japanese bicycles would disintegrate under such treatment.

'But why did he ride into the post in the first place? Surely that doesn't say much for "sixth sense" martial-arts awareness?' I asked Paul.

'Well, it was after he'd been drinking with his cronies. He was probably dead drunk at the time.'

Everyone accepted that Kancho was an alcoholic. It was all part of the myth, like the fact that he used to smoke a hundred cigarettes a day and could still perform amazing feats of physical endurance. He was the closest I'd come to a living Tesshu; he shared Tesshu's predilection for drink, though he wasn't a poet.

But now he had turned seventy-eight, was often in hospital, and most probably dying of lung cancer.

Out of respect for the fact that he was the founder of the Yoshinkan school, its living connection with the master Ueshiba, a tenth-dan, Japan's greatest living martial artist, and not to mention being a mean mother who'd killed people with his bare hands, no one talked openly about his illness. Sometimes people whispered in the dojo kitchen about his health, but that was all.

What was talked about was his collection of clocks. Kancho

only had two interests in life: aikido and clocks. His house was full of them, ticking and tocking away in every room, countless wall clocks, grandfather clocks, carriage clocks and cuckoo clocks, setting a perfect rhythm, measuring out his life. He spent his time moving from clock to clock, adjusting the time, winding their springs, listening to their varied chimes, watching the pendulums swing back and forth, waiting for nothing, or death; a dying man obsessed by the passing of time.

I only saw Kancho once, from behind, crowded out by bowing teachers when he made his final visit to the dojo. He was very frail and his formal dark suit was as small as that of a child.

The top foreign teacher, Robert Mustard, had one question he loved to ask, to snap out at unsuspecting beginners: 'What's the most important thing about Yoshinkan aikido?' There was only one answer: 'Spirit.' Mustard was very big on spirit. If a beginner showed spirit it didn't matter that his technique was poor. A third- or fourth-degree black belt without spirit would be ignored by Mustard. He would simply refuse to teach them. I was worried that Mustard might refuse to teach me if I was inadvertently disrespectful, so I went the other way, getting up when he entered the tea room and fumbling with the drinks machine to get him a mineral-enriched Pocari Sweat soft drink. Being respectful made conversation a little one sided.

'You know I once gave up aikido?' he told me, offering me a Hi-Lite ultra-harsh Japanese cigarette, the only brand he smoked.

My voice didn't always sound like my voice when I spoke to Mustard. It sounded fake, even to me. 'Why did you give up?' the voice demanded.

'Politics. I was getting caught up in the politics of the dojo, so for about a year I didn't train. Maybe once a month or less. I gave up *trying* to do aikido. I just came in and messed around. Then something strange happened. All of a sudden I was dropping people with no effort at all. I'd finally worked out what it was about.'

41

The voice seemed fated to ask dumb questions: 'What *is* it about?'

He smiled, and flipped the worn end of his black belt on to the table. It was Mustard's way of answering stupid questions. In a gesture, it meant train harder.

'That year I taught at a junior high school. I saved a bunch of money. I got a nice five-room apartment.' He stubbed out his cigarette. 'You know, at my level, if I was a boxer I'd be a millionaire by now.'

'Right, right.' I nodded.

'If I had a kid I wouldn't let him do martial arts. I'd get him pitching baseballs from the moment he could walk.'

'Get him to earn the million!'

'Exactly. There's no money in aikido, not if you're honest, not if you want to teach people the real thing.'

'Right.' *The real thing* – that phrase again. It was what the voice wanted. To be accepted as real.

'And I'm not getting any younger. I'm thirty-eight, and it gets harder and harder.' He paused and took out another cigarette, not offering me one this time. 'But in other ways I'm getting stronger. In aikido terms I'm stronger now than I've ever been. In this place there's only one person stronger than me.'

I wondered why he was trying to convince me. I'm already a believer I wanted to say, but the voice wouldn't let me.

'Right,' I nodded earnestly. There was an uncomfortable silence and we both looked away. When I turned back Mustard was popping his Hi-Lites back inside his dogi jacket. Then, for a brief moment, he gave me a look which meant: you don't know what the hell I'm talking about, do you?

Mustard's sentiments were the same as Tesshu's: 'If single-minded determination is absent, one will never advance, regardless of years of training.'

Chida Sensei was the top teacher now that Kancho no longer taught, but Mustard was an expert showman. He knew how to excite beginners by giving them a glimpse of the powers of aikido. After classes he would stand around until someone asked him a question. Then he would call for an *uke*, a volunteer attacker, and the show would begin.

The *uke* would try to punch him and Mustard would move fractionally out of the way, turn, then toss the attacker across two or three mats. This was a helicopter throw. Or else Mustard would instantly move in, avoid the punch, and smash *uke* flat with his palm to *uke's* jaw, transferring enough power to bounce the attacker's body off the ground.

Mustard had 'it', 'the magic', the ability to throw people very hard and seemingly without effort. Kancho Sensei said, 'If aikido doesn't look a little fake then it isn't real aikido.' That fakery was 'the magic', the ability to utilize full body power to produce an effect of startling magnitude. No big arms, no weightlifter's chest, but a sense of timing and a co-ordination of body weight so perfect that an attacker would be lying dazed on the ground before he knew what had hit him. This was another definition of 'it' – the 'what hit me' sensation, the feeling that the power felt to be exerted is severely disproportinate to the effect on the attacker.

Tesshu's explanation of magical abilities was almost dismissive: 'It's nothing – if your mind is empty, it reflects the distortion and "shadows" present in others' minds. In swordsmanship "no-mind" allows us to see the perfect place to strike; in daily life it enables us to see into another's heart.'

Once you had *felt* a technique you usually became a believer, someone who gave at least some credence to the idea of magical powers. In the end, you saw, and felt as *uke*, so many displays of magic that it became normal. When you performed magic for the first time yourself, then, said Mustard, there was no turning back. I asked him how long it took him before he 'had the power'. 'Two years after I finished the police course, ten years after I started aikido.'

Ten years was a long sorcerer's apprenticeship.

He seemed much older and wiser than thirty-eight. There was

something heroic about him, an old Norse god in a heathen land, an anachronistic Thorin Oakenshield. He seemed frightened of nothing except his teacher Takeno and the wrath of Carol, his tiny girlfriend. She banned him from smoking, which he now did in secret, hauling on a high-tar cigarette in the tea room before classes.

Sometimes Mustard would offer up his body for ritual examination:

'Here, feel this.'

He put his thick bony wrist in my hands and twisted it about. It felt like gravel crunching around in the joint. Then he rolled up his sleeve.

'Check out the elbow.'

His arms were not straight, but bent backwards at the elbows. The right elbow was bent even more alarmingly than the left. It simply meant Mustard had taken more hard throws on the right. He had broken, bruised, cracked or strained virtually every bone in his body. He considered it a worthwhile price to pay.

Each year, at the All Japan Aikido Demonstration, Mustard had been the chosen *uke* by Chida Sensei's rival, the monstrously powerful Takeno, who some believed to be the strongest aikidoka in the world. Takeno and Chida had both been students under Kancho, though Takeno had, a few years before, broken away to form his own dojo, practising a faster, more spectacular form of aikido than Chida at the main dojo. Takeno was known to be brutally tough. 'A few knockouts are healthy, it clears the brain,' he used to say. Live-in students would often last just one day with Takeno, climbing out of the locked dojo at night never to return.

Uke 'receives' the master's aikido. In short, *uke* attacks and gets beaten up. No one had been beaten up more than Mustard. And he chose this path because of a single-minded belief that the only way to be good was to 'feel' the master's technique and try to copy it: 'Kancho took Ueshiba's *uke*. Takeno took Kancho's *uke*. I took Takeno's *uke*. It's a direct line. It's the ony way to get the real power.'

That was one of his favourite phrases: 'The real power.' And though it was melodramatic, he sucked you into his world, the world of pain and humiliation at the hands of a great master, the only way to learn, or so he made you believe.

Mustard accepted the latent racism of Japanese martial arts. He accepted it but it had made him bitter. He had been kept at fifth-dan when there were seventh-dan Japanese he was superior to. That rankled. After all, it was him Takeno preferred to use year after year, not a Japanese.

At his fifth-dan test Kancho had said, 'Good face.' At that level of aikido, where mere technical brilliance is presumed, this was the highest praise. 'Good face' meant more than just a fierce expression. In the semi-coded language of the martial artist it meant Kancho took Mustard seriously as a fighter. It meant that despite the artificialities of the test Mustard had not looked foolish, rather he had maintained the inner dignity necessary for a warrior, a man prepared to die at any moment.

When I was six I wanted an older brother, and my cousin, who was ten, fitted the role. Like older brothers everywhere he took pleasure in tormenting his loyal sidekick. He made me bury my Action Man in the compost heap, calling it a 'camouflage operation'. He set fire to an Airfix model plane we'd both painstakingly made and threw it out of a second-floor window. 'It's been shot down,' he explained. On holiday in Cornwall he forced me to walk barefoot with him across a hot gravel car park. I did it because I wanted to be like him, though at the time I remember thinking, Why am I doing this?

This need to imitate my elders continued when I started writing poetry. I followed a fairly usual path, copying Keats then Hardy, Eliot, Pound, Yeats and Auden. Now I was copying Mustard, except the only thing about him I could really imitate was his walk. I pulled my shoulders down and tried to root myself to the ground with every step, the way Mustard did. With him it gave an impression of easy power, but I realized I wasn't quite getting there when Frank shouted from behind, 'Looks like a strained pelvis to me.'

We were in Ken's restaurant when Mustard stretched out his legs under the tiny table and became expansive. Ken was Hawaiian Japanese, and his wife ran the restaurant. They served perfect horse mackerel with fragrant rice and were the only restaurant around which didn't dose everything with *ajinomoto*, Japanese monosodium glutamate.

Mustard held a chopstick in one hand, wedging it between his fingers, the middle finger underneath the chopstick and the outer fingers on top.

'People talk about *ki* – but what is *ki*? Training is not about *ki*, it's about giving everything, about being prepared to die. When you come into the dojo you have to cultivate that frame of mind.'

Suitable noises of encouragement and support came from the assembled diners.

'If I see someone who doesn't have respect for the teacher I'll just walk away. I won't teach that person. Takeno Sensei would punch them out, but I just walk away. Without respect there's no teaching.'

I remembered how Frank had shown slight disbelief when Mustard was demonstrating something after the class. Instinctively Mustard did the technique on Frank using full, unrestrained force. Frank picked himself off the floor, grinning apologetically and rubbing his shoulder. It took a month for the shoulder to heal.

Mustard held up his chopstick. 'Watch this.'

He broke it easily.

I tried to do the same but only succeeded in giving myself a severely bruised middle finger. A chopstick is easy to chop, or break, but snapping it using only the restricted power of the finger and not the hand is difficult.

'There's no "correct" technique for this,' chuckled Mustard. 'Only years of practice.'

He then broke two chopsticks at once. Then three. He grinned at our expectant faces and said, 'There's only one Japanese teacher I know who can do four.'

In my mind Mustard had a heroic quality I had long been looking for: a kind of macho dignity that I guessed he'd learnt from his Japanese teachers. He was also a masochist, a hard man, a drinker and a sentimentalist. He often talked nonsense and I knew it was nonsense – all that stuff about warrior spirit and being prepared to die at any moment – but then and there it made sense, it flowed into a void within me, the namby-pamby valueless void left by years of sensible education and warnings to wear a crash helmet when riding a bicycle. This was wild stuff and a grown man was speaking it. He was also a master – he could walk the talk all right. Such men wield considerable power and I would later appreciate just how deep a decision it is to commit yourself to hero worship of such a man.

One day Mustard asked me casually if I was going to do the Riot Police course. I was too surprised to be able to answer. In the end I mumbled out a 'maybe'. Until then I had believed that a prerequisite for the course was a black belt at least, if not in aikido, then in another art. Mustard had already been a third-degree black belt when he did the Riot Police training eight years before.

By starting aikido in Japan at the headquarters in Tokyo, I could slide in the back door. If I applied for the course from outside Japan the requirements would be more stringent. But if I continued to train hard (ie., every day for the next six months) they would let me do the Riot Police course.

But was I really good enough to sustain eleven months of hard training, five hours a day, five days a week? I didn't know. I really didn't. I asked Darren, a former bouncer from Australia, who'd completed the police course in Paul's year. Darren was as tough as anyone in the dojo, but he was open and self effacing, which made him easier to talk to than Paul. Darren would be one of the *shidoin*, assistant teachers, for the next senshusei course. 'If you want to do it, you will,' he said. 'It's as simple as that. You just have to want to do it. Mind you, when I finished the course I thought I'd never jog again, my knees were that bad . . .'

Riot Police students were known as senshusei, trainee specialists, and at the end of the year they gained a teaching licence. But during the year they are treated as the lowest members of the dojo. They are stripped of their black-belt status and forced to wear white belts during the course as a symbol of humility. They have to clean the toilets and showers and treat the teachers like gods.

The method of teaching has changed little since the days of the Imperial Japanese Army, of which the modern police force is the spiritual successor; the Japanese army, or Self Defence Forces, were more closely regarded by the American occupation forces and more thoroughly purged of Japanese-style militarism.

The teacher has no worries about attracting students or even keeping them. He can be as hard and as brutal as he likes and he will still receive a salary from the dojo's sponsors. Sponsors of the Yoshinkan dojo included the Sasakawa Corporation, which was known to have traditional, if not ultra-nationalist, sympathies. Sasakawa himself had been imprisoned as a category A war criminal from 1945 to 1948.

Both Kancho and his father had been members of the ultra-nationalist Black Dragon society, a secret pre-war group to which Sasakawa had also once belonged. Yoshinkan aikido derived its insistence on 'Spirit' from the same philosophical underpinnings as the ultra-nationalists, though the direction, since the war, had been to make 'Spirit' a personal striving rather than a nationalist ethos. Kancho, I'm sure, was not much interested in politics, but his thinking was more amenable to the right than the left. If the police needed someone to imbue their officers with 'Spirit', Yoshinkan aikido was a perfect vehicle, with its pre-war credentials of nationalism, and its postwar success as a tough and systematic martial art.

'Spirit', then, was a fairly recent cultural import into the study of aikido. Unlike the various schools of swordfighting, aikido had, until the late nineteenth century, been a largely secret form of jujitsu. It had been passed down through noble families, taught only to loyal retainers and the sons of aristocrats. *Yamato Damashi*, Japanese Spirit, was a broad-based cultural idea which had existed throughout Japanese history but was only fused with aikido in the nationalist era of the 1920s and 30s. Even then it was only Yoshinkan aikido which maintained this link. Other forms of aikido reflected the philosophical beliefs of their top practitioners. Ueshiba, the founding father of modern aikido, increasingly blended his aikido with the nutty religious cult of Omoto. Tomiki, who founded 'sport' aikido, was more influenced by the pedagogic approaches of Waseda University's education department. It was only Kancho who remained true to the pre-war notion of 'Spirit'. Learning 'Spirit' was what the Riot Police course was all about.

I had become fitter during my recent aikido training. I supplemented this by joining an expensive gym full of women in sexy leotards, an indoor running track and jogging machines. Though body building is considered a waste of time by most serious aikidoka it felt good to put a bit more muscle on. I practised flipping on the foam exercise mats that were laid down. Flipping, I knew, would present problems. I could do a forward roll, but a flip, which is an acrial forward roll, was hard for me to master. Everyone said that if you can't flip before you start the course you'll be in serious difficulties, because the training requires so much flipping. And if you can't flip out of a throw you take a real beating.

I started running, leaving Fuji Heights in the early evening and running along the railway tracks to nearby Shakujikoen park. I ran around the lake in the park several times looking for the cayman which local TV reported had been spotted lurking there.

49

I never saw it. Neither did I see the duck with a crossbow bolt through its neck, another recent refugee, according to the press.

This park was one of my few connections with nature. In parts it was almost wild, which is perhaps why the story about the cayman got started. There was a small shrine built on pilings out into the lake. In the autumn, before it got dark, mist would lie on the lake and swirl around the base of the shrine. A man who played tenor sax often sat on a bench next to the lake playing Mozart. The music and mist hung over the lake as I pounded round the lightly wooded slopes.

I regarded the others who had signed up for the course with suspicion – were they tougher than me? There was little Agastino, a Chinese-Portuguese Australian who told everyone he'd been an unarmed combat instructor in the Australian SAS. Agastino, or Aga as he liked to be called, had scars all over his body, even his testicles, but I didn't feel I knew him well enough at this stage to question him about them. Aga was into positive thinking and Nuskin health products. He recruited poor fools to help sell their overpriced sports foods. The truth about Aga was more banal: he was actually an accountant who, as a member of a territorial signals unit, had been on exercises with Australian Special Forces. Aga had thin wrists, tiny bones, but overbuilt pecs. He talked big, too – bullshit mostly. I got this from Danny, his mate, who had been in the same unit and was also doing the course. Danny had a big grin, a permanent toothy smile. He was the kind of guy who would have gone to Gallipoli and not come back. But Danny had the wiry, super-fit kind of body that has no problem with stamina. I didn't think Aga was that tough, he just talked tough, but Danny, despite his boy's interest in dolphins and dangerous spiders, looked like the business.

William Howell, my American friend, had also persuaded himself to do the course. Before coming to Japan he had been a trawler deckhand and a deerhunter in his native Washington State. Will was well mannered and good looking, but he also revered book learning. He was always asking Chris to recommend a good text, and sometimes he'd read it. Women liked Will but he'd brush them off with automatic ease. He was mystically hyped up about the course: 'This is our Vietnam,' he used to say. At other times he was more prosaic: 'It was either this or law school.' Would Will survive? I thought so, he had invested all his pride in completing the course.

Will's friend Adam also signed up for aikido and the course. Fat but gymnastic, heavy and bendy, Adam was the kind of guy who was always getting beaten up by people who took against his face and his Robin Williams patter. After spending some time with him I began to see why. He alternated weedy passivity with a tendency to bully when he could get away with it. He'd married a Japanese girl when he was eighteen and she had become pregnant. Now he was twenty-two and his wife had taken the little girl with her to America. Adam saw the course as some kind of therapy; if he could complete it then it would prove he wasn't a complete failure. I was convinced Adam would give up after a week. He was unfit, despite having been a pro-skateboarder, and he had an old knee injury that still gave him problems.

Fat Frank wanted to do the course but his visa situation wouldn't allow it. He'd lost weight and with his huge calves and bull neck would easily be tough enough. I tried to persuade him to con his way on but we knew that Paul, the assiduous English cop, would sniff him out. Chris was encouraging but gnomic: 'I have deep reservations about the way of teaching of the Riot Police. But you won't regret it if you finish it.' He was also honest about himself: 'I'm not sure I could complete it myself. I'm too accident prone. And from what I've observed, a major part of it is injury management.'

It was harder to compare myself to the current foreign senshusei. I didn't know what they looked like at the beginning. Halfway through the training they all looked super fit. Only Nick, an Englishman I'd seen being bullied by Mustard, looked ill at ease and was still making the odd mistake in the basic movements.

They avoided talking to regular students and sat, grim and unsmiling, in the locker room between lessons.

I only saw the Japanese police students after lessons. They were all young-looking guys with thin wiry bodies. One had a cockatoo-like quiff which seemed pretty outrageous for a Riot Cop, but probably most of the time it would be hidden under his helmet.

I knew that if I did start the course I would not be able to give up. Too much pride was at stake. And if I was honest, I wasn't so different from Adam, using the unbelievably hard training as a way of proving that I counted, that I really did exist.

I thought about the rest of my life. What had I got to lose? It was only a year, after all. If a comparison was possible, the equivalent basic training at Tesshu's school had lasted for three years. A kind of inevitability had been developing over the months. I'd talked about it so much, meditated on the injuries I was likely to receive, brainwashed myself with the idea that the course was the only way I would really progress in martial arts. The big decision had been watered down over months of agonizing, of an unconscious process of convincing myself I could really do it. When I paid over my money and handed in all the forms, including one which signed away all responsibilities for injury or death, it didn't seem such a big deal, after all. Whenever Mustard saw me he'd laugh derisively and say, 'You're mine! You're mine!' Which should have been a warning to me.

Three months before the senshusei course started there was an 'international party'. All the foreigners who did aikido and the Japanese staff at the dojo attended.

I talked to Nick, who had now decided to quit the course two months before it finished. He had a long face and nervously extinguished his cigarettes in a piece of melon. Under the stress of the course Nick had developed asthma. During a *hajime* session (continuous training without a rest) with a Japanese teacher who had a reputation for being merciless, Nick started to hyperventilate. The teacher saw he had stopped training and came over and started shouting at him. Then he hit Nick in the face.

Nick told me, 'I was really scared. I mean, this is Japan, I had no comebacks, I didn't know what he was going to do. He could have done anything . . .'

After hitting him the teacher forced him to do several rounds of the ubiquitous 'bunny hops' (*usagi tobi* – a standard punishment in Japan, and somehow typically Japanese in that it looks cute and silly but is actually very strenuous). *Usagi tobi* are banned in Japanese high schools as a punishment because of fatalities. They are probably not the best cure for hyperventilation either. It left Nick in an ultra-tense and nervous state. When his girlfriend became pregnant it was the final straw and he quit and left Japan.

Another teacher, Shioda junior, son of the founder, was known to be especially tough on non-Japanese. Some said it was a result of his enforced three-year stay in England during the 1980s, sent there by his father, who was laying the groundwork for a worldwide network. In those years the young Shioda had found England a miserable place to be. Young women, perhaps, had laughed at his curious, mutilated English and, like his literary forebear, Natsume Soseki, he languished in the cold damp of the English climate.

His vendetta against gaijin, foreigners, because of his experiences in England, was said to be especially strong against English nationals.

It all sounded too ridiculous to be true, but when he came up to me at the winter dojo party his manner was oddly aggressive, though his English was very good. With his clipped, almost hysterical mode of questioning, the younger Shioda, at forty-three, seemed the very picture of the sadistic Japanese Army officer circa 1941.

'Why do you do the senshusei course?' he interrogated.

'I'm very interested in Japanese culture and I believe aikido is good Spirit training.' It was a standard reply.

'Ah, Japanese Spirit. This is very important.' He peered at me with defiance. 'Japanese Spirit is the most important thing!'

'Japanese Spirit is very interesting,' I said. He nodded curtly and went away.

'He likes you,' said the hugely muscled Israeli girl sitting next to me. Like a lot of ex-military Israelis she had drifted into martial arts and was as able as any man at dishing out the rough stuff.

'How do you know he likes me?'

'Because he smiled.'

'He didn't.'

'Apart from his sadistic laugh, the closest he comes to smiling is when he nods. That nod is a smile. Believe me, if he doesn't like you, you really know it.'

Adam, the other would-be senshusei, was also interviewed by Shioda at the same party. 'That guy's really nasty,' he said, moving his head slightly to indicate where Shioda junior was now sitting. 'He told me I was too overweight to do aikido.'

'You are a bit on the overweight side.'

'I know, but it was the way he said it, like he was planning to have me skinned and roasted for lunch. There's something cannibalistic about that guy.'

After the sit-down part of the party we moved on to a nightclub in Shinjuku san-Chome, the red-light district of Tokyo. On the way to the station Oyamada Sensei shoved Mike 'Stumpy' Stuempel's head into a privet hedge using an aikido move. Stumpy was a current senshusei, and at six foot two he towered over Oyamada. But Oyamada was the teacher, so Stumpy could only grin sheepishly. I noticed him picking bits of privet out of his ears for the rest of the evening.

At the nightclub, a reggae disco called MC 1000, I met Roland 'the Terminator' Thompson for the first time. An

Australian by nationality he was of Scottish and Irish descent, with a bit of Chinese and Aboriginal blood thrown in for good measure. He was known to be the only person ever to have resisted Kancho's *nikajo* wrist lock. They called him 'the Terminator' because after one lesson with him you felt, we were assured, so completely terminated you didn't want to continue. I asked, in my innocence, if he had any advice for a beginning student. Roland laughed with a mocking irony I found disconcerting. He was the same age as me, but with his red hair and pitted potato face, sloping shoulders, big wrists and six-foot frame he seemed older, uglier and infinitely tougher. He had a quiet, charmingly vague manner when sober. After a few drinks he became rougher, ruder, more terminal.

Current senshusei students offered their advice. Mike 'Spike' Kimeda, half Canadian, half Japanese, whose father was a famous aikido teacher in Toronto, said, 'Always make sure there's someone worse than you. That's your insurance policy. If someone cracks it will be the guy at the bottom, not you.'

'Stumpy' Stuempel, another Canadian, told me: 'You can't prepare for the course. The whole thing is designed to push you further than you could go on your own. You can't prepare for doing six hundred press-ups, or an hour of *jiyu waza*, free-style attacking practice, that exhausts after a few minutes.'

Both Stumpy and Spike would be course assistants, *sewanin*, in the senshusei course I would be doing. At the top was the teacher, then came the *shidoin*, then the *sewanin*, and at the bottom the senshusei. Everyone bullied the level beneath. And the senshusei were bullied by everyone.

John Coffey, an American and another hard man (he was a third-dan and had done the course three years previously – his brother was the top ice hockey player Paul Coffey), was more philosophical and softly spoken. He gave me a look reminiscent of Marlon Brando in *Apocalypse Now*. 'I remember after I finished the course I went up to the mountains to a kind of retreat. It was run by Zen monks and the whole atmosphere was very ascetic, very austere. We were given very little food and deprived of sleep. We stood under icy waterfalls – that kind of thing. After a few days I was standing in this icy water and a sudden realization flooded over me. I suddenly knew my body was a piece of shit. It wasn't an idea – I knew it. Just shit, waste, garbage, nothing special at all. And knowing this I knew I could make my body do anything. If I'd know that before doing the course things would have been ... easier.' He smiled and I noticed the various small scars on his face.

I decided to leave the foetid thumping racket of the nightclub. I felt I needed fresh air. A lot of fresh air. As I said a hurried goodbye Roland fixed me with his grey watery eyes. 'It's dangerous stuff, this aikido. You call kill people with aikido.' He wasn't smiling. 'Thanks, Roland,' I said, and hurried towards the exit wondering why I wanted to become like them.

Foaming at the Mouth

'Tether even a roasted chicken.'
From the seventeenth-century Samurai manual
Hagakure

April

For the first time in my life I was about to wilfully inflict damage on myself.

The school bully, the one who punched me in the face with a cricket glove, had also liked damaging himself. He had a curiously malformed thumb, a stump of scar tissue that stopped at the first joint. Sometimes, during lessons, he would stab himself in the thumb stump with the sharp point of his compasses.

I can remember other friends deliberately cutting themselves with modelling knives. The most barbarous folly was performed by the naughty boys at the back of the class who gave themselves blue-ink tattoos with a fountain pen and the ubiquitous pair of compasses.

My parents, when they got the chance, smothered me with kindly concern. I think that if I'd tried to toughen myself up with self mutilation they would have taken me to a child psychiatrist. In Britain, in the 1970s, only skinheads and the deranged welcomed a beating to build their own resistance to further torture.

The first day of the Riot Police course was, appropriately, April 1. There was an inaugural ceremony held in the dojo under a huge Rising Sun flag that hung from the wall.

The police would start a month later. They had been running a month late, ever since the Royal Wedding of the previous spring.

Ito, the head disciple, issuing commands in the same voice as Chida, his mentor, lined the international contingent up for the inauguration and made us kneel for ten minutes while a former foreign minister made a long speech. All the VIPs I noticed were seated in chairs. As well as the huge Japanese flag hanging over the shrine there was a purple Yoshinkan eagle flag hanging from a tripod in the corner. When a senshusei name was called out that student had to jump to his feet as fast as possible and shout out his name and nationality. It was good form to shout as loud as possible. Riot Police don't mumble, we were told. Kancho was too sick to attend. It was the first police course ceremony he had missed in thirty years.

After the ceremony we stood around at a bit of a loose end. There were two Canadians, both called Nick. The smaller and younger of the two was an Armenian Canadian and told us his name was not really Nick but we ought to call him Nick because everyone else did. Later he told me his real name, but I forgot it. Little Nick had problems writing, despite having been sent to an expensive private school. He had scars on his arms from knife fights. There was something sharkish and cold about his black eyes.

The older and bigger Nick was jovially keen to shake everyone's hand. He was a few months younger than me, so I was the oldest on the course. He had been an outdoor activities instructor in Canada and had studied 'Outdoor Leisure' at university. 'My God,' quipped Will, 'the guy's got a degree in lighting campfires and putting up tents.'

Ben and Craig were both Australian. Ben was well over six foot tall and without embarrassment told everyone he had studied ballet back in Melbourne. Ben looked floppy and relaxed, used to a painfree existence. I guessed he would only last a month. Craig was watchful and quiet. He had a bulky body and pale skin and had trained at karate and iado, the art of drawing a sword. He had an Ian Botham style haircut, short at the sides with a mane down the back. Virtually everyone else had either shaven or crew-cut hair, which was the expected senshusei hairstyle.

R'em, the Israeli, was to be my training partner for the first three months. There was something Tiggerish about him, a bounciness that was appealing. He had a mop of frizzy hair and round glasses which he never removed, even during fist fights, he said. He sold silver rings for a living and told me he had two girlfriends, one Japanese and one Israeli. 'But I am Yemeni-Israeli, and Yemenis are allowed two wives!' he said, winking at me. His English and Japanese were both poor but he rarely stopped grinning. Fat Frank didn't appreciate R'em's jokes: 'He tries to make out you're just as dirty-minded as he is – I don't like that.' Before coming to Japan (via motorcycle across India) he had served as a captain in the Israeli paratroops. He was thin and wiry. He told me he'd always liked fighting.

It was then I realized that we were a kind of foreign legion within the senshusei course. Foreigners who had washed up and were at a loose end, dropouts even, who sought salvation in the punishing discipline of dojo life. It was too late to worry that I was running away from life, too late to think of all the freedoms I would have to give up. For the next year we were all the property of Yoshinkan aikido.

The senshusei course starts from zero. It presupposes no knowledge of aikido apart from a few basics. For those who are already black belts the idea is to strip out bad habits by going back to fundamentals. The course proceeds very fast. In a year we would do more training than someone practising an hour a day four times a week for five years. The dojo demanded a certain level of competence before starting so that the high speed of learning could be kept up.

There would be four tests throughout the course. The third

59

test would be for black belt, the final test for an instructor's licence and a police course completion certificate.

We were all given a manual, translated from the Japanese, which outlined a rough diary for the year. It also told us our duties. In each seven- or eight-hour day at the dojo we would spend two hours cleaning, attending meetings, writing up our diaries and hurriedly eating meals. When we weren't at the dojo there were training camps to attend, as well as excursions and demonstrations.

Twice a week we started at 7.15 a.m. so that a half-hour Japanese lesson could be fitted in before the first aikido lesson.

All aikido classes were an hour or an hour and a half long, though this would be stretched to two if the teacher was feeling vengeful. There were three such classes each day. Including warm-up time and sitting to attention in *seiza*, the painful kneeling position of all would-be Samurai, we would spend five and half hours a day, five days a week, for a year, doing hard physical training in the same hard-matted thirty-by-fifteen-metre room.

At either end of this room, the dojo, were two clocks. They had to be checked every day, sometimes adjusted several times a day since they were always either slow or fast. These clocks ruled our lives.

The first lesson was widely advertised as the hardest. In previous years people had given up the senshusei course after the first lesson, some of them giving up aikido for good as well. I wondered who would be the first to crack up on our course.

The first month was used as a way to weed out those who couldn't adapt to senshusei-style training. In one year the number of foreign students had gone down from sixteen at the start to four at the end. The previous year had lost seven people throughout the course. The Japanese rarely gave up, except through injury. Foreigners were not always so tough. But they were not doing it on a salary, like the police.

One twenty-three-year-old Canadian had given up after three

days. This was the previous year. He told me he just didn't like being shouted at. But instead of fleeing in shame he stayed and trained twice a day in regular classes. And though a senshusei black belt is held in higher esteem than a regular black belt, he passed the test at the same time as those doing the course he had quit. This was the plan that Chris and Fat Frank aimed to follow. With luck, all of us would pass black belt at the same time, though I would still have to complete three more months of instructor training.

We were lined up kneeling and waiting for our first senshusei teacher to arrive. It was an early class so we knew it would be a foreigner. A minute before the class started five or six other Western teachers knelt down along the same line as us. These were either witnesses or assistants in the mayhem that would follow.

As the clock struck the half-hour, Roland 'the Terminator' strolled in. We went through the bowing procedure and then jumped up to attention to await orders.

The lesson was very simple. Everyone was told a spot they should run to and when the order was given everyone had to get to their spot as fast as possible. And then we had to run back to the line. And then back to the spots. And then back to the line. And then back to the spots. AS FAST AS POSSIBLE.

Quickly, Roland's voice became hectoring and hysterical as people made inevitable errors. Every mistake was punished by a round of *usagi tobi* (the bunny hops, which look like fun things to do, but after fifteen or sixteen rounds the novelty begins to wear off).

When we had learnt how to get to our spots we practised going into *kamae*, the basic fighting stance of aikido. First we went into right-side *kamae* and then we went into left-side *kamae*.

The shouting by Roland and his five assistant tormentors was like nothing I had yet experienced. It was pure boot camp. I could hear people being abused all around me. 'One more

61

fuck-up and you're out,' Roland shouted at Adam, who had even less experience of aikido than I did. Again and again we bunny hopped around the dojo. It was ludicrous and yet exhilarating. Roland came over and started bellowing in my ear. 'Lower your weight. Lower. LOWER!' I got confused and he sensed the victim in me. He came closer and shouted louder. Somehow I realized I had to get it together or his bullying would never stop. It was back to the school playground. I concentrated fiercely and projected defiance. As if things were now working on an instinctual level he backed away and started picking on someone else.

By now the bunny hopping was becoming a little lacklustre. We were assaulted by more shouts and insults to get us moving again. Everybody's lungs were bursting for air. People started falling over as they hopped.

Now the 'assistants' moved in. They gathered round those who looked like they might be fading and heaped insults and abuse on them. It felt like there were bombs going off all over the place, that I was back in some nightmarish First-World-War scenario, that I could run but never escape the mortar attack of bellowed 'instruction'.

Only at one point did I suddenly think: What the hell are you doing here? Why don't you just walk away? I banished the thought quickly. I knew I couldn't afford the luxury of such thinking if I wanted to stick it out for the whole year.

Compared to the others, I seemed to be doing OK. Adam was having the most problems, but then he seemed to get a second wind and started bunny hopping madly like a suicidal wind-up toy.

And then with a shouted 'ya-me!' (stop) it was all over. We stood at attention wheezing and dribbling like grandads. Roland gave us barely a look before dismissing the class.

Half an hour to prepare for the next lesson. I drank a litre of water and collapsed on the floor of the changing room. Stephan Otto, one of Roland's assistants, and a former power-lifting champion of Bavaria, came up and patted me on the back. 'You did well out there. I was kind of surprised. But it was good, good.'

The next lesson was taught by Chida Sensei. We all expected the worst. Instead, Chida gave us a lecture. He lined us up and laughed at our height. 'Too tall for aikido,' he said. 'All the top people like Ueshiba, Kancho Sensei were small.' He told us we were anticipating commands rather than following them. 'This is mental inflexibility. A man who anticipates cannot stand still. He cannot wait. His timing is always out. He telegraphs every punch and his opponent knows exactly what he is thinking. You cannot plan a fight!'

We all looked shamefaced. In our last lesson we were told we were too slow. Now we were too fast. What we had to learn was the correct manner.

We were trying too hard. Or trying in the wrong way. The problem was how to try hard in the right way. How to try without 'trying'. Because, in the end, trying hard is not enough. You have to get results. You have to win the fight, since losing may mean death. How do you win without caring too much about who actually wins?

We made mistakes and Chida said, 'This is not the regular class. In the regular class we say something and people forget, so we say it again. In senshusei training we only say it once. In senshusei training you cannot forget. You are taught once and you learn straightaway.'

He said this without a shred of irony in his voice. He paused after he'd said it and the warning hung for a moment in the air like a threat. He continued in a soft voice: 'When I joined the dojo and became a disciple I made my will. I knew that at any time I could be killed by Kancho Sensei. I made my will because I wanted to be prepared to die.' There was another long silence as this final pronouncement was made.

Chida finished with a series of stamina-building exercises. One of the exercises was simply sitting on the floor with the feet raised and outstretched in front. We were all shaking and quivering with fatigue after five minutes. Chida was forty-five years old and completely unperturbed after ten minutes of keeping his feet up. Indeed, he gave the impression, constantly, that he could go on for ever.

I later discovered there was a trick to this physical feat – just as there is to most displays of amazing strength or endurance. The trick is that when you tense the stomach muscles you involuntarily tense all the surrounding muscles as well. Some of these pull in the opposite direction to raising the legs so that you are actually working against yourself. This serves to tire out the stomach very quickly, however strong you are. Indeed, the stronger you are the stronger the counterpull of involuntary muscles. Instead, you must relax the stomach and concentrate on the hip tensor muscles that connect the femur to the pelvis. For this the back must be straight. Aikido, since it teaches a high level of body awareness and requires the ability to isolate and relax certain muscles, makes it easier to perform such 'miracles'.

The early weeks of training were designed to test *konjo*, or guts. It was a traditional Japanese training method. If you were asked to do two hundred press-ups it was for moral rather than physical reasons. The Japanese teachers were not interested in working up to something gently. *Konjo* demanded that they threw us in at the deep end.

The first lesson had been on a Saturday. Training restarted at 7.15 on Tuesday morning. I had two days to rest before the real onslaught began. Frank observed my attempts to stay immobile in a sleeping bag with amusement. Chris had stronger views. When he suggested a curry rice at the Murakami brothers' establishment around the corner he was annoyed that I rode my bike the hundred or so metres to the restaurant. As the Murakami brothers, cheery identical twins in their sixties, fixed identical bowls of curry with a topping of red pickle, Chris outlined the necessity of not using the course as an excuse for epic laziness whenever I wasn't training. 'But that's the only way I'll survive,'

I protested. 'Then you won't learn a thing,' he snapped back. Frank was conciliatory, 'He's only just started, give him a chance.' 'Yeah,' I joined in, 'give me a chance.' Chris stabbed at his curry rice with a none too clean Murakami spoon and said nothing.

I lay around in the apartment with aching limbs and wrote up my 'senshusei diary'. We had to hand the diaries in each month. They contained detailed explanations of each technique and an assessment of our feeling towards the training. At that point I couldn't summon any feeling so I wrote everything down in dry technical jargon.

By Tuesday morning I was still so stiff I could hardly climb the dojo stairs. Senshusei were forbidden to use the lift.

Once in the dojo we were assigned our cleaning tasks. Adam and I were given the toilets 'for at least the next three months'. It was definitely the worst job but it had one advantage, providing a chance to properly warm up by vigorously scrubbing the urinals and polishing the pipework. The toilet-roll dispenser lids had to have a mirror finish and so did the electrical socket covers. Adam mopped the floor. Paul had told us that cleaning was an integral part of the course. 'It's good training,' he said. 'I tell you,' said Adam, from his position behind one of the toilet bowls, 'we're going to be the meanest fuckin' janitors in the world when this is over!'

By the second class Adam was to my left and shaking with exertion. His whole body shook violently as he leaned out over his front knee, arms extended, as if in pathetic homage to the gods. We were doing a basic turning movement which starts in the *kamae* stance and ends with the body leaning forwards with almost all the body weight on the front leg. The arms reach forward too. The exercise is usually practised a few times before class. We had been at it for an hour, with long intervals holding the position over the front leg. People screamed with agony. Adam, Craig and Big Nick were the most vociferous – they were also the heaviest, which meant they were putting more strain on the front knee.

The howling and shouting was so bad that some of the *uchideshi* (live-in Japanese disciples) came out of the office to watch. They concluded we were the noisiest senshusei course ever.

By this time Adam's defiant shouts had become a low whimpering interspersed with the odd moan. I noticed a quantity of white spittle-like substance around his chin: it was the first time I'd seen anyone literally foaming at the mouth through physical exertion.

Shioda junior seemed unconcerned. From time to time he turned his back on us and looked out of the window at the building site below.

Stumpy, the Canadian *sewanin*, former senshusei and now course assistant, ran around trying to 'encourage' us. 'Use the pain!' he shouted. 'Ben, get up, don't cheat yourself!' The one constant chorus was: 'Come on, senshusei – where's your spirit!'

Adam's spirit was about to desert him. The moans became a yodel of anguish as his whole body rose up in a convulsive wave of shaking. His face had gone bright purple, though his hands were bloodless white. Then he fell to the floor, shook twice and lay completely still. Dead still. My God, I thought, he's died. He's had a heart attack and died.

Eerily, no one moved from their spots, though a certain lightening up was noticeable, as if Adam's supreme commitment had earned everyone else a holiday.

Stumpy shouted at Adam, who remained unmoving on the floor. Shioda was looking at the clock and had not noticed Adam's seizure. We had been told to never move without being ordered to move. I looked at Will. Will looked at Adam, who was inert and if dead, at least released from the physical pain we were all enduring.

My training partner, R'em, could stand it no longer. He broke ranks and rushed forward to Adam, who gurgled as R'em put him into the recovery position. Stumpy came over, followed by a bemused Shioda. All my frustration was directed at Shioda. Are you happy now? I thought. Now that you've killed someone? At the same time it was intensely interesting.

But Adam wasn't dead. Stumpy ordered R'em back to his spot and then lifted Adam up. 'Don't throw me out!' Adam gurgled deliriously. 'Let me stay! Don't kick me off the course!'

Adam was dragged to the side and Shioda ordered Stumpy to take him outside for some fresh air. But Adam wouldn't go. He clung on to the wall bars, whimpering and begging to be allowed to stay. He really believed that if he left the dojo they'd never allow him back in again. Shioda shrugged and Adam sat in a heap, his face covered in blotches.

Adam had given everyone a ten-minute rest. The last twenty minutes of the lesson passed in a kind of limbo, the howling reduced to a muted minimum.

Adam even joined us towards the end of the lesson, stumbling along with the proud dignity of a wounded veteran. After the lesson he told us how he had started to hallucinate, imagining that 'they' were coming to get him. 'They' were the dojo staff, whom he held in superstitious awe.

'They won't throw you out for fainting,' said Danny.

'That wasn't a faint,' retorted Adam. 'That was a colossal head rush of fear. That Shioda guy really scares me.'

'You went an amazing purple colour,' I said.

'I thought you'd died of a brain haemorrhage,' said Ben.

Adam looked thoroughly pleased at the suggestion. As a lover of attention he had certainly got more than his fair share. Even the teachers made comments. In a pep talk before classes, Stephan, the German assistant teacher, remarked on Adam's fortitude. In his Bavarian English he chided us for not trying hard enough: 'You know, like in ancient Greece, they had these wrestling matches. Sometimes to the death. Sometimes a guy died because he was trying so hard. And that guy would be the winner, not the other guy. Because you have to give everything. That's what the ancient Greeks believed, and it's true. And right now Adam here is trying the hardest, because he trained so hard he passed out. That is the right spirit. That is senshusei spirit.'

The next day, in Oyamada's class, Adam threw up. He rushed from the dojo with just enough time to make the basins in the toilets.

Dojo protocol was that you didn't need to ask permission to throw up. If you failed to make if off the mats you had to put your head inside your dogi top and throw up there.

In a Chida class Adam's nose exploded in a spontaneous nose bleed.

The first week ran into the second, and then the third, and it seemed that Adam had run out of attention-getting devices. He still moaned softly while we sat kneeling in *seiza* for any length of time. He claimed that a skateboard injury had left his knees skewwhiff and it made kneeling very painful. Probably it did, but by now everyone was beginning to have their own hurts and was becoming less sympathetic.

Suddenly Adam would pop up from a low to a high kneeling posture, spoiling the symmetry of the line. People groused and told him to sit down. The Japanese disciples were snickering and Adam was letting the side down. Reluctantly he would lower his weight back on to his knees, a true martyr to aikido, his unselfconscious whimpering echoing in the large airy dojo.

As Chris never tired of pointing out, pain is personal, pain is subjective. You should never judge another man's pain. Not only is the amount of pain subjective for any given injury, so different people are sensitive to different pains. It is difficult to conclude that someone has 'a high pain threshold' because he may tolerate a migraine without painkillers but scream blue murder if his finger is nicked by a penknife.

The area is further muddied by imagination – indeed, this is the major contributor to an over-reaction to pain. It's not the pain in itself, it's what the pain *means* which is so distressing.

It is one thing to be able to suffer pain. It takes a second level of stoicism to ignore the damage that the pain signifies.

People take hard knocks, break bones, cut themselves badly, tear ligaments, pull muscles in rugby, wrestling, surfing and horse riding, to name but a few sports. And they suffer these injuries with few complaints, usually anxious to be back doing the thing that did for them in the first place.

On the senshusei course it was different. The teachers emphasized that we would be in pain a lot of the time, indeed the foreign teachers (who were more masochistic than the Japanese) hinted that learning to live with pain was a large part of senshusei training. That created an atmosphere of clenched-teeth heroism, which had little to do with good aikido.

The Japanese teachers were more matter of fact. They gave no outward sign of pain or injury and expected none from us. But they were not judgemental. The Westerners chided us and scolded us, the Japanese simply ignored us and yet gave us no rest. What characterized the Western teachers was impatience. They wanted us to be good immediately. They wanted us to be tough immediately.

Perhaps it is the ability to choose that makes a wounded rugby player take to the field and laugh at his injury. We had no choice in the matter. The rule of the course was to keep training whatever the pain. We had yet to discover how bad an injury had to be before it earned you a holiday.

And we were scared of getting hurt too badly because we knew we'd have to be there the next day, and the next day, and the next day for a whole year. It was either that or give up. There was no halfway house.

As I lay awake at night, unable to sleep because of chronic knee and elbow pain, my mind worked to find ways to heal myself. I should walk less and cycle more, since cycling, with its low-strain, low-level exercise of the legs, had proved to be therapeutic. I should try Stumpy's patent hot towels on the knee joints before going to bed. I should massage the joints with Deep Heat. My mind raced on in the opposite of Zen mind

69

detachment and acceptance. This was not Zen mind, it was survivor's mind.

Others had their own ways of coping. After the first week, Nick the Armenian told Big Nick, his partner, that when the going got tough Big Nick's eyes seemed to pop out with intensity. 'You've got a real mad-dog look, all right,' agreed Paul, who hung around the tea room, spying on us, I thought.

'Mad Dog,' said Big Nick. 'I like that. You can call me Mad Dog if you like.'

There was a moment of embarrassment. It was a bit much to ask for a nickname, but no one said anything. We were all quite formal and polite at that early stage.

'Mad Dog – more like sad dog,' said Ben, as we went into the next class. I didn't say anything. I didn't feel secure enough in my own performance to start insulting other members of the group. Ben was not malicious, he just didn't care that much. He was a natural loner whereas my survival strategy included using the group and not fighting them. That was the plan, anyway.

Will was the other loner. From the start he had taken against Aga. 'What a bullshitter that guy is,' he complained to me. 'What's that shit he's always trying to sell? Nuskin? Forget that, have you seen how expensive their sport drinks are?'

Aga's main problem was that he wanted to be the leader. He wanted it so badly everyone caved in and let him become the unelected spokesman. His first idea was to push for an International Senshusei jacket. He brought in colour charts and lettering charts and pretty soon everyone had been bamboozled into agreeing to pay for expensive black bomber jackets covered in loud badges.

'I don't like Aga,' said R'em. 'I know his kind from the army. He is a selfish.' I was surprised by this because R'em rarely had a bad word for anyone. But Aga was a curious mix, because he did genuinely want the group to succeed. He was considerate of his partner, and yet you knew he would rat on you if a teacher questioned him. I began to revert to the playground way of

70

judging people – who'd blab, who'd try and get revenge, whom I could trust to be a 'best friend'.

Two weeks into the course and they decided to toughen us up a bit more. We'd suffered the slow anguish of muscular pain, now it was time to suffer the sharp pain of physical blows.

The strikes and blocks in aikido are meant to have force, but their role is to distract and soften up an opponent rather than to finish a bout, boxing style. Strikes in Japanese are known as *atemi*. Shioda senior, who learnt his streetfighting in the vice neighbourhoods of pre-war Shinjuku, had pronounced that 70 per cent of an actual fight was composed of *atemi*. Obviously it was no good having weedy civilian-style *atemi*, we were senshusei, so the *atemi* training would be hard.

Darren, the diffident Australian, was assigned the task of knocking our strikes into shape. Unlike Paul and Stephan Otto, the other assistant teachers, Darren sometimes admitted there were aikido moves he wasn't that good at doing. I knew that strikes wouldn't be one of them. Strikes were, in fact, one of Darren's specialities. Back home in Australia he'd practised for hours bashing his forearm against tyres, trees and even steel. 'Reckon it's pretty strong now,' he used to say. 'Probably break another man's arm with it.' He talked dispassionately about his forearm, as if it were a tool or club, a blunt instrument and not a part of his living, breathing, easily mangled human frame.

Repeatedly striking the forearm against a hard object, like a wooden post, or against another forearm, causes further calcification of the bone and a deadening of the nerves in the arm. Along the way you are supposed to discover the correct way to strike, which is with a relaxed arm. No one told us this because this lesson wasn't about learning to strike properly; it was about willingly inflicting pain on yourself. Not knowing the correct way, we all struck with arms as stiff as iron girders and, after the first few blows, it hurt, with a very uncomfortable dullness, like an extreme ache.

In karate, practitioners deform themselves by repeatedly

71

punching *makiwara*, or punching-boards. In kung fu they drive their hands into hot sand. Scarification and nerve damage follows in both cases.

Turning your hand into a nerveless club of battered flesh and bone seems a low-level approach to martial arts. It is the simplest way to improve the odds if one has little faith in speed and technique. Many tai-chi masters eschew it as primitive. Others find the prospect of chronic arthritis at the age of thirty hardly worth the trouble of growing a huge distended knuckle.

Forearm strikes are more sophisticated. A strong strike sets up the correct feeling for an aikido technique. Strike training is also a good way to build up resistance to pain. It is only of secondary importance that you can break down doors and decapitate Doberman Pinschers with one deft swing of the mighty forearm. Or so the theory goes.

Tesshu, as a traditional warrior, believed that any blows received were a good opportunity for self improvement. He instructed early morning tradesmen visiting his house to give him a punch 'anywhere on his body'. Eventually the tradesmen complained to Tesshu's brother that they were actually hurting themselves by having to punch Tesshu's hardened body.

We lined up facing each other. R'em's black eyes glinted with mischief and I couldn't help grinning at him. We swung our right arms behind our heads and smashed them together in front of us. This was a *shomen* strike, a front strike. Darren kept the count: '*ichi, ni, san, shi, go,*' and the strange half-strangulated noise he made when saying '*roku*' with his Australian accent.

We did ten on the right, then ten on the left. Then ten on the right and ten on the left. Every now and then R'em's bony wrist would hit mine. Fortunately it seemed to be hurting him just as much as me. I began to search for different parts of the arm which were relatively unbattered. Darren put a stop to this: 'It's not an elbow smash,' he said, and demonstrated again by clubbing Aga a few times for good measure.

R'em winced with pain and I struck him more lightly. 'No!

Harder!' he hissed. 'If we go easy now it will be too tough later on.' He sounded as if he was talking from experience, maybe the Israeli army did things the same way.

Darren looked on with wry amusement. My arms were bright red from the beating they had received. I noticed an ominous blue bubble about the size of half a tennis ball raising itself on the inside of my left arm. Had I burst a vein? No more looking, I decided, staring instead at R'em's face; too much looking at battered flesh is bad for morale.

We now did twenty strikes against our partner before switching and striking the next man. Another twenty strikes and we moved on again. I became aware of a roaring, bellowing noise from farther up the line. Aga was yelling demonically like a trainee soldier doing bayonet practice. The racket was infectious. It's easier to convince yourself it doesn't hurt when you are shouting. This is the distraction-method of fighting pain, the preferred Western way. The preferred Eastern way is detachment. But this was no time for Buddhist reflection. I started to yell too. What the hell, I thought, I might as well let some steam off.

I faced Will, who looked steadfast, and we gave each other a respectable beating. There was no time to even check my exploding veins before Aga was in front of me. He seemed to have completely lost control. He was not even keeping to the count called by Darren. His face was contorted and his eyes were streaming with tears.

Darren urged us on. Stumpy urged us on. We urged each other on. Stumpy urged us some more with his favourite battle cry: 'Come on, senshusei, dig deeper!'

I received a methodical hammering from the iron-hard arms of Little Nick, whom I also suspected of being a covert tree thumper. I wondered how much longer I could keep giving 'sincerely hard' thumps as opposed to cosmetic swipes. But I was saved from this dilemma. Darren told us to stop.

For some reason everyone started grinning at each other. Huge grins of lamentable stupidity as we stood there rubbing our sore arms. The only people not grinning were Little Nick and Aga, who was still weeping. I later became used to these collective displays of emotion, but at that time it was still strange. I think we were grinning to show each other the aggression was not 'really us'. In fact we were like schoolboys who become the best of friends after a punch-up.

After the trauma of the forearm-strikes lesson Danny suggested, in his simple, unaffected, but somehow batty way, it would be more 'spiritual' if the group leader (which circulated each week) said '*otagai ni rei*' (all bow) and at the moment of bowing we all shouted 'oos!' in a loud voice, bowed and slapped the ground in front of us. Surprisingly, everyone agreed. I agreed too, but not for spiritual reasons. It gave the end of a lesson something of a high point, drawing us together. We all slapped the ground in unison like worshippers at a spiritualist gathering in the deep South. It was a Western thing to do, an adaptation of a passive Japanese politeness into a form of rugby-team bonding. And how 'in time' the group floor slap was gave an indication of how much the group was 'pulling together'.

The saying of 'oos' at every conceivable occasion is common to most Japanese martial arts. To ignore an 'oos' is the height of bad manners. A senshusei 'oos' was supposed to be loud and full of vim. A frequent criticism of Adam was that his 'oos' lacked commitment. He had been taught Japanese by his wife and a certain feminine style of pronunciation infected all his communication in that language. The dojo disciples mimicked his way of speaking, finding it a hilarious joke, but the teachers were harsher. They made Adam 'oos' endlessly, but it still came out with a startled squeak as if someone had just pinched his behind.

After the collective bow and collective 'oos' we all ran – senshusei did everything at the double – to get the brooms to sweep the dojo floor, which was swept after every class. As we gathered our brooms people showed each other the terrific bruising on their arms. Ben's arms were already black, with sickly

74

yellow edging. I didn't want to look at the blue bubble, but I risked a quick glance and it had subsided a little.

Aga had completely recovered his confidence; he shamelessly re-established his leadership of the group. It was as if he had never wept at all. 'Yeah, I don't know what happened, somehow I just lost control of my eyes out there.'

My body was changing. I was changing. The physical shell that surrounded me was growing, hardening, getting more defined by the month. A residual layer of waistline had melted away, tendons began to stand out for the first time in years, muscles began to bulge. A quick pose in front of the mirror while cleaning the locker room: nice, very nice, the body as it should be, *Homo-activus* rather than his sofa-seated cousin *Homo-sedentarius*. I was careful not to be caught posing, though I knew we were all at it, checking ourselves out with ambiguous ardour, loving our new mirror images, the plates of muscle that connected our creaking joints together.

And I had grown to like pain. A certain sort of pain, a pain that was almost a pleasure. 'Not a brandy and cigars kind of pleasure,' as Mustard put it, 'but a pleasure all the same.' This pain was the pain you get from having a shoulder pinned to the ground at the end of an aikido move. Your partner held your arm and twisted it up behind your back, grinding your face further into the mat. The pleasure came from knowing that nothing was being broken, that you could 'take it', that the shoulder was being stretched, taken to its own limit and then released just when you tapped out on the mat. Only teachers ignored a tap on the mat, bad-ass teachers like Chino who liked breaking limbs, but partners never did; one rapid tap was enough to get you away from the worst kind of shoulder pin. I was learning. I was becoming a connoisseur of pain.

When one of Tesshu's old commanders heard that Tesshu had the temerity to start his own sword school he flew into a rage. He burst into Tesshu's house and beat him around the head

75

with his fists. Tesshu did not flinch, or even try to move away. Eventually the man tired of hitting Tesshu and left in a huff. When asked the reason for his non-resistance Tesshu explained: 'It is essential to harden our bodies and this incident was simply another form of training. It was a contest of will, matching the pain in my head with the pain in his hands. Since he was the one who gave up, I am the winner.'

Police Academy

'A Samurai's underwear should be made from the skin of a badger. This way he will not have lice. In a long campaign lice are troublesome.'

From the seventeenth-century Samurai handbook
Hagakure

It was a mistake to have forgotten my bike lights but it was an even bigger mistake to let Fat Frank ride on the back. His hundred-kilo bulk, perched on the fragile carrying rack, squashed my 'shopper' rear tyre flat. As the bike rolled forward it made a noise like chewing gum being unstuck from something. We were on our way back to Fuji Heights from the video store. It was a journey I'd made countless times.

There was a small hill before the railway level crossing and the relentless clanging sound of the alarm bell meant a train was about to pass through. The barriers were still up so I stood up on the pedals to get some extra power. Speeding down the hill I timed my zig-zag under the descending barriers perfectly. Then I saw the policeman. The nearest policebox was round the corner. Normally the police never strayed more than five metres from the entrance to the box. What he was doing on the other side of the tracks I didn't know. He moved imperiously into our path, his arm outstretched. He shouted a command to stop, and in my dojo-trained way I almost did; after all, riding without lights was an offence, but it was hardly major. Then I remembered Frank was on the back. Strictly speaking he was an illegal alien. If caught he'd be sent straight back to Iran. I stood up on the pedals again, swerved viciously and took off down a side alley. 'He's coming after us!' Frank shouted in my ear. Lumbering up

77

a slight incline I could hear footsteps and a voice behind us. 'Dry riverbed!' yelled Frank. We bumped up the curb and through a gap in a chainlink cyclone fence. Skidding down the concrete curved wall we started to bomb along the paved bed of the river, which was no more than a trickle. On this smooth downward gradient we soon picked up speed, winging our way under small bridges in almost total darkness. On and on we went until I was completely out of breath. We skidded to under a dark bridge. There was no sound of running. We returned to Fuji Heights following on foot the darkest alleys and back streets. Only when the flimsy front door was locked behind us did I at last relax, knowing we had escaped the long arm of the law.

Aga stuck his head into the tea room. 'The cops have arrived,' he said. 'And they look like a right bunch of poofs.'

The others charged out to have a look. I put my can of heated coffee into my footlocker so it wouldn't get stolen or knocked over, and followed them.

We looked into the dojo where the riot police were self-consciously warming up. Some of them wore brand new yellow-ish dogis, indicating their beginner status. Others wore judo or karate dogis. Karate dogis are thinner than aikido dogis; judo dogis have a seam down the back. Their kit gave some indication of their previous training in martial arts. All of them had to be at least first-degree black belt in two arts, or third-degree black belt in one art. Stripped of their Kevlar body armour, their plastic 'Samurai' helmets that intentionally mimicked old-style helmets, their nasty side prong batons and automatic pistols, they still looked fit and wiry. They joked continuously with each other, and when we introduced ourselves, greeted us warmly. They wanted to be friends, that much was obvious.

Mustard's mentor, the great Takeno, used to say that checking someone out, asking yourself, 'Can I take him or not?' is the first and weakest fighting posture a man can adopt. The second stage is when you ask yourself, 'What if he throws a punch, what if he tries to kick me? What do I do then?' The final stage, and the only really strong mental posture, is when you say with a smile on your face, 'Come on, try your hardest, give me your best shot.' As the Japanese shopkeeper says, '*Irasshaimase! Irasshaimase!* Welcome! Welcome! Come on in!'

We were all obviously still stuck at the first stage, for we bitched and gossiped about one thing: just how tough did the Riot Police think they were? When we hit the mats who would 'have' whom?

It was good to have something new to talk about in the tea room, where conversation had for quite a few days revolved around the disappearance of Craig. Craig's application for a cultural visa had not gone smoothly and he had been ordered by the authorities to return home to Australia to wait for his new visa there. It would mean missing a lot of training, maybe up to a month. If he stayed away longer than a month I seriously doubted that he would return to the course.

Ben, too, was having problems. In the ramen shop patronized mainly by the Isareli contingent he showed R'em and me his arms, which still had huge black bruises extending from the wrist to the elbow joint.

'I don't think I can take much more of Danny,' he said, as I ordered another round of soft drinks and a beer for myself. 'He keeps whacking me as hard as he can.'

'Whacking?' queried R'em.

Ben turned on him with sudden vehemence. 'Hitting me, *shomen* strikes, whack, whack, whack!'

'Hit him back,' said R'em mischievously.

'I can't. It hurts too much. Anyway, I don't want to.'

'It's whack or be whacked out there,' I said.

'It's not right. We've only just started. He used to be in the army. He's a bit mad . . .' Big Ben trailed off inconclusively.

'He ought to go a bit easy on those arms, at least,' I agreed. 'It's no use making them worse until they've got better. A bit.'

'Danny is a simple,' said R'em. 'He only knows his way.'

'He may be "a simple",' said Ben, 'but he's also a real arsehole.'

It was a mistake, but I decided to have a word with Danny. We were sitting in the tea room the following day after training.

'Coffee?' I asked.

'No thanks,' said Danny. He looked at me with his wide open face, his prominent teeth giving the impression of a perpetual grin. I once asked Chris what he thought of Danny. He paused and replied, 'Too many teeth.'

Danny was so straightforward it was easy to be straightforward back.

'How about laying off Ben a bit?' I said.

'It's good for him,' said Danny with finality.

'He's only a kid,' I said, disliking my complaining tone of voice. 'He hasn't done anything like this before. You should work up to it more gradually.'

'He's got to learn.'

'Look, you've been in the army. You've done martial arts before—'

'You lot talk like he's some kind of baby,' Danny was angry now. 'He isn't a baby, he's a fucking seven-foot giant ... and you lot, "his mates", have got it wrong. He signed up for this course.'

'But even so—'

'Even so what? The harder I am the better it is for him.'

'And for you too?'

'And for me too.' There was an uneasy silence. 'This is bollocks.' He got up and stormed out of the tea room. Oh well, I thought, I tried.

But Ben had not yet given up. Now the police had arrived we would have a chance to train with them, reducing the stress of working with the same person day after day.

Of the new course intake, I already knew Sato, Sakuma and Hal, the three civilian Japanese senshusei. Both Sato and Hal were skilled at aikido, especially Sato, who was a *nidan* (second-degree black belt).

Sato was twenty-five and wore a 1950s-style greatcoat, and a homburg on his shaved head. He looked like he was about to walk on to the set of a period martial-arts film set in nineteenth-century Manchuria. He had trained as an acupuncturist and also knew shiatsu massage and joint manipulation. When senshusei got injured they always went to Sato for advice.

Hal was a law student at Waseda University, who cut all his classes to study aikido. Waseda was the top private university, more social than Todai (the number-one public university) but still a difficult place to get into. His friends called out his name during lectures so that he would be credited with attendance. At night he copied up their lecture notes.

He was cheeky and puckish and came from Osaka, which in Japan is a licence to act the fool, since most comedians come from the Osaka area. It's a bit like coming from Liverpool in Britain. 'He carries himself like a boy prostitute,' said Fat Frank. Both he and Sato were doing what was necessary if they wanted to become *uchi-deshi* disciples and follow a career in aikido.

The third civilian Japanese, Sakuma, was not a policeman and yet it was inconceivable that he could be planning a career in aikido. Sakuma was fat. Not just overweight, but fat. He had a big body and a big head and was tall, maybe five foot ten or eleven. He had started aikido four months before the course began. He had asked to join the senshusei course, and the teachers, snickering behind his back, and sometimes openly in front of him, agreed to let him try out. He wasn't a policeman and he wasn't a *uchi-deshi*, but they let him join the police course because they believed he would drop out very quickly.

In Japan, people don't like to exclude you openly. If you're not wanted they will make life so difficult that you will leave out of choice. Sakuma's presence would give the more sadistic teachers and *uchi-deshi* a chance to show how to get rid of an unwanted student.

Sakuma fascinated me. Here was a kid, eighteen years old, who had a dream: to become tough and strong by training with the police. His handicaps were immense, both social and physical. Despite being a big kid you could see that he had been ignored or bullied at school – probably because he was the proverbial fat kid in class. He did not seem to mind the endless ragging he received later on, or being ignored completely, as he was at the start of the senshusei course.

At first, it seemed as though none of the Japanese liked Sakuma. The foreign senshusei, however, perhaps because of this, took to him immediately. Right from the start he had trouble keeping up with the rest of the police, who had trouble keeping up with the rest of the foreigners. We had a four-week headstart and it took two and a half months for them to catch up.

Sakuma became a kind of mascot for the foreigners. After a tough lesson people would pat him on his sweaty back, congratulating him on getting through the lesson.

True to their policy of weeding out the weak ones at the beginning the Japanese staff were particularly tough on Sakuma. The *uchi-deshi* kicked or slapped him when he failed to move fast enough.

I would later observe Fujitomi, a dwarf-like *uchi-deshi* who looked half-asleep most of the time (he had circulation problems and was always cold, like a lizard out of the sun), stand over Sakuma and his partner for a whole lesson. Every time Sakuma finished the technique and got up to scuttle back to his place he received an almighty kick up the arse, which sent him flying back down to the ground again. This made him late in starting the technique again and subject to more abuse from the teacher, who, of course, ignored the way Fujitomi was waylaying the fat kid. The arse kicking happened each time Sakuma did the technique. It continued for the whole hour and a half of the lesson. Sakuma did not give up. Nor did he become angry. He just kept getting up.

He was bawled out more often than he deserved, and was made an example of for mistakes that everyone made. Not once did I hear him complain. I never saw him shed tears – though with the quantity he sweated in the first month of the course it was hard to tell.

A Japanese who joins the *Kidotai* has to study a traditional martial art full time for a year. Those who select aikido come to the Yoshinkan dojo we attended. They give up most rights over their own lives. Only serious injury will get them a rest from training – but too long a break results in failing the course and consequently blowing their career prospects. One policeman who suffered a mild heart attack during training was sent back from the dojo with a curt 'weak' written on his report. There are no desk jobs for the *Kidotai*.

The dojo's brief from the higher echelons of the police force was to toughen the police up. The year's training was designed to be a kind of boot camp. The police encouraged the dojo to treat their young officers badly. Their attitude was rather like a parent sending their child to a prep school without central heating: make the kid suffer, and if he rings home sobbing and begging to be taken away you know that at last he's learning what life's all about. The police were not concerned parents who would complain if their offspring was maltreated.

There were many stories of police students being injured by the Japanese teachers. Chino Sensei, 'the country boy', had the worst record for dojo fractures. With his squat body, protruding jaw and bad teeth, Chino, at thirty-one, was a deeply feared teacher. He had broken the elbow of one police senshusei and the injured man had six weeks away from active training to recover. In the cop's first session back Chino broke the same elbow again.

Everyone was told they had to do a turn for the 'Please Welcome the Riot Police Party'. The assistant teachers got excited about the whole affair. I asked Paul what 'turn' he had performed when he had been a senshusei, two years before. 'I blew up a condom and put it on my head,' he said, grinning with slight embarrassment. 'Oh, that sort of turn,' I said, deciding immediately to write some kind of rude and amusing poem, something I'd tried and tested before.

Only Adam was determined to push back the boundaries of comedy with something new. He stood on his hands, put his dogi on upside down and put a tailor's dummy head between his legs. With Will as a bellowing instructor he performed the basic movements we did each day. The grotesque inversion made it very funny – the police loved it and so did the teachers.

We all sat in tracksuits in a big horseshoe made of low tables on the dojo floor, the teachers at the hoop end of the horseshoe. There was plenty of Japanese beer and I quickly had that pleasant expansive feeling of warmth inside me. The cop next to me, Onizuka, was also tight, his face brick red from the alcohol. Chino Sensei, the hardest nut in the dojo, was not drinking. He covered it up by carrying around a huge *sake* bottle and unsmilingly forcing drinks on cops and senshusei. Just as he liked inflicting pain on others he seemed to relish giving them hangovers as well.

Onizuka spoke little English, despite having studied it for five years. He was simply too embarrassed to speak a word of it apart from loan words like 'pitcher' and 'homerun'. He came from a family of fishermen in Kyushu, down in the south of Japan. He liked to laugh but would wait to see if I found it funny too. If I did then he would open his mouth and chortle and show me his teeth, which were in a terrible state. His first name was Shiroku, so I nicknamed him Sherlock, which pleased him. He told me one of his ambitions was to go to a desert island for a month with a huge stack of pornography. I could tell he had decided to be my friend. It was a little too arbitrary for me but I knew that was the way things worked in Japan – your friend was the person you were seated next to, and when you were no longer seated next to each other you were no longer friends. Usually.

Sherlock was called up to do a turn. He sang a rude song

which involved doing a series of gestures that all the cops knew but the foreigners didn't.

Another cop went up, and after pulling one arm out of his tracksuit sleeve, he linked the sleeves together so that it looked like he really had two arms outstretched and clasped together in front of him. The other arm he kept inside his tracksuit, and pushing it down the front of his pants he made a huge penis bulge that grew and grew as the outstretched arms massaged it. He sang an out of tune song as he did this.

Sato, the completely bald student of acupuncture, went up and sang a song in Chinese, which was a very classy thing to do.

The irrepressible Hal had dressed as a woman in a bra and panties. Though muscular he looked fetching. He pranced and pouted and stuck his bum out while singing a very vulgar song, about, as far as I could understand, the problems of menstruation. The finale came when he turned around and there was a tea-bag with a cardboard tag hanging down from his panties. Everyone roared with laughter.

Really, the entertainment was better than Japanese comedy on the TV, where comedians often break into giggles during the performance of a sketch. It's not nearly as professional as in the West. Sometimes, as a result, it's funnier, but usually it's not. I realized that the gap between professional and amateur was far smaller in Japan – Hal being every bit as good as the people on TV.

My poem, being mostly in English, went down like a lead balloon. Everyone just talked through it. There was no respectful silence, which is what, I think, would have happened in the West. I realized that the content of the performance was immaterial. It was simply performing that was the important thing – humiliating yourself in front of your fellows in order to build a stronger bond. At least you never got booed in Japan.

Because of this poem I had to live with being known as the poet. The midget *uchi-deshi*, Fujitomi, found it especially amusing. 'Yoshinkan Aikido Poet! It's too strange!'

85

In my 'poem' I introduced all the Westerners, except myself, in a series of rude limericks. When I'd finished, Chida, surprising me that he had followed the whole thing, said, 'What about you? Why do you spare yourself?'

Sakuma went up last. There was an extraordinary diffidence about the way he moved, stooping as he passed the last man at the end of the table to pick up a lighter and a cigarette pack. He lumbered up to the upturned crate on which people had been performing and surveyed the assembled crowd. There was a lot of noise: jeering and cheering that were indistinguishable from each other. Sakuma looked mournful but not hopeless. He fumbled for the cigarette pack and tore off the lid. Then, quite surprising everyone, he set fire to the lid and held the flaming cardboard between finger and thumb. There was a sudden silence as the crowd became transfixed by the fire.

Without waiting for the flames to die down he shoved the whole fiery mass into his mouth, where it stayed. He did not blow the smoke out of the sides of his mouth, or out of his nose. He just stood there on his crate looking sheepish, hissing gently from the flames extinguished by his wet mouth.

Until then I had been convinced that Sakuma would be the first to give up. But with no skill or artifice the man had eaten fire. Just to be accepted he had burnt the whole of his mouth. And the doleful doggedness of him made me reconsider: Sakuma was made of tougher stuff than everyone imagined.

After the party Paul arranged the number-two party. In Japan there are usually a succession of parties in one evening, the constant change of location serving to thin the numbers down to the serious hard-core.

We went to a small bar near the dojo. Ben and Danny had temporarily signed a truce over the excessively hard arm strikes they were giving each other. As Danny had predicted, Ben had become stronger and could now give quite as good as he got.

Everyone was stormingly drunk, the more so for an impromptu display of comic pro-wrestling by two of the cops before the party left the dojo. Indeed, we were all getting a little too excited and Chida appeared and gave one word of command. There was immediate silence in the dojo, everyone shocked to hear, in such a short burst, such a completely commanding voice from such a seemingly gentle figure. The noise stopped. Then he smiled to let us know there were no hard feelings. But it had done the trick and we quickly left the building.

In the bar Oyamada Sensei spoke his queerly accented but competent English. He applied locks and grabs to Hal, who squealed with pain, but with a kind of do-it-again complicity. He also applied the same painful locks to Sato, whose expression never changed however painful the arm lock was.

Several glasses of beer were knocked over. Hal whispered something into Oyamada's ear. Oyamada Sensei then turned to Paul and asked with great seriousness: 'Paul, do you like cunnilingus?'

'Er, yes, it's all right ... how about you?' Paul was always a little stiff and on his best behaviour around the Japanese teachers.

'Yes, I like it,' said Oyamada, a slick sheen of sweat on the bald front of his head. Then he turned to Hal and tortured him some more.

Hal was fully living up to his reputation. He told us Sato was 'Cherry boy for two years!' Sato said, 'My partner is crazy!' and rapped Hal playfully on the head with his knuckles. Hal screamed so Oyamada punched him a few times for good measure. And then, as an afterthought, he twisted Hal's nipple through his shirt. Hal obligingly wriggled and squealed for help. 'Are you cherry boy too?' Hal asked Paul.

'No, but I bet you are,' said Paul.

Oyamada revived for a moment from the semi-stupor he had fallen into. 'Do you like cunnilingus, Paul?' he asked again.

'It's all right,' Paul repeated defensively.

Oyamada grinned benignly and then his head lolled forward. Hal pretended to chop him on the back of the neck while he wasn't looking.

Then we settled the bill. As Oyamada took his leave we all bowed respectfully to him. When his back was turned Hal pretended to kick him up the arse. Then he made a series of rude hand gestures at the departing back of the sadistic teacher.

'Did he hurt you?' I asked.

Hal rolled up his shirt in answer. His nipple was severely bruised.

'He's a bastard,' said Hal. 'He always hurts you.'

At the number-three party, in a noodle shop, I talked with Sato. He told me I was frightened to use power. 'There are two kinds of foreigner,' he said. 'One is frightened of power and the other loves it too much. In Japan it is more complicated. Here we have *form*. By learning form we can forget power until we are ready to use it. But you must not be frightened.'

The cops' nickname for Sato was 'Grandad' because of his old fashioned way of talking. I once saw him wearing a 'legalize marijuana' t-shirt. His sister had brought it back from California. I asked him if he knew what it meant. 'Oh yes,' he said. 'But I have no interest in these things.'

I asked him why he never let pain show on his face.

'If I show pain, I feel a different kind of pain, a kind of pain that tells me to stop. But if I keep a clear face then the pain is not so bad. We called it "the face of Kannon", a face like the Buddha.'

When we trained with the cops the Japanese teachers liked to mix foreign and Japanese senshusei as partners. If you weren't quick you'd end up with Sakuma, because no one wanted to train with him. It wasn't that he was especially bad, though he was, at the beginning, appreciably worse that everyone else, it was just that you'd be forced to partner him in all his humiliations at the hands of the *uchi-deshi*.

Most of the time I trained with Sherlock. He liked training with me because, unlike Little Nick and Mad Dog, I did techniques only as hard as he did them to me. Sherlock didn't want to get hurt and neither did I. Whenever a teacher walked by we'd both crank it up a little, and then we'd relax again. Sherlock could take punishment when it was necessary, unlike Gimpy, who was always getting hurt. We knew the cops' names, but somehow their nicknames, once given, stuck fast.

Gimpy wore bandages on both wrists. He was the weediest-looking of the cops – he looked like a college student. His real name was Yamaguchi, but he became known as Gimpy, or Elfman's brother.

Elfman, Fujie-san, had an oddly pointed head and large ears. He was nervous and earnest. He was often partnered with Gimpy. Together they were the Elf twins. Elves, but also cops, and though their faces were often creased with pain, they never gave up.

Because their spots were near mine I often ended up with the Elf twins when I wasn't training with Sherlock. They were good to train with because they were not obsessed by strength and power. They just wanted to get the form right.

Other senshusei held the Elf twins in scorn. By now the reverential note had left conversations about 'the Riot Police'. Soon they were just 'the cops'.

I don't know what I'd been expecting before the course – six-foot man mountains covered in scars and bulging muscles? Hard-eyed cops who'd spent too long with people on the wrong side of the law? No-nonsense tough guys like Paul? This bunch were disciplined all right, and as a group they were more impressive than us. But man for man they weighed less and comported themselves with more irony, less committed *madness*

The physical frailty of Elfman and Gimpy was deemed their fault in some way. We were tacitly encouraged to 'beat up a cop today'. But even Riot Police aren't indestructible, and because of Gimpy's weak wrists it was compassionate to take it easy on him.

Little Nick disagreed. Whenever he got the chance he gave Gimpy a good beating. Some teachers were complicit in this. During one lesson Gimpy was reduced to doing techniques on one side, as not only his wrist but also his elbow had been damaged in some way. The technique we were doing was *hijishime*, an elbow lock, the only technique in aikido where the lock goes against the joint. In this technique the elbow is extended and pressure put on the back of the arm. If you don't escape fast enough the elbow can be broken or badly strained.

Chino was teaching, walking around and from time to time putting his killer lock on people. I was training next to Little Nick and Gimpy when I heard an audible crack from Gimpy's good elbow. He broke off and shook his arm in pain. Chino saw everything and grinned his gap-toothed smile at Little Nick and gave him the thumbs up. The elbow was not broken, but for a week it was in a sling. This was the stuff Chino wanted to see.

Chino was not criticized for this. All teachers, apparently, went through a 'tough' phase and the cops were considered fair game by everyone, including their paymasters.

Even Ando the merciful had once been known as 'the little devil' (it sounds better in Japanese) sparing no one in his aggressive style of training. After he got married, Ando became merciful, and it was always a relief when he was teaching. The shortest and fastest of the teachers, his freestyle aikido looked similar to Kancho's. Ando liked jokes; when Chino was a disciple and gave him a lift on the back of a bicycle, Ando put his hands over Chino's eyes as they plummeted down a steep hill. Of all the teachers only Ando had any kindness in his face.

Because the cops were victimized they looked after each other very well. Perhaps the victimization was designed to bring out this group spiritedness, but the 'professional' aikidoka sneered at the way the police spared themselves.

There was no doubt the foreigners were more obsessed about training than the Japanese senshusei. The atmosphere of obsession was fostered by the teachers. It was transmitted by example and by the encouragement of the *sewanin* assistants, Mike 'Spike' Kimeda and the big-boned 'Stumpy' Stuempel.

In Japan obsessive behaviour is normal. But it is a low-key

kind of obsession, very self-effacing. It isn't gung-ho, Western style. And whereas the Japanese could be hard and at the same time friendly, the foreigners could not. To be friendly meant you weren't serious.

The foreign senshusei were more at sea than the cops. At least the cops knew what *budo* meant. Literally, *budo* means 'the way of war', but it has connotations far beyond this. It connotes a way of life involving sacrifice, honour and pain. The cops knew about *budo* and rejected it. Even Kancho had said, 'Modern aikido is more physical exercise than *budo*.' But the foreigners hankered after the old ways, the pain and the honour. They wanted bona fide *budo* or nothing.

Fat Frank and I decided to go out to Enoshima Island. It was only a few hours by train and the walk across the causeway to the island reminded me of childhood visits to Mont St Michel in France. We climbed past the many shrines to the peak of the hill on the island and drank a beer overlooking the waves crashing on rocks beneath us. 'Where do you think the next land is?' asked Frank.

'Japan – I think we're on the curve of a bay here.'

'No way – the next land from here is America. California.' He pronounced California with languorous relish, as if emphasizing its promised-land status.

We called in on some friends who lived on Chigasaki beach next to Enoshima. They were Japanese friends, a brother and sister, and their father lived with them. He was as close as you come to a 'macho' Japanese – hard drinking, ebullient, always the boss. Walking back with him from a late-night sushi bar, Frank, who was a few steps in front, was not his usual observant self. Perhaps it was all the *sake* we'd been drinking, but he didn't notice the policeman until he was pulled to one side by his sleeve. Without a pause Father butted in with his cheery laugh. 'What are you doing?' he demanded of the young copper. 'This man went to Cambridge University! Cambridge University, do you hear?' The policeman gave a sycophantic smile and wished us a good evening. As we walked away Frank whispered to Father, 'I never went to Cambridge.'

'Didn't you?' said Father, his eyes wide with mock astonishment, and then the old man started laughing hard and loud, not stopping until we'd walked all the way home.

Zen and the Art of Being Really, Really Angry

'Confucius was a sage because he had the will to become a scholar when he was fifteen years old. He was not a sage because he studied later on. "First intention, then enlightenment."'

From the seventeenth-century Samurai handbook
Hagakure

Fat Frank was going further afield these days, following his own routes around the best garbage pickings in town, weaving through high-income neighbourhoods at dawn in a leather jacket with a torn lining that became one huge pocket for the convenient stashing of finds. One day he came back with the complete works of Mishima bound up with string, the outer copies damp and wrinkled from the early morning dew. On another occasion he found a pachinko machine that only needed to be plugged in to work – the books stayed but the machine was too big and had to go. A constant theme was his lighter collection, which numbered hundreds; mostly plastic, some grotesque – one that Chris favoured was puce and moulded with knobbles, like a bizarre sex accessory. None of the metal lighters were gold, though he did have several engraved Zippos, but again nothing worth very much (I despaired that he'd ever find anything of real value). Every few months there were news stories of housewives who found fortunes, hundreds of thousands of yen, in manilla envelopes left on dustbin lids, destined for collection by some official in the continuous brocade of bribery that is an indissoluble part of Japanese public life. Maybe Frank would get lucky one day and solve all our problems with cash.

Chris had found a new niche for himself as a 'character' model. He answered an ad in the *Tokyo Journal* and visited a model agency that only wanted 'Western character models' (i.e., bizarre and distinctive looking). At the interview young people with perfect figures and film-star looks were turned away as being 'too common', but they welcomed Chris with open arms. With his beard, round glasses and bald head Chris was perfect for roles as a doctor in vitamin adverts or as an engineer in car commercials. Then he landed a plum job: as a Jesuit missionary in a Japanese docudrama series. In one scene all his converts were crucified by the local Samurai warlord. The director told Chris to act 'suitably shocked' when he heard the news.

Meanwhile Frank was pursuing his own path to martial-arts excellence. He had gone back to the source and examined Kancho's autobiography for tips. Kancho claimed that one of his most significant insights came while watching the way a goldfish swam through a group of fish coming towards it. The goldfish never retreated, relying instead on its ability to move from side to side but always keeping forward momentum. That is why there are no backward steps in aikido. He also commented that a goldfish starts every move by turning its head in the direction it wants to go. 'If you want speed, and balance, use your head to start the turn,' said Kancho.

He also trained with large dogs. The dogs were taught to keep on attacking him as he swiftly avoided their lunging, spinning out of the way and cuffing them – how hard, history does not record. (Not too hard, I hope. It's one thing to have beaten up men in pursuit of ultimate fighting superiority, but it's a little shameful to have beaten up dogs as well.)

Frank talked about getting a dog. Wanly, without conviction. He knew he was on delicate ground. 'Even a small dog is absolutely out of the question,' said Chris. He was right. Where would a dog live? Under the sink with all the roaches?

Then he produced an oblong fish tank with only a slight crack which he'd mended with black masking tape. 'How about a fish, lads?' It was time to put *kingyo no mitori geiko* (goldfish watching) into practice.

There was a friendly bear-like geniality to Fat Frank. I had never seen him angry, though Chris warned me it was a terrible sight when it happened. Cited as evidence was 'the battle of the gas station', where Fat Frank had singlehandedly defended his relatives from a lorryload of disgruntled road menders at an Iranian petrol station. Armed with iron bars and spades the road menders had been stunned into submission when Fat Frank tore someone's arm off. 'Tore it off?' I questioned Chris, who had been in Iran at the time but not actually present at the fight. 'Put it this way,' he said. 'It was so dismembered, one shoulder was in the other armpit.' Frank was modest about his anger and described the battle in terms of necessity rather than violence: 'When this guy swung his bar I knew I had to jump higher than I'd ever jumped before, and I did.' The thought of Fat Frank's hundred-kilo bulk leaping high into the air was indeed terrible to contemplate.

We had the tank, which stood on the dresser, requiring us to move all Chris's papers on to a chair, so now all we needed were some fish. Ben solved the problem for us at a local street fair. Using his immense height he was able to lean right over the counter of a stall that gave goldfish as prizes if targets were knocked down with corks shot from an airgun. He held the gun at arm's length, only inches from the target, and scored a successful knockdown. At a normal distance the airguns were so leaky and ineffectual that it was pure chance if a wayward cork hit a target. The prize was a sickly looking goldfish we immediately named 'Little Kancho'. Ben won two more healthier specimens for Kancho to 'fight' against before he was banned from the shooting stall.

Back at Fuji Heights goldfish watching became a compulsive pastime. Kancho, the real Kancho that is, was right: goldfish don't swim backwards – but they do swim back and forth a hell of a lot. They sometimes brush fins, but they have a loathing for

95

collision. They swim as if they will collide, but they never do. Humans, on the other hand, often have a need to 'show' that they won't collide by giving a wider than necessary berth to someone moving towards them. Over-reaction is as bad as under-reaction – it spoils the organic nature of a conflict, breaking your connection to your opponent, inserting 'thought' where your best guide is instinct.

Tesshu claimed he was at last fully enlightened when 'no-mind' or instinct, rather than intellect, became his sole guide in swordsmanship and in life. This lesson had been taught not by a warrior but by a successful businessman who told him: 'Merchants should never be timid or concerned with victory or defeat, profit or loss. If one only thinks about making money, his heart pounds with anticipation; if he fears taking a beating, he will shrink and cower. Nothing can be accomplished by worrying about such things. It is best to keep one's heart clear, face the work at hand directly, and act boldly.'

Darren gave a modern update on this: 'I generally act as if I'm going to get hit and then I'm surprised when it doesn't happen. To be over-worried about being hit is the wrong frame of mind.'

Sometimes what was said only sank in long after it was heard, in situations unconnected with its utterance. At other times, an event and some words relating to it occurred close together, and a lesson was learnt.

The greatest difference from a Western lesson was the one-shot lesson, where you did one thing to excess. I think now that it was the one-shot lessons that really changed us. They used pain, and relief from pain, to etch the subject being taught deep into the brain, so that you could never really forget it. Pain heightens the memory of a lesson, enabling you to relive it in detail. In the West a lesson is just information; in Japan it is an experience.

'It was over 400,' said Little Nick.

'Maybe,' said Mad Dog (after all, the higher it was the better for everyone), 'but I made it 350.'

'It was 328,' said Will, trying to look backwards over his shoulder at the raw flesh in the middle of his back.

'Nah! It was more than that,' came a chorused reply. It had to be more than that.

We had just finished the '600' back breakfall class with Chino Sensei. When Chris, Fat Frank and I started aikido we couldn't even do one.

The back breakfall is simply falling backwards on to the arse and then the back. As your bottom hits the ground you kick your legs up and this takes the force out of the fall. Some momentum has to be retained though so that you can stand up again in one smooth move. The getting up requires the feet to pop under the buttocks as you spring to a standing position. Swinging the arms helps you to spring up easily. Done quickly, back breakfalls are very tiring.

I'd worked up to about 100 during the past few months and that, I felt, was my absolute limit.

Chino gave the count and we started: '*ichi, ni, san shi, go, roku, shichi, hachi, kyu, ju*'. He got to ten and started again. I squinted surreptitiously at the clock. Forty minutes to go.

After ten minutes people were beginning to tire. The cops started to shout encouragement to each other:

'*Yoshi.*'

'*Faito.*'

Sakuma, I saw, had a blood spot on the back of his dogi. This and the backside were the parts which were rubbed raw by continuous back breakfalling.

'*Faito.*'

The direct translation of the ubiquitous Japanese word of encouragement, '*gambatte*', is 'fight on'. This had entered Japanese sports in preference to *gambatte*. But in its loan-word form it was pronounced '*faito*', which sounds amusing to native English speakers. It was a sure sign that the foreigners were making fun of their Japanese counterparts when they joined in the calls of *faito*. This time no one did.

Chino was a master at establishing a group rhythm. All the Japanese excelled at this, and when a group rhythm has been established your endurance is multiplied six or seven fold. No Western teacher could establish a group rhythm. Paul was particularly good at the opposite – constantly breaking any natural rhythm that was set up.

I was sure that one reason the Japanese sensei liked mammoth training sessions, where two hundred press-ups or an hour of *hajime* were done, was that during these sessions a rhythm could take over. Somewhere, dimly, I glimpsed mastery at aikido as the ability to use rhythm to your advantage: fit your defence around the rhythm of another's attack, or make your attacker dance to your rhythm.

Twenty minutes in and I had lost count. My backside, just above the crack, was decidedly sore. We were going neither fast nor slow. Chino had established a killer rhythm. Most senshusei were keeping up. Sakuma's back had a huge sun of red on it. Will, too, I saw was bleeding profusely.

I watched Chino as if hypnotized, and then I suddenly noticed – he was cheating! When he went down he spread his feet apart. This meant that in the initial squat his backside would almost touch the ground, so taking all the strain off it hitting the ground and rubbing raw. When he stood up his feet were together, which was why I'd missed his trick earlier.

I immediately copied his style. It was much easier. But when I snapped my feet together coming up I caught my balls between my legs. Nasty!

I went back to the 'correct' way, concluding that Chino must have had the rumoured lack of endowment down below. Either that or he had mastered the ancient Sumo trick of sucking the testicles into the body at will.

Fifteen minutes to go and my legs felt like jelly, close to total collapse. Only the rhythm kept me going, and the sight of Sakuma, whose face was a river of sweat, his body bouncing as it hit the mat, a prelude to the frantic wobble that was his way of getting up.

All the cops and the foreign senshusei were groaning and grunting; there was blood on the mats and sweat pouring off everyone's face. Then it happened. Five minutes before the end something clicked inside me. For the first time I felt my mind concentrating more and more inwards, focusing on a tiny point with increasing accuracy, rather than diffusing, spreading and flailing. A new door had been forced open in my brain and I knew I could keep going and going.

The clock chimed but Chino did not stop. The tension was palpable. How long would he overrun the lesson? After each fall Sakuma was now struggling to his feet with pitiful desperation. A trickle of blood ran from his feet down between the two mats in front of me.

Two minutes over, three minutes over, then, at long last, Chino gave the order to stop. There was a sort of shuddering down through the gears as everyone came to a halt. He told us to relax. Immediately my legs collapsed. We crawled off the mat and knelt and bowed to Chino in relief.

In the changing room Danny's dogi trousers were held up for inspection. The arse part was suggestively bloody.

'You been up to something with Aga you haven't told us about?' said Mad Dog. Locker-room humour – all part of the package.

In one lesson Chino worked us incredibly hard for an hour and twenty minutes. Then he ordered everyone to lie down and look at the ceiling. It was pure bliss. It was a dream come true – the chance to actually rest in a lesson. Adam said later, 'I was sweating so much that when we lay down my eye sockets filled with water – it was like looking out of a goldfish bowl.' Ten minutes of heaven. Someone actually moved and Chino ordered them to lie still. After it was over he said simply: 'When you work, work. When you rest, rest.'

*

A break in training came when we made the annual pilgrimage to Iwama, Ueshiba's shrine, aikido dojo and farm. Next to the farm was a mountain. I'd read about it in Kancho's memoirs. It was on the steps going up the mountain at Iwama that the young *uchi-deshi* had fought with swords at midnight. Wearing white '*banzai*', *hachi-maki* towels on their heads as their only visual guide they had cut and thrust in the perilous stepped darkness.

'Steps up a mountain is a bit funny,' said Ben, when I told him the story.

'It's probably a Japanese molehill,' said Will. '*Yama* means anything from a slight bump to Mount Fuji.'

'No, this is a real mountain,' I said, though I had no proof.

I had imagined a place far more rural, but as the train to Iwama passed further and further through the suburban country-side north of Tokyo I slowly realized this was as rural as it got. No matter how far you went from Tokyo it seemed the countryside always looked more the same than different. Grey buildings with faded red signs, dusty grey-green trees, small roads busy with cars, masses of overhead wires, more grey buildings, an absence of wind, more overhead wires. Wherever you went the overwhelming impression was of the overhead wires.

I sat with Ben and Will on the train and Ben returned to a constant theme: how the whole course was just brainwashing.

'But you knew that at the beginning,' I countered.

'I know, but it's different from how I imagined.'

'How?'

'It's working. I didn't think it would work, but it's working. I think I'm becoming a violent bastard.'

'Don't worry,' said Will, 'you're still a wimp.'

It was a compulsory trip for the foreign senshusei, but because it coincided with payday for the police they were allowed not to come. For some reason the police had to appear in person to collect their pay and this once-a-month holiday was the cause of wry resentment amongst the foreigners.

When we got to the station we had to run from the platform

to the farm, which had now become an aikido centre. The farm was a cluster of low wooden buildings surrounded by cedars and pines that gave off a pleasant odour of resinous sap. There was a kind of longhouse for a dojo, with sheds and outhouses with steamed-up windows – kitchens and dormitories, I guessed. The senshusei were the only people in suits.

Half an hour later R'em arrived on his motorcycle incongruously dressed in a suit and a pair of motorcycle boots.

Darren was the assistant teacher in charge and he was grimly annoyed: 'Where the hell have you been?' he said.

'I ride my bike,' he grinned.

'You were meant to come by train.'

'I know.' R'em continued to grin.

'Stop fucking grinning about it.'

R'em looked abashed, though I doubt if he knew the word 'grin'.

R'em had been late for training once. They made him kneel in *seiza* for an hour as a punishment. If you were late three times on the course you were out. But R'em never made excuses to the teachers. He reserved his excuses for us.

'I think today no training so I don't wake up. Then, oh my god, it's eight o'clock. I have to take the bike. 180, 190, I go.'

'How's the suit?' I asked. I had lent him a suit as R'em didn't have one himself.

'Look at this,' he said. 'The button is coming off. But don't worry, I'll get it fixed and I'll get the suit cleaned. It will be like new.'

I found myself thanking him for wearing my suit.

'How long do we have to wait before lunch?' asked Little Nick.

'About two hours,' Spike smirked.

There was nowhere to sit down, so we had to spend the two hours standing in a crowd with the other aikido pilgrims, watching a Shinto ceremony in front of the pagoda-like shrine.

Priests in white robes intoned and warbled with the 'flat'

harmony of traditional Japanese music. They swished and bowed and placed cedar sprigs on a small altar. Each sprig necessitated more intoning. When I thought it was all over they started to take the sprigs one at a time off the altar. I realized with horror that we would have to continue to stand through the whole ceremony in reverse.

There was a little light relief. Ueshiba's son and heir to the leadership of the Iwama sect, Kisshomaru, performed aikido with no real attacks or throws.

'It's fake,' said Little Nick, disappointed. And he was right.

After an hour and a half, one of the Shinto priests got cramp from kneeling down in *seiza*. He had to get up and shake his leg out. It was the first time I had seen a Japanese person suffer in *seiza*. 'It warms your heart to see that kind of thing, doesn't it?' said Will.

The shrine shelf was overladen with fruit and vegetable offerings. Halfway through the ceremony a large cantaloupe fell off and hit the floor. 'Oops!' said Adam, 'the shrine had to do a dump!'

And even when the ceremony seemed to be over there was always just one more chant, one more sprig of cedar to lay on the altar, which I now knew meant there would have to be removal time budgeted in as well. In a way the whole thing was like a metaphor for the senshusei course, for my time in Japan: just when you think it can't get worse, it does. Then, suddenly, it's all over.

But truly, nothing goes on for ever – not even a Shinto ceremony. By mid-afternoon we were sitting under the pleasant trees at the back of the farm eating a packed lunch that contained shrimps, which R'em couldn't eat for religious reasons.

After lunch I set off to find the mountain. The ceremony had been an empty experience for me. I hoped to gain something more from visiting the famous mountain. Fortunately it was signposted, and I trailed along roads and through bamboo groves until I reached the foot of a hill.

It was definitely more of a molehill than a mountain. I started to jog slowly, my waterproof rubbing noisily, change rattling deep in one pocket.

Climbing up even the most obvious-looking path, I was not surefooted. I was pausing to find suitable places to walk, not my usual spirited canter up any old mountainside. Even at this pace I was passing other walkers: families in red plastic, the children carrying Mickey Mouse rucksacks; middle-aged men with metal-framed glasses and long camera lenses; an attractive couple, unsuited to rough terrain and looking, I suspected, for a leafy and private glade for their own enjoyment.

After half an hour my lungs, heart and whatever other organs are involved had 'clicked in', were working smoothly together. I had caught the rhythm of this particular hillside. I had remembered my old, quick way of ascending. Surprisingly, I think it was aikido that had spoiled my balance. There is a natural jazz involved in fast, difficult footwork. There's no time to think, or rather no time for thoughts to travel from the feet to the head and back again – by that time the square of turf has crumbled, the stone slipped, the exposed cable of root snapped. The feet have to think, have to be forced to think by putting them off balance. Then one foot restores balance, pushing the other off balance a little, and so it goes on. If you search painstakingly for a firm foothold, like a pensioner on an icy path, each time you will find disappointment and make no progress, or very slow progress. You have to engage in the dynamic of ascent. The best analogy is running on duckboards across swampy ground: move, move, move or drown.

Aikido exercises, which were a prelude to aikido, the raw, pure aikido which knows no rules except the natural laws of the body's movement, these exercises practised *ad infinitum*, repeated to the point of tedium and out the other side, had conditioned my mind into searching for stability, sure ground, a flat-footed resting place. There are no such places in the hills.

To learn the principles of running free, perhaps you need flat, safe ground. The safe ground of aikido was the form we so endlessly practised. It had made me cautious. This was the lesson of Kancho's mountain, force yourself on through caution to the outer edge. Not as far as folly, the wide scary zone of pure risk (I'd been there in my rock-climbing days; pushing luck to its furthest extent and then further), but closer in, where caution is forgotten and *involvement in the fun of it* kicks in.

At the top, where there was a Buddhist temple, I searched for the famous steps. I found them on the other side of the hill. They led down to a car park. There were hundreds of them, very steep, and the ledge of each step was narrow. Trees over-shadowed the steps making them damp and shady. The steps followed to some extent the contours of the hill, now steep, now more shallow, but always sharp edged with only enough room for one foot.

I imagined Ueshiba and Kancho and the other students dashing up the steps with white headbands and brandishing swords. You'd have to be mad to do something like that. Mad, or really into it.

I stared down the steps and then out across the countryside crisscrossed with power lines. Despite the trees all around me the countryside below looked littered, like a park at the end of a summer's day. There were no more clues at the top of the mountain. Descending the tiny steps was hair raising. I forced myself down them at speed, my legs just short of a tangle. I went faster, so there wasn't enough time to think. Then I was moon leaping, taking several steps at once. I slipped twice but had enough momentum to regain my footing. At the bottom I met Ben.

'Is that where they fought, up there?' he asked.

'Yes,' I replied.

'Is it worth going up?'

'Your feet are too big,' I said. 'This mountain is for size sevens and below only.'

*

Towards the end of the 1930s Kancho became caught up in the colonial ambitions of Japan. Attached to a military commission, but still a civilian (in Japan at that time there was such a rank as a civilian colonel), he arrived in Shanghai to look after obscure business interests.

Before leaving he went to his master, Morihei Ueshiba, to pay his respects. Ueshiba told him: 'Shioda, do not let anyone defeat you. What I taught you – now put it into practice.' For Kancho this was like receiving his '00' rating – licensed to kill. 'Nothing could have made me happier – until now Sensei had always been unfailingly rude to me. For the first time he recognized me.'

Prowling around Shanghai, Kancho described it as a place where 'murders were common and part of everyday life'. As oppressors, the Japanese were not that popular and Kancho must have felt this. One night he got into a quarrel with a street-corner pimp in the French quarter. He was out drinking there with his *kohai*, junior colleague, who was also a martial artist. What the quarrel was about Kancho does not explain, but the argument escalated and soon the pimp's gang had chased Kancho and his friend into a bar.

'I realized that to start a fight in such a place meant that we could not leave alive unless we won. For the first time it was a case of fight or die.'

Trapped in the bar, Kancho held the door shut as they heard steps hurrying down the stairs towards them. 'Holding tightly on to a beer bottle I controlled my breathing. When the first opponent was on the point of opening the door I pulled it open first and he fell forward, losing his balance. I hit his head as hard as I could with the bottle. Then I thrust the broken bottle up into his face and twisted it. Immediately the next man entered and aimed a kick at me. I moved sideways and brought my open hand down on his moving leg. Such a counter requires perfect timing, and this was the case. He went crashing to the floor, groaning in agony. I learned later that his leg was broken.

'Two people were under control already and at that moment

a strange sensation arose. Inside my head a voice was repeating, "You are strong. No one can defeat you." I gained a kind of absolute confidence and a strange calm came over me.

'There were still two attackers. My *kohai*, who was expert in judo, took one and I took the other. I was so calm I became aware of the attacker's intention. It was as if I could not lose, knowing, almost by premonition, what he was about to do. He came straight at my face with a punch. I moved inside his body to avoid the punch and in a variation of shihonage [a core aikido technique] I locked his elbows and shoulders. I threw him hard and there was a sound of splintering bones.

'The last man was being thrown by my junior, but every time he was thrown he just got up again and carried on the attack. I stepped forward and in a powerful jump I punched directly into his rib cage. This one strike was particularly effective as I had my centre well forward in total harmony with the punch. From this one impact he was destroyed and did not get up from where I had felled him.

'Surveying the scene I found it hard to believe what had happened. Body and mind had been in total accord with technique and through an explosion of "*kokyu rokyu*" [concentrated power requiring correct breathing] I had seen the truth of aikido. At that moment I thought, "I made aikido mine."

'This, truthfully, was my aikido enlightenment.'

Back at the dojo, another religious experience was in store for us a few days after our visit to Kancho's mountain. Somehow I knew something was up just by the way 'the Terminator' strode purposefully in, bowed to the shrine, swivelled and bowed to us, who were already kneeling in anticipation. I had become hypersensitive to the sound of each teacher's walk, reading good or bad moods into the very rhythm of their footfalls. It was important that the teacher wasn't angry, so I looked for signs to reassure me that he wasn't, a predictable psychosis for those who suffer at the whim of the all powerful.

In the previous year, Nick, the hyperventilating English senshusei who'd quit the course, had become so obsessed by which teacher would be taking the class that he'd ask all the assistants before the lesson. In the Japanese fashion of withholding information they wouldn't tell him, so he'd start his own elaborate conjectures based on whose turn it was likely to be. Then he became convinced that he was being picked on. I knew that feeling, it was especially strong for me when Mustard took the class.

The story of Nick's hyperventilation and beating from a teacher was held up as a kind of warning to senshusei. I asked Spike, who had been on Nick's course, about it.

'Nick was going OK but then he lost it.'

'How do you mean?'

'He lost it. He stopped training but he was still standing up. That's what made the teacher mad. He hadn't passed out or anything, so he could have carried on training.'

I made a mental note to pass out before giving up.

'Right,' said the Terminator, 'this is going to be *kuro-obikai* – a one-hour *seiza* lesson.'

We sat in two lines facing our partners, getting tentatively into the dreaded kneeling position. This was going to be a long haul, and how you start in *seiza* determines how painful it will be.

Correct *seiza* is not just kneeling down. You have to remain motionless and expressionless as well. For foreigners who have never spent any time kneeling before they start aikido it is always a trial. It's not being able to move about and release the tension in your knees and feet that makes it so difficult.

We were aware this class was going to happen, we just didn't know when. It was one of the famous 'killer' classes, what everyone talked about when they wanted to impress people just starting aikido. We'd talked up the pain of *seiza* and now we were going to feel it.

It would have been nice to have just sat in silence, but Roland had other ideas. We would each in turn give a speech on what the senshusei course meant to us.

I looked at R'em and he grinned. I grinned back. We were probably the only people grinning. It felt like bravado.

Mad Dog started the speech making. He talked lugubriously about how he had come all the way from Canada to study aikido in Japan. 'I really think we are so lucky to be here training with all the top senseis.' Then he named all the teachers individually, which took up a bit more time. He went on to say 'it was the hardest thing he'd ever done'.

Will came next. By this time I could feel my legs going numb. Just let them go numb, everyone said, remember the secret of *seiza* is not moving. Once you move the blood starts flowing and then you're in pain.

I expected Will's speech to be almost witty, but it wasn't. Despite his talent at repartee Will was drawn into the dreary self analysis like everyone else. It was like being in a cultural revolution and having to criticize ourselves.

'This was a chance to be good at aikido,' said Will, adding, 'it's the hardest thing I've ever done.'

Aga's speech was a clever construct of aikido clichés. But I couldn't blame him. It would tax even the most creative mind having to think of something original and sincere to say when all you wanted to shout was, 'What the hell am I kneeling down for!?'

During my speech, a pitiful account of how the course was psychologically more demanding than physically demanding, Aga started to curl forward and groan. I was surprised. Aga had, until then, always cut a rather boastful figure, a man for whom the word pain had no meaning. Then I remembered the psycho-outburst during the forearm strike training. I wondered if he was going to lose control of his eyes again.

He groaned a little louder.

'Aga! Sit straight!' commanded Spike.

Aga sat up and then collapsed forward again, his face bright red.

'Internalize the pain, boys,' said Roland, soothingly. 'Don't let the pain show on your face.' I could tell Roland wanted to keep the tone religious rather than authoritarian.

R'em's speech was the most memorable for me simply because it was so short. It was also mercifully free of the propaganda – the words and the phrases bandied around the dojo, picked up by the *budo* magazines, then recirculated back to the dojo, losing all semblance of a connection with reality.

'This is not the hardest thing, but it is a very difficult thing,' said R'em. 'Because no one tell you to get up, and no one tell you to come in each day. That is the hardest thing. The thing you choose.'

Aga was squirming badly on my left. Adam was squeaking and rolling his eyes. A general level of agitation had set in.

I looked around for something to concentrate on. For a while I stared into R'em's face, then I found myself looking around again. I started making faces now, grimaces barely controlled to show how much I was suffering. But I knew if I was on my own I wouldn't make such faces. Everyone else was making such a meal of it I felt somehow it was necessary not to be too stoical. By this I mean I still had some slack left, but not much. If I'd been completely in control I would not have moved at all.

My hearing was impaired towards the end, or rather my concentration was gone. I heard Little Nick drone on and I hardly took a word in. He had a soft, portentous voice anyway, which was hard to hear above the raucous, upscale noises of the dojo. But I was in no mood for listening.

Having spent so much time with the same group of guys I realized that everyone had a 'speech' that they repeated as often as they could. It contained their worries, hopes, fears and preoccupations. It revealed their inner selves. This speech was like their mission statement. Adam's included long excerpts about his criminal father and sister and drug-addicted mother.

He even managed a fleeting reference to this during the *seiza* session – 'This is something I want to finish. I think I'd be in gaol if I wasn't doing this course.'

Amid much scratching the floor and screwing up of faces, Roland, impassive as ever, made his own speech.

It was still hard to believe he was the same age as me, he seemed so much older. Age and authority are interchangeable. I wondered if Roland de-aged when he got home to his wife and kid. Did he pull off a rubber face mask like the villains in *Scooby Doo*, shouting, 'Darling, I'm twenty-nine again!'? Or was he set at fifty permanently?

Roland told us: 'One time I was standing in *kamae* and Kancho just came up and touched me in the small of my back. That one adjustment taught me more about the correct way to stand than hours and hours of training.'

For a moment the fidgeting stopped as people contemplated Kancho Sensei's masterful touch. Then Aga broke down and started yowling and banging his head gently on the floor. For the first time, I thought, maybe it really is that bad, maybe he's not faking after all. Unperturbed, Roland continued to the heart of his speech.

'What is it that makes a senshusei? What is senshusei spirit? One time, a few years back, I watched a senshusei student being corrected by a teacher. This student was unable to do what the teacher said. He kept trying and he couldn't do it and the teacher just kept correcting him and correcting him.

'And I could see that the student was immensely frustrated and becoming angry, angry at himself and angry at the teacher. I thought, in fact, that he would' (here Roland paused, as if searching for the right word) '*strike* the teacher. And yet he kept trying, he kept that anger under control. And that's how I see senshusei spirit. Pure anger, controlled anger, waiting to be used. Find that anger, boys. Find that anger in yourselves!'

For a few brief moments we all became angrily inspired and

no one cried out. But then Aga broke down again and we all became shamefully noisy.

As Chris had pointed out, it's very hard to judge someone else's pain, especially when you're going through the same outward experience. But come on, I kept reminding myself, we're only kneeling down. We're not suspended on meathooks by our genitalia in a Gestapo cellar.

Dimly, I could already grasp there were two levels of pain. Pain (1) was the actual sensation. It was on the level of an objective observation: 'I have been stung by a bee. There is a pain in my upper left forcarm.' Pain (2) is the subjective reaction: 'Ow! It hurts! It really hurts!'

Young children only experience pain (2). It hurts and hurts and hurts and then it's over and they stop crying.

The basic character of pain, and almost indistinguishable from it, is the desire for it to go away. A masochist doesn't want it to go away. This serves to neutralize the pain (2) content of the experience, since pain (2) is the 'It hurts!' side, when it seems as if the pain is everywhere and not localized, as if it is attacking your brain directly, and is indistinguishable from the desire for it to stop. In a way pain (2) is 'please stop now'.

Growing older increased the domain of pain (1). We may experience chronic pain, for example, which won't go away. We either become miserable or we cordon it off, localize it, objectify it ('there is a pain'), and then we learn to almost ignore it. Almost.

Slowly I was beginning to see that the senshusei course was a lot about coping with pain, about losing the pain (2) experience and getting pain under control on the pain (1) level. If you train until you faint then you have lost the pain (2) element. If you stop when 'it hurts' you may be doing the safe thing, but you are not commanding your body, it is commanding you. There may be a time when your life depends on who is in command.

The Terminator looked at the clock. We had been fifty-five minutes in *seiza*. He held us in suspense no longer: '*Ya-me!*'

111

No one could walk at first. There were two schools of thought on the best way to overcome total leg numbness. One held that you remain sitting as long as possible stretching and massaging your legs before getting up. This was the gradualist school. The other school believed in jumping up and stamping the feet hard to stimulate circulation. The shock was greater but the 'jump' school boasted a quicker recovery. Stephan warned against jumping up too quickly: 'Sometimes when you have no feeling in your feet your toes bend backwards and you can break your foot.' He showed us by bending his foot backwards under the ankle. After that I was always a little careful about jumping up with numb legs.

When the gruelling *seiza* lesson was over, the conversation in the tea room turned to religion.

Everyone except Ben and I had experienced some form of hallucination during the long stretch kneeling down. Mad Dog and Little Nick had had the most acute illumination experiences:

'It was like a white light – like in *Close Encounters* – and suddenly I couldn't see Mad Dog's head, like it was all inside me . . .'

'In mine,' said Mad Dog, 'it was like a photo negative, everything that was light went dark and everything dark went light.'

'I was staring at your face,' said R'em to me, 'and it go very very small. It was like looking down telescope.'

Everyone spoke about their visions in awed terms. If we hadn't had to leave for work I'm sure a religion would have started there and then.

I kept quiet, but Ben was unrepentantly sceptical: 'It's all crap,' he said.

But it was odd how quick people were to label their visions 'spiritual' and to regard them with hushed respect. Half remembered scraps of a religious education mingled with re-runs of David Carradine's *Kung fu* were apparent in this quasi-spirituality.

112

Everyone wanted something special to happen, and sure enough it did.

We escaped the retelling of visions and went to the nearby graveyard to eat lunch. This was my favourite place, damp and shady, a haven tucked away from the noisy street. Every now and then a salaryman on his way home would stop at the graveyard shrine, clap his hands once and ring the dull, unmusical bell that hung by a thick rope. Head bowed for a moment I wondered what prayers he was uttering, what wishes he was making – a new car? A pay rise? A simple desire to become a better man?

'Enlightenment:' a Zen priest told me when I first arrived in Japan, 'there are two kinds depending on your type. One type of man has many mini-enlightenments. The other has one big enlightenment.' 'What if you have no enlightenments at all?' I asked. 'Such a man does not think to ask this question,' he said.

Our food was laid out on the mossy stones in front of us. The graveyard had been empty for a while. A cloud of mosquitoes buzzed in and out of the sunlight. Graveyards are good places to eat lunch, much better than cemeteries, which I always find depressing and creepy.

A multitude of ants hurried across the moist gravestones scavenging for the crumbs we dropped. Ben massaged his still-sore knees. Neither of us spoke for a long while. Eventually the silence became palpable; finally it was broken as another salaryman in white shirt sleeves tugged impatiently at the bell rope, making it toll its flat, tone-deaf sound.

Challenge

'Me against my brother. Me and my brother against my neighbour. My village against your village. My town against your town. My country against your country.'

Fat Frank, re-telling a Persian proverb

'When faced with a crisis put a little spittle on each earlobe and exhale deeply through the nose. Then break a chopstick. All nervousness will disappear instantly. This is a secret matter.'

From the seventeenth-century Samurai manual *Hagakure*

'Cup of tea?' I asked Frank innocuously.

'Yes, please.'

I handed him the cup without a pause. He didn't look up from the book he was reading.

'Challenge,' he said, as he took hold of the cup.

'YOU TWO!' shouted Chris. 'I told you that "challenge" was banned in this house!'

It was no good. We couldn't stop. 'Challenge' is an addictive Iranian game of diabolical simplicity. Every time you receive something from another player you have to say 'challenge'. I give you the car keys, you have to say 'challenge' as you accept them. You hand me the paper, I say 'challenge' as I take hold of it. Between good players, i.e., the obsessively competitive, a game can last for *years*. Fat Frank's dad had several games going at once with different people. One had been running for *seven* years. Seven years without ever forgetting the magic word, or seven years of remembering never to receive anything from anyone? It amounted to the same thing – an atmosphere of tension and suspicion – just what we didn't need at Fuji Heights.

'After a month or two it can get pretty heavy,' said Frank. 'You'll probably start avoiding me.'

'How?'

'You'll find a way.'

He smiled his serene, knowing smile. Damn him! I wasn't going to be beaten at some half-baked Iranian parlour game.

'Have a cigar.'

'Challenge.'

We'd been playing for a week.

Shioda junior was taking the lesson; Shioda the cruel, Shioda the short, Shioda the hated. We'd been taught by him only a couple of times and already he was feared and disliked by everyone. We knew that Chida the masterful did not get on with him, and with Kancho Sensei nearing death, everyone was taking sides for the final scrabble over the remains. Now his son was about to take us for our first *hajime* lesson.

Hajime just means 'begin' in Japanese, but to senshusei it had particularly terrible overtones. *Hajime* training involved doing the technique as fast as possible, again and again and again.

All techniques in aikido are practised in pairs. When the first pair have finished the teacher commands '*hajime*' and everyone has to do it again. This meant that those who were slowest slipped further and further behind and could not benefit from the rhythm that was set up. If you finished first you sometimes got a micro-second of rest between finishing and the teacher noticing that you had finished. This was the incentive to be first.

We had all heard about the horrors of *hajime* training – the vomiting, the passing out, the heat exhaustion, all the things the previous generation tell you to make you scared.

'*Hajime*.' '*Hajime*.' '*Hajime*.' Twelve pairs of men in a dojo striking and grabbing and swirling and administering the final chop to the head, which is the end of the technique – needless to say there was always lots of shouting.

The technique Shioda selected for this particular *hajime* was '*katate mochi shihonage*' – the most famous takedown technique in aikido. It was the one Chris had reconstructed from a manual back in Fuji Heights before we'd even started lessons. Ueshiba had a student who *only* practised *shihonage*. Ueshiba said, 'All of aikido is in *shihonage*,' meaning, I suppose, that all the body-movement principles trained in aikido are present in this technique.

The basic form is deceptively easy. Your wrist is grabbed and instead of breaking free you consolidate the attacker's grip *while at the same time* ducking under his arm and turning so that his arm is bent back over his shoulder. You now either throw him or drop to the ground taking him with you. We were doing the most basic form where you drop to the ground taking him down on to his back.

Shioda demonstrated the technique hurriedly on his assistant, bringing him down to the ground with an almighty thump. The assistant broke the fall by slapping the ground hard with his outstretched arm.

If *shihonage* is done fast enough it is possible to knock the attacker out by hitting the back of his head against the ground. A special breakfall was taught at the dojo so that a lot of the force of the takedown could be absorbed. Of course, Shioda did not show us the important points of the breakfall, he just told us to get on with it and practise.

Practice after one demonstration is the old way of teaching martial arts. The aspiring student had to be quick to catch the secret of the technique because things would not be repeated. Ueshiba used this method: as he wandered around he would not criticize students but simply congratulate them on doing so well. Shioda junior left out the congratulating part. After showing us the technique he wandered around sniggering at our efforts.

I had, before starting the course, been briefed by Steve, an amiable Australian who had started the same police course as Paul. After six weeks he gave up with swollen, bruised arms and injuries sustained through doing an incorrect *shihonage* breakfall.

I got him to teach me the correct fall and I was grateful to have learnt this prior to endlessly repeating the technique.

At that time I didn't know that the only recent death in the dojo had been during a *shihonage* class.

While practising in a regular class a Japanese student, a married man in his forties, had told the teacher he was suffering from a headache. The teacher told him to continue. At the end of the class the student remained on the mat. His partner looked shamefaced, and no amount of stern comment from the teacher could make the lazy student get up. He was dead, of a brain haemorrhage sustained during the back-of-the-head-to-the-mat takedown.

His wife's reaction was unusual by Western standards. She expressed no complaint, only a gladness that he had died at the dojo, 'which was a place that he loved very much'.

After we had been practising *shihonage* for a while Shioda junior announced that we would, for the last twenty minutes, perform the technique *hajime* style.

We set to with gusto. Mad Dog, I noticed out of the corner of my eye, was taking a hammering from Little Nick, and his eyes were bulging with Mad Dog bravado. Not only were they doing the technique fast they were also trying to do it well. No such consideration entered into R'em's and my performance. In a confusion of flying limbs and hasty smacks of the mat we went as fast as we could, not caring if the technique fell apart or not.

I started to get tired. Sloppily tired. The kind of tiredness when you slow down immensely but you believe that you are still doing things just as fast as you were before. I used to sometimes get it when jogging – you'd imperceptibly slow to an ungainly limp, but it would feel as if you were still powering along. The clock suddenly took on an overwhelming importance. But from where I was my shortsightedness made the clockface a blur. I did not want to squint and draw the wrath of the teacher. So we laboured on, dragging our limbs as if they were old logs, lungs heaving and sweat everywhere.

Then the call came to stop. We all drew to attention in the *kamae* stance: arms in front, as if on-guard, leaning slightly over the front leg. It was the start and end posture for all techniques.

But this *kamae* was different. People were quivering and shaking from exhaustion. Sweat dripped in huge puddles on the floor. Mad Dog seemed to be sobbing.

We gave the bow and did our circle 'oos' and limped over to the place where the brooms were stored. Out of earshot of the teachers I gave Mad Dog a friendly pat on the shoulder. We were respectful of his tears. Did it mean that he was close to the breaking point? 'I just gave everything I had to give,' said Mad Dog when he had dried his eyes. 'There was nothing more and we had to keep going. That was so fucking tough.'

Mad Dog had been doing aikido for five years, but he was overweight. In the first three months of the Riot Police course his weight dropped from 92 kilos to 76 kilos.

After a *hajime* class, or in the summer, any class, we would drink two or three litres of liquid. The senshusei favourite was to buy powdered Pocari Sweat, an aptly named Japanese sports drink, and mix it with tap water in a two-litre bottle. After another lesson it was all sweated out again and you had to drink another three litres. In the height of the summer people were taking in and sweating out over six litres a day. Urination levels remained normal, it was all coming out as sweat.

When I was partnered with Sato for *hajime* training, who I had never seen sweat, and whose technique was dynamic and powerful, I was worried that it would be my turn to pass out. He just kept going, like a machine, or a tireless animal on a treadmill, and I got weaker and weaker. My strikes became pathetic apologies for violence. My lungs heaved for oxygen.

Then I saw it on the end of his nose. A bead of sweat. Sato was sweating. I was jubilant. From somewhere I got a second wind. My technique picked up. Now I could feel that Sato was getting tired too, less so than me, but he was tiring like a normal human being. At the end of the class Sato gave me his normal curt bow. Then he smiled as he wiped the sweat off the end of his nose.

Petty, long-running arguments had started to break out in Fuji Heights. I had taken to storing a whisky bottle in Kancho's aquarium, trying to reclaim some of the space that had been occupied. Frank thought it unhygienic, but I put this down to an Islamic suspicion of alcohol. Chris remained loftily above this dispute but was still heavily against our ongoing game of 'challenge'. Chris was also annoyed at the lack of respect the senshusei showed the regular students. 'You're so bloody rude,' said Chris. 'And it's not as if your aikido is that good anyway.'

Perhaps he was hoping for a rise. When Ben came round, usually to cut our hair with his clippers, I'd have an ally. Then we could say, 'You guys just don't understand. Only people on the course understand.'

We were special, dammit, and we weren't going to let anyone forget it. From being one personality, Fuji Heights had fractured into three distinct 'family' roles. Chris was the mum, caring for injuries and cooking good wholesome food. Fat Frank was the dad, telling me off for not helping Chris out by doing the dishes, but not doing them himself either. I was the teenager: errant, lazy, selfish, vastly misunderstood and, like a teenager, I realized it was high time I got a girlfriend.

Not that I had much energy for sexual hi-jinks, or even lo-jinks, somehow the constant training had perished my sex-drive to a survival minimum.

The Victorian emphasis on sports to keep a young man's mind off sex was a proven strategy. For months I'd hardly thought about women. Perhaps it was the warmer weather but increasingly I now saw the advantages of wrestling with a girl rather than a sweaty Israeli paratrooper or Japanese Riot Cop.

There was theoretically no shortage of women. Basic prudence kept me away from the high-school girls I taught. On odd evenings I also did part-time work at one of the many ramshackle conversation schools in Tokyo. A constant stream of office flowers, attractive female office workers, paraded through my classes. I observed other teachers picking up their students with consummate ease. At one school, teachers would loiter on the stairs waiting for the most attractive students to leave. This might have contributed to the school's recent bankruptcy. Attractive men with young, blond looks were in highest demand. At one university a sexy twenty-two-year-old handed her phone number to a teacher I knew with a direct: 'You, me, play. OK?'

I was not one of the fortunate few whom the Japanese female population chased after in undisguised lust. I didn't seem to like the ones who liked me – Madwoman for example, who when I spurned her advances threatened to run me down in her 7-series BMW. I was a lackadaisical Romeo at the best of times, lacking the unflinching eyes of the salesman and brutal indifference to rejection that Patrick assured me were necessary for sexual success.

Patrick was thirty and married to a Japanese girl of twenty-two. They lived in an apartment with a lavatory devoted to beer cans. One thousand and forty-seven cans to be precise. He was slowly making it into a shrine dedicated to all the beer he had drunk. Three walls were covered with cans, stacked from floor to ceiling, and he was now working on the fourth. I wondered what he would do when he ran out of wall space in the loo.

Patrick was incredibly laid-back. He spoke such slow English in such a deep voice I thought, at first, it was due to some speech inpediment. Later, I concluded it was all the years he had spent teaching English in Japan. His own Japanese was poor, and his wife chided him about this. 'It's embarrassing at first,' he explained, 'not being able to speak to your inlaws. But after two years it's fine. The embarrassment just goes away.'

Patrick was tall and looked like a young and unshaven Roger Moore – if Roger Moore had gone to art school. He was the kind of guy pop stars would talk to in the first-class lounge, assuming that someone cooler than them must be worth talking to. He was a successful teacher because everyone liked him. He made you feel calm, and, since most Japanese are excitable, he was greatly valued.

He was touchingly sentimental too. 'Rob,' he'd say, 'you're my mate, my mate. We must down some beers together. We mustn't lose touch.'

Patrick's advice was to get someone to set up a date for me. 'My wife's got loads of friends,' he said. 'And *omiai*, matchmaking, is the Japanese way.' I wasn't too sure about Patrick's wife's friends, so I left the offer open.

Of all the 'Outsiders', people who weren't studying or teaching the course, I found it easiest to talk to Nonaka Sensei, a sixty-five-year-old teacher at the high school. I took to sharing my lunch with her in amongst the filing cabinets and metal desks of the teachers' room. She was impressed that I did aikido, but you had to be careful with Nonaka Sensei because she was also adept at flattery. In the end I learnt a sort of code, knowing what was meant to be taken in and what was simply there to oil the conversation. 'I have a student who does aikido. She is a most superior student. I know it is not so vigorous as senshusei, but it is also aikido. Many foreigners want to study Japanese subjects, sometimes they do better than Japanese!'

I tried once to question Nonaka Sensei about the war but she snapped back, 'The past is past.' And then she smiled sweetly and poured me another bowl of green tea. I later discovered her family home had been bombed in the war and she had lost two of her brothers. Nonaka Sensei was more interested in talking about the present and the future. When I complained about my senshusei injuries, she would say, 'You must be strong!', and then she'd hand over several bags of fruit, chocolate cake and Japanese snacks, to help me stay strong. Sometimes her generosity could be overpowering. She knew I didn't have a girlfriend and she tried to fix me up with a young Japanese teacher at the school. It was doomed from the start, Miss Yoshida being a pleasant enough creature but really not my type at all, nor I hers. Her hobby was learning English – mine wasn't; she liked tennis and I didn't; her father was an eminent dentist and her mouth was full of what seemed to be gold experiments. Miss Yoshida sat with me through a number of painful lunches whilst Nonaka Sensei gave us time on our own, busying herself with the tea things. Miss Yoshida chided me for wearing a raincoat with a torn epaulette, and then offered to mend it for me. Things were going too far. I told Nonaka as politely as I could that it wasn't working out. 'Of course, I know,' she said, her eyes sparkling with amusement. 'Miss Yoshida is . . . a white elephant!'

Mr Wada's desk was next to mine and when he didn't have any Virginia Slims he offered me boiled sweets. I never saw him eat at school, except boiled sweets; he never went to the school canteen.

Mr Wada told me he had never had a girlfriend.

'Never?'

'Unfortunately I live with my parents. But I would like a girlfriend. Do you have a girlfriend?'

'Yes,' I lied. I felt it was the answer he wanted.

'Is she Japanese?'

'Er, yes.'

'May I ask her name?'

'Junko.' A common enough name.

He thought for a moment.

'My cousin's name is Junko.'

'Really?' I said. 'Well, I don't think she's your cousin.'

His face clouded with embarrassment.

'It is difficult to get a girlfriend in Japan,' he said.

Perhaps he was right. Anyway, I had more serious matters to contemplate – such as my inability to flip. I'd always loathed forward rolls, even as a child. It was one reason I never took up judo, and, along with handstands, it was the part of gymnastics I never liked. It seemed so bloody unnatural to want to turn the body upside down. What was natural, to me, was to want to

122

protect the head, not put it in danger by elaborate anti-gravitational manoeuvres.

But you can't avoid forward rolls in aikido. And after you become adept at rolling you have to come to terms with 'the flip'. This is like a forward roll except you don't get to use your arms, or arm, to land on first. You launch yourself forward, spin in the air and land on one side of your back and shoulder. 'It's like a big banana landing on the floor,' said Paul, and I thought of those giant plastic blow-up yellow bananas that English football supporters used to wave on the terraces.

Instead of a big banana, I felt more like a tower of bricks, upending itself and then crashing to the ground in clouds of dust and noise. As your back hit the ground one arm was supposed to be outstretched slapping the mat to take the impact out of landing. The effectiveness of the slap was all in the timing, and mine was *bad*.

The flip is a key part of Yoshinkan aikido. Sometimes, when you are thrown too hard and too fast, there is no time to do a safe forward roll. And there are some techniques, wrist throws for example, where, if you don't flip, your wrist or arm or collarbone is broken.

Dopey, a big lumbering cop with a doleful expression, whose stiff and unyielding movements ensured various jibes by teachers and foreigners alike, had real problems with the flip. He would go over and come crashing down and the whole sprung floor of the dojo would reverberate. It was painful to watch.

Sakuma and Ben also had difficulties, but when it came to flipping, I was the real dunce of the class.

I couldn't get the hang of the flip. I could do one but it was ungainly, wooden, too rapid and hurt like hell when I hit the mat. I was caught in a negative loop. Because I didn't like flips I did them too fast, which messed up the timing of slapping and hitting the ground. Because I was frightened of being upside down I tried to dive as close to the mat as possible. Sometimes it felt as if I was trying to dive *under* the mat. But the closer you

123

are to the mat the harder it is to land safely. It seemed grossly unfair that the solution was counterintuitive, that in order to be safe you had to be as high off the ground as possible. With me I was often so close I could feel my hair brushing the mat as I flipped over. A nasty sensation – what if my head was a few centimetres lower? It might get jammed and torn off completely. I didn't like thinking about it, but I had to. There was no escaping the flip because all the advanced techniques required the attacker to flip out in order to escape a throw. Flipping was what gave aikido its characteristic gymnastic appeal. Flipping was what made aikido look difficult, for the good reason that flipping *was* difficult. I could tell it was going to be a problem right from my first day. My own personal little problem. My cross to bear. My burden. It was odd how I instantly knew whether I could do a thing even before I did it. I knew the techniques performed on the knees would be no problem just by watching others do it. Yes, I thought, I can do that.

But flips were different. And the more I was cajoled, advised, abused, shouted at, the worse they became. And as I got more and more bruised and beaten up I began to lose the ability to even do a decent forward roll and its big brother, the diving forward roll.

The trouble started with Oyamada. There was something tough about Oyamada, but also camp. I could never forget his interest in cunnilingus, even when he was torturing me. He was the only teacher who had not done the senshusei course. Some said this was what made him so hard on senshusei students. Certainly his lessons were paragons of boredom, his favoured teaching method being repetition after repetition until the hour and a half was up.

Oyamada lined us up against one wall of the dojo and ordered us to do continuous forward rolls to the other side. And then back again. And then back again. It was fun at first. A nice break from heavy physical exertion, but then it became obvious he meant to keep us at it for the rest of the lesson.

124

After ten minutes I was severely bruised on the bony 'knobs', the tips of the ilium that project slightly on either side of the fifth lumbar vertebra, just above your backside. For the next eleven months these bruises were never to go away. The bony projections built up layers of calcification which just made it worse. Sometimes they swelled up, sometimes you thought they had gone away and then you'd crash-land on one and you knew they hadn't.

Will christened them 'knobbies' and the name stuck. It was an injury peculiar to senshusei students – a combination of hard mats and excessive training – and something never suffered by any of the regular students. Like a wound stripe or a Purple Heart, it was something you could only get by going into action.

Some people got knobbies so bad they had to have acupuncture to cure the pain, others invented curious and generally dangerous breakfall techniques in a desperate attempt to land on anything except those two sensitive spots.

'You've got to be careful,' said Paul, 'because sometimes the bone gets infected.'

Infected knobbies! What could be worse? In our narrow universe of four walls and a hundred hard mats I could imagine nothing worse than an infected knobbie.

Oyamada was the handmaiden of the painful breakfall, but Robert 'the bastard' Mustard was the one who completed my de-education in how to flip with ease and grace.

'OK, lads, get the mats.'

We would race to the corner of the dojo to pick up the two mattress-like mats that were intended for those learning how to flip.

We had to line up and Mustard or Stumpy would grasp you by the hand and then you had to flip. 'Good. Good. Good. No good,' Mustard would comment as we went over. I was always 'No good.' Maybe it was his way of encouraging me. It had the opposite effect. I began to long for the magical words: 'OK, lads, put the mats away.'

We graduated to being thrown and then one afternoon Mustard said, 'Right, let's have some fun.'

He took a *jo* from the wall rack of wooden swords and knives. A *jo* is a hardwood stick of roughly the same dimensions as a thick broomhandle. The police at Narita airport are armed with *jo*, a multi-purpose quarter staff, club and vicious poke stick, though I noticed they also carry guns.

Mustard stood on the mat and instructed the first man to grab the end of the *jo*. He then jerked the *jo* upward and forward so as to throw the man. Letting go, the man flipped and landed on the soft mat.

I could see the problem would be in when to let go. Too early and it would show it was not a committed grab. Too late and I would have no arm free to break my fall.

In the end I concentrated so much on the stick that my flip was a half-assed affair without enough life. I caught my head on the mat as I went over. There was a sickening crunch from my neck, which twisted sideways. For a second I blacked out. Then I knew I had to get up. I rejoined the line with wobbly knees.

'Break your neck and you're out of the course!' Mustard shouted from his position with the *jo*. Then he walked over to me and held up a finger. 'How many fingers?'

'One.'

'You're all right,' he said.

I didn't feel all right. I had torn a neck muscle. What was worse was my confidence had dropped to an all-time low.

'You bounced right on the top of your head,' Adam whispered to me in the line. 'It looked kinda weird.'

I was glad that Mustard told us to put the mats away before I had to flip again. It was good, because I was beginning to think he had it in for me. When he announced he was going back to Canada for a trip I half hoped he wouldn't come back.

With diving breakfalls I had a little more luck. Four or five people would crouch in a line and you had to run and dive over them and do a breakfall. It was a hard trick, and even the

126

miraculous Sato once crashed into the last crouching man. I saw him shake his head in disbelief as he picked himself up.

My technique was to run like hell, give a warlike shout and hope that the last man wouldn't mind too much as I crash-landed on to his back. But even I managed to clear the obstacles once in a while.

I was feeling beaten up but so far I hadn't been injured. Apart from Gimpy and his elbow the cops also had a cleanish bill of health, and so did the rest of the foreign senshusei.

The first person to break something was Danny, and it was during a lesson where we were repeatedly flipping. He landed awkwardly and broke his toe, which is a small but very painful bone to break.

On the way to the dojo that morning I had already suffered a minor bike crash into a scooter and was habouring a premonition that things would get worse.

Since re-reading Robert Graves' war memoir *Goodbye to All That* before the course, as a way to keep things in perspective, I had become a firm believer in employing ritual to ward off evil. In one incident in the book a soldier makes a hubristic comment and they all 'touch wood', except one poor fellow who is killed.

I rationalized touching wood by telling myself, and others, that it simply focused my mind on a potential hazard and was just a technique for raising awareness. On a purely psychological level I found touching wood defused anxiety about what I had predicted or inadvertently said. If such anxiety was allowed to fester I convinced myself I'd suffer some painful wish fulfilment, deathwish fulfilment, if you like.

But superstition could go too far and I was beginning to give roadside trees a hearty slap as I cycled past them.

After my near miss of a bicycle accident I was left with a feeling of unease. I approached the dojo and immediately touched wood on a fence pole outside the front. I heard footsteps and looked round to see if anyone had seen me. It was Ben. That was OK, I admitted my weaknesses to Ben.

'You want to be careful today,' I said. 'I've got a bad feeling about it – and we are doing *kotegaeshi*.'

In this technique the attacker's arm is bent back against itself, but out to one side rather than over the attacker's shoulder. If you continue to bend someone's arm and wrist in this way it will eventually break, unless the attacker, who is now the defender, does a flip. This unwinds his bent arm and leaves him on his back on the ground.

In the first lesson I had almost forgotten my counsel to go carefully, when there was a strangulated cry from where Ben and Danny were training. I looked round. Danny was lying on the floor. By trying to avoid landing on a 'knobbie' he had caught his toe awkwardly in his dogi trousers. Quickly he was carried to the side. Paul told us to carry on training. From the sidelines I heard him say: 'I'll pull it back into the socket in no time – that's not broken, it's only dislocated.'

Ben managed to persuade Paul to let him take Danny to a doctor before attempting this vigorous home cure. Paul, still convinced it was not broken, reluctantly stopped himself from jerking the bone back into its socket. He agreed that they should go to the bone-setting clinic next door to the dojo. Most of the customers at the clinic came from the dojo. It seemed a little macabre to me but at the same time somehow reassuring. Fortunately Danny had medical insurance.

Danny came back to the dojo later in the day. His toe had sustained a ninety-degree fracture. If Paul had tried to pull it back into the socket he would probably have succeeded in simply pulling the toe right off. Ben, who still had faith in teachers that extended beyond their narrow area of demonstrated expertise, was shocked at the casual and careless treatment of Danny.

'It's only his toe,' I said. 'It's not life or death or anything.'

'If it had been anything more serious I'd be even more worried. This is a sign that they don't care,' Ben said, heatedly. 'I'm telling you: if I get hurt, keep me away from the teachers –

just get me straight to the hospital. I'm not even convinced by the bone clinic next door.'

Danny had told me weeks earlier that he had failed to get into the Australian SAS because he pulled a ligament in his knee while training for the test. I now saw a pattern emerging. Danny would get injured so that he would have a tailor-made excuse not to finish the course.

As he was helped on to his bicycle (which he rode one-footed) he said, plaintively, 'You may not see me here tomorrow, chaps.'

'You must not be sad,' said Nonaka Sensei. 'You must always keep one happy thing in your head, and when you feel sad, think of that thing.' I told her the course was getting me down. 'It is your choice,' she said. When the teachers' room was empty she would sometimes grip my hand and, waggling her thumb, taunt me to pin it down with mine. However hard I tried she always beat me at thumb wrestling, pinning my thumb with her bird-like ultrafast movements. She never lost. 'Now you are *down!*' she said, when she inevitably won. Being beaten at thumb wrestling by a sixty-five-year-old woman always cheered me up immensely. She was gleeful in victory: 'Why do I win? Of course, because you think too much. You are much too intelligent to beat me!'

Steve, the Australian who had given up the course the year before, was back in town. He came round to Fuji Heights and told us about the geological survey he was doing in Laos. It sounded fascinating, a million times more inviting than the claustrophobia of the dojo.

'You're doing better than I expected,' he said, in his blunt yet friendly way.

'Thanks,' I replied.

'But you'll give up before the end,' he added, taking a sip of tea.

'Why?' I was genuinely shocked.

'Because I did.'

Right, I thought, Challenge.

Despite his plaintive comment Danny did come in the next day. He limped to the dojo office and informed the diminutive Ando Sensei about his broken toe. Expressing matter-of-fact sympathy Ando told him he had two weeks to recover. Of course, he would still have to come in to the dojo, but he would sit in the chair and watch each lesson.

For the senshusei there was little possibility of convalescence. As soon as the injury healed you had to get back. If the doctor said take a month off, the dojo teachers said take a week off, or sometimes they encouraged you to train through injuries. The more time you took off the further you fell behind and the more likely you would be re-injured when you started up again. And unless you couldn't walk you had to attend the dojo every day and watch every training session. If the injury was to the upper body you had to sit in *seiza* throughout each lesson. That's four and a half hours of *seiza* each day, enough to give you an injury in its own right.

If the injury was to the lower body then *seiza* was not required, but there was a special senshusei way of sitting on a chair (ramrod straight back, feet together – not crossed and flat on the floor) and this way of sitting was not conducive to recuperation.

The harsh policy on senshusei injuries was another traditional way of 'building spirit'. The idea was to produce fighters who could acquit themselves well whatever the state of their bodies. The aim was to break the subjective link between how you feel and how you perform. Instead, it sought to replace it with a decided goal and achievement of that goal using the body, rather than the body dictating what the goal should be. In going to sleep when you feel tired, eating whenever you are hungry or fighting when you get angry, the body dictates the goal and not the other way round.

When we started the course Stumpy came round and asked

each senshusei about former injuries. It was taken by most to be an excuse for scar showing, Adam winning with all the multiple fractures a misspent youth on a skateboard had given him. R'em was the only one who asked why we were being asked. 'So that the teacher will know what your possible weak points are and what your limits are and how far they can push you,' came the reply. Adam's inability to sit still was partly sanctioned by his tale of woe about breaking his knee when he was fifteen. R'em said: 'Regarding this course I have no old injuries to report.' I realize now that this was the best policy to follow, admitting old injuries always allowed a let out, an escape route. R'em had allowed himself none.

I had definitely regressed. The extra discipline of training did not carry over to the apartment. When I wasn't arguing, or playing 'challenge', I spent a lot of time sleeping. Even when we hired videos I'd often fall asleep in the middle. Rewatching one Steven Seagal movie I said, 'The next bit's really good ...' Then I started snoring – even the good bits couldn't keep me awake.

Fat Frank and Chris were still training every day at the dojo and slowly making their own way towards a black belt. If they continued regular '*kenshu*', intensive, regular training in daytime classes, they could test for black belt at the same time as the senshusei.

'It will be interesting to see whose aikido is better,' Chris would needle. 'I'm still not convinced the course is about aikido, it has more in common with a crude initiation rite or simple survival training.'

Fat Frank was more impressed. 'I don't think I could put up with the shit you guys put up with.'

Fat Frank had still not found a job and spent a lot of time washing dogis and clothes in the washing machine. One day there was a minor drama when his special Iranian underpants were stolen from the line. We knew they had been stolen because suddenly there was light in the apartment. The underpants, which were huge, brown and elasticated, had been handmade by his mother, and when they were drying on the line they blocked out all light through the kitchen window. I got used to the darkness. When light suddenly entered the apartment I rushed out to see what had happened. The mammoth pants were gone! There was no sign of a thief. Perhaps a freak gust of wind had torn the huge flapping garment from the line. And though panty theft, female usually, is common in Japan, I found it inconceivable that anyone would actually want to possess such a monstrous pair of brown Iranian undies.

Chris was quite harsh about the whole affair. 'At least I can read without putting the light on now,' he commented.

Despite being 'mum' Chris was now the major breadwinner at Fuji Heights. His acting career had petered out, the decisive blow coming when a red-headed midget was chosen to present a new energy drink, rather than Chris who had specially worn wacky big glasses and a luminous green suit to the audition. He decided to give up the insecurities of showbiz and now spent long hours at Mitsubishi, Itochu and Mitsui, teaching highly intelligent salarymen. In these top companies Chris had wangled a job teaching those singled out for promotion abroad and he found it far more stimulating than ordinary English teaching.

The job had come through Patrick. Whenever I met him he'd ask, 'What is this aikido stuff anyway?' I'd show him some locks and he'd say, 'Very nice, very nice – in theory. But what about in a real fight?'

Outsiders were all the same. They wanted to know if you could duff up Mike Tyson if he gave you a funny look in a bar. Sometimes I explained the implicit fallacy at length. Sometimes I just said, 'I may not be able to dish it out, but I know I can take a hell of a beating.'

It was around six o'clock in the evening and a glorious blue twilight was setting in. Car tail lights contrasted a brilliant red against the deep blue of the evening sky. I was riding my shopper bike past the local school when I saw them snagged on the high fence behind a cedar tree. On closer inspection the truth was obvious: it was Fat Frank's underwear. Standing on the parked bike's saddle it was easy to unhook them. I bundled the immense garment up and rode home in triumph. Without thinking I dumped them down in front of Frank, who was seated watching a Japanese quiz show.

'Hey,' he said, 'thanks. Where did you find them?' He handled his dear garment and at the same time we realized the same thing. He had received something without saying the talismanic word.

'You just lost!' I said. 'Challenge!'

Good Cop, Bad Cop

'It is bad manners to yawn in front of someone. If a Samurai licks his lips while his mouth is closed the yawn will go away.'
From the seventeenth-century Samurai manual *Hagakure*

I told Nonaka Sensei I had made friends with some of the Japanese police. 'I think it is hard to be friends with a Japanese man,' she said. 'He will always want to show a foreigner his favourable side.'

The cops lived in the sho-dojo, a small room next to the main dojo. I went in to get a cigarette from Sherlock; I was always on the verge of giving up, so spent half the time without cigarettes. I opened the door and was hit by a waft of smoke. All the cops were lying in sleeping bags. Seven or eight of them were smoking. They had a TV and a video player and I noticed a stack of porno videos, though they weren't being watched at the time.

'You guys live pretty well,' I said to Sherlock. He gave me a big grin, revealing his mossy, corroded teeth, quite the worst teeth in the police group.

'Take it easy,' he said. 'There aren't any teachers here! Here, have a pack.' He gave me a new pack of Mild Seven, the salaryman's preferred smoke, from a ripped-open carton. Two or three of the cops, and Sakuma, were sound asleep. Sato was reading a book.

'Stay for a bit,' said Sherlock. He introduced me to the 'gorilla', Maeda-san, who was the group comedian, and whose main interest was pro-wrestling.

'Do you know Tony St Claire?' he asked.

'Afraid not.'

'Gally Lineker?' asked Saito, another cop.

'Yes,' I said, 'the gentleman of football.'

'But you are the real English Gentleman,' said Sherlock, showing his awful teeth again. 'You always eat Japanese noodles with no noise!'

In the dojo Sherlock was my new 'mate'. Before training we would swap a few friendly words, explain our latest injuries. If I forgot this ritual Sherlock would sneak up behind me after the lesson and pinch my backside. I'd seen boys do this at a junior high school I had taught at and assumed it was just a way of showing friendship. It was still hard to square with images of macho Riot Police, though. Somehow I couldn't see them pinching bums at a SWAT training centre or at Special Branch HQ.

Amongst the foreign senshusei a hard punch to the stomach signalled affection, a desire to be chummy. In the tea room people put locks and holds on each other and were boisterous, unless Robert Mustard was there, when the mood changed to deferential, even obsequious.

The tea room contained two drinks-vending machines, a row of shelves for our shoes and named spots on some more shelves for our food. It was a grey room hung with posters of the top Japanese teachers executing dramatic aikido throws. Every so often people would go up to a poster, point at the victim of the throw, whose features were usually obscured, and ask, 'Who's that?' Then everyone in the room, diverted for a moment from the tedium of everyday chit-chat, would turn and shout the answer. Or, in another variation of this game, someone would go up to the poster and say, 'Is that . . . Takeno?' Or 'Is that . . . Mori Sensei?' I even found myself doing it from time to time, quite unconsciously; somehow the posters compelled it.

Twice a week at 7.15 a.m. the tea room became our classroom. Mrs Hasegawa, the wife of a former foreign minister, would arrive downstairs to be met by the 'shinkoku person', the group monitor for the week. Standing outside in the busy street in

135

white pyjamas, embarrassed because of a white belt, wearing sandals, as shoe-shod salarymen walked past to work, it was always tough if Mrs Hasegawa wasn't her usual three minutes early.

The greeter would bow deeply to Mrs Hasegawa. She would giggle and bow back. Stilted Japanese conversation was then made as she was escorted to the lift and up to the dojo. Escorting Mrs Hasegawa was the only time senshusei were allowed to use the lift. It was the only perk of the job.

Mrs Hasegawa was our Japanese language teacher, though I'm afraid the senshusei were not the best of students. Our Japanese ranged from the fluent (Will and Adam) to the stumblingly incompetent (Danny and Mad Dog). I was somewhere in between, having taken lessons for six months when I first arrived in Japan. But everyone already knew what we had to know: aikido Japanese, the barked orders and commands that had been learnt the hard way very quickly: understand or face physical punishment. Mrs Hasegawa never punished anyone, she was far too nice for that. Unfortunately this meant no one took her lessons very seriously.

Twice a week she came and twice a week we diligently worked through huge lists of verbs and nouns. I even learnt from Mrs Hasegawa the correct Japanese character for wild boar. Aga was the most insolent student, treating Mrs Hasegawa as if she had nothing of value to teach. It was an odd contrast to the alert obsequiousness he showed to the aikido teachers. Danny was the worst student, always breaking out into irritated English, 'I just don't know the answer, OK.'

As soon as Mrs Hasegawa had been escorted back outside, the tea room was used for a hurried breakfast before cleaning duties started. Unlike the laid-back, sleeping-bagged feeling of the cops' sho-dojo, there was always an atmosphere of frenetic tension in the tea room. Ben had once laid his head down and Mustard had told him that if he wanted to sleep he should quit the course. We were banned from listening to Walkmans by Paul.

'It's good training,' he explained. 'The whole time you're in the dojo you're on the alert, ready for action.'

When the atmosphere in the tea room became too oppressive I hid in a toilet cubicle and caught fifteen minutes' sleep between lessons. It reminded me of one primary school I attended, where I hid in the toilets during playtime to escape the humiliation of not being picked to play football.

One person I didn't want to have to spend time with was Mustard. Just being around him made me nervous, expectant of a rebuke or harsh criticism. 'If you can't take it, go home,' was the one everyone hated, with its built-in implication that we were all weaklings. After one severe berating from Mustard, when he told the foreign senshusei that we were wasting our time and might as well give up, Mad Dog was choked up with emotion, he hated so much to be on the wrong side of the teacher.

Sometimes, I could tell that the hero worship got Mustard down. From time to time he yearned to be just one of the lads. He tried, unsuccessfully, to be matey, but no one could forget his rank and the fact that he wanted respect just as much as friendship. I don't think he was prepared for the loneliness of being at the top. Kikuchi, the most easygoing of the *uchi-deshi*, told me that Kancho Sensei only had four intimate friends, who went drinking with him most evenings. None of them did aikido. They probably didn't even discuss the subject.

Perhaps in imitation of Mustard, Mad Dog had started smoking again and so had Adam. Mad Dog had not smoked for five years. He had given up by going on a wilderness canoe trip for ten days with only his dog for company. 'Sometimes I got so desperate I rolled up leaves and smoked lichen,' he said. Mad Dog was fearful of his wife: 'If she finds out I've started again we're definitely talking divorce here.'

I liked Mad Dog and his little homilies. Whenever ice was applied to an injury he would parrot (on the subject of how many minutes to keep the ice on the injury), 'Twenty on, twenty off, or it'll do no good.'

Startling rumours would start from nowhere in the tea room. At one stage everyone convinced themselves that the man who delivered the juice refills for the vending machines was the great Takeno himself.

'Look at the poster if you don't believe me,' said Little Nick.

When Mustard heard this he guffawed with laughter. 'When Takeno comes to this dojo none of you bozos will have any doubts. He's got a space around him that causes pure fear. You guys'll be shitting yourselves.'

Patrick had arranged an *omiai*, a matchmaking introduction. We were to go to watch a TV quiz show being made. Patrick's wife was one of the contestants. One of his wife's friends, Mariko, was coming along too. She had expressed an interest in meeting a Western man. I was that man. Patrick and I hurried around the Imperial Palace on our way to meet his wife and Mariko at the TV station.

'What's she like?' I asked.

'Very nice,' said Patrick, looking at his watch and striding ahead. We were half an hour late.

'What's she really like?'

'I already told you – very, very nice!'

'No, what's she really like, come on?'

'All right – she's a real old dog. Any other questions?'

Patrick's wife, whose name was Noriko, looked striking and glamorous sitting with the other contestants. The game was hosted by a celebrity presenter, a 'tarento' as the Japanese say, a direct and inappropriate transliteration of the English word 'talent'. The format was simple and involved answering questions for cash. I sat next to Mariko who sat next to Patrick. Mariko was very attentive and asked me lots of questions. She was nice looking. Her face looked very clean. She was Noriko's age, which is to say she was twenty-two.

At one point the *tarento* spotted Patrick and me, the only foreigners in the audience. To get a cheap laugh he spoke his worst schoolboy English. When he discovered Noriko was Patrick's wife he asked her to say something in English. She blushed and said, 'Why were you so late?' The cameras zoomed in on Patrick. There was a long pause, as if Patrick was thinking of something especially witty to say. But in the end all he managed was: 'Sorry, Nori.' But the audience thought the rhyme was intentional and were so primed to react that an insane laughter took hold, making this domestic wrangle sound like the punchline of a hilarious joke.

But the joke was really on the other contestants. They were all genuine, having applied to join the show and passed an audition. Noriko was only on it because she knew the director's wife. They needed a pretty face to balance the dedicated and bespectacled looks of the other participants. That morning the director had rung her up and asked her some questions 'purely for practice'. These turned out to be the actual questions and, as he had corrected Noriko over the phone, she got most of them right. He even told her one 'wrong' answer, which she dutifully repeated on air. The audience roared with laughter as it was obviously wrong. Noriko looked baffled, her grip on general knowledge never strong at the best of times.

Noriko came second after a male postgraduate student, a real brain box who triumphed despite the handicap of being a genuine contestant. Noriko's prize was $750. She and Patrick generously agreed to take Mariko and me out. We went to a restaurant that served, amongst other dishes, roasted sparrows. I ate seven or eight sparrows, which tasted like charred leftovers of bony chicken.

After the meal we went to a karaoke box. I made the grave mistake of singing 'Bridge over Troubled Water'. It only has a weak piano backing track and my voice quavered and fluted, hideously nude without the usual mush of sound to protect it from ridicule. I said goodbye to Patrick, Mariko and Noriko feeling the evening had gone pretty well. A few days later I rang Patrick up and asked him what the feedback was.

'You're in with a chance,' said Patrick.

'How do you mean?'

'She definitely likes you . . .'

'Yes?'

'But she's not so sure about the aikido, she's worried about whether you'll ever get a proper job or not.'

'Hold on, we're not talking marriage here, are we?'

'You never know.'

'Well, I do know, actually. I am definitely not talking marriage at this stage.'

'You can never rule it out completely—'

'I just have.'

'Oh, well. What's the message?'

'I don't mind another meeting – but marriage is out of the question.'

Patrick later reported there was no reply to my message.

With Mustard in Canada Paul was driving us mercilessly towards the first test. This would be an examination in basic techniques, like *shihonage*, and all the basic movements. It suddenly hit me that I could fail. It was unlikely, on this first and easiest of tests, but it was still possible.

Paul trained hard but without any of the psychological games that Mustard played. His insults were straightforward, designed to be taken on the chin. When he wanted to be rude he compared us to the cops or the regular students.

Every morning, before a Japanese teacher took over, Paul would pound into us the same techniques, again and again and again. Day after day the routine hardly varied. One lesson, something clicked. 'Keep it going,' shouted Paul, 'the power's starting to come.' It was a group improvement, instantaneous and absolutely discernible. I *felt* something I'd only intellectualized about before: the power of the team, which was more than a sense of belonging, it was the knowledge of a collective effort dragging you to a level you could never reach alone. We would be much better than the police, who were still a month behind, and Paul was determined we would look very much better.

All this time Danny looked on. After two weeks his toe was still very painful but the swelling had gone down. He negotiated another week's reprieve, but towards the end of the week he started training again, half-healed broken toe and all. 'It still hurts,' he said, 'but what else can I do? You chaps are leaving me behind.'

The test involved standing alone with your partner and doing five basic techniques selected from the fifteen or so we had learnt. The Japanese teachers looked on with clipboards, ticking our mistakes.

During his test I watched Danny from the sidelines as he struggled through a basic movement that involved pivoting around his bad foot. His teeth were exposed in a rictus of concentration, or pain. I knew even then that he wouldn't fail the test, however many mistakes he made. He was showing the most important thing already, what Sato called 'the Spirit that conquers imaginary ghosts'.

For everyone apart from Danny it was an easy test. After doing our techniques we were summoned by Chida and told that everyone, police and senshusei, had passed.

Some of the regular students asked us what had happened to Danny. Will was offhand with them as soon as they started to talk about their own injuries. 'I saw myself in the mirror the other day,' he told me, 'and I've developed that look, that real cold look that last year's senshusei had. When ordinary people talk about aches and pains I just give them that look, the senshusei look that means, "Don't talk to me about pain, you don't even know where pain *starts*, brother."'

Mr Wada told me he had, at long last, found a girlfriend. I offered him a Lucky Strike and he took it experimentally.

'How old do you think I am?' he asked.

'Oh, hard to say,' I said. And I really didn't want to say. To preserve the elaborate ritual of our conversation I didn't want to speak my mind in case he was offended. Was he young and wanted to appear older, or was he actually older and desperately wanted to look youthful? I guessed he might be twenty-eight, but to cover both possibilities I said, 'About thirty?'

'I am thirty-four years,' he said, gravely.

'You don't look it,' I said. 'You look very young.' He was pleased by that. 'And now you have the contact lenses you look even younger.'

Inexplicably Mr Wada had started wearing contact lenses. I now saw that it was part of his campaign to get a girlfriend.

'Sometimes I have tears,' he said, referring to the lenses.

'Where does your girlfriend work?' I asked.

'In an office,' he said.

'She's an office lady,' I said.

'Yes,' he said, doubtfully.

'How old is she?'

'Twenty-five.'

Perhaps he wanted to talk about girlfriends in general rather than this specific girlfriend.

'It's good you've got a girlfriend at last,' I said.

'My girlfriend does not always agree with me,' he said.

'Right,' I said.

'But because I love her I must try to see her point of view.'

'Good idea.'

'So, my way of thinking is changing.'

'How?' I asked.

He started to speak and then shook his head.

'This is strange for me,' he said.

There was a burst of noise as a group of girls came round the corner of the corridor laughing and shouting and brandishing their toothbrushes. After every lesson girls spent time cleaning their teeth, as if hysterically trying to reverse the Japanese reputation for poor dentistry. The group split into two and swirled past us, seamlessly joining together again on the other side. The girls were not our students and ignored us as they passed. For some reason both Mr Wada and I were transfixed by the passing group of girls. Together we watched them in their innocuous energy and zest, racing along to the large steel sink to clean their teeth.

The Hottest Summer Since 1963

'It is better to live on your feet than to die on your knees.'
'Proverb'

'A Samurai will use a toothpick even though he has not eaten.'
From the seventeenth-century Samurai manual *Hagakure*

Heat. The rainy season had not been rainy at all. But it had been hot. It was more like the steamy season. Back at Fuji Heights the roaches had staged a comeback, one even hitching a ride with me to the dojo in my bag. It escaped out of my locker and ran across the changing-room floor right under Stephan Otto's eyes. He screamed a Bavarian obscenity and ordered us categorically to stop bringing food into the changing rooms. Then, no doubt feeling very righteous, he examined the showers and found mould growing on the walls. It was a bad start to the day, the showers were Adam's and my duty to clean. We had been shifted off toilet duty when the cops arrived. Showers were better than cleaning up after the collective shit of a dojo, but we had grown lax about cleaning the shower walls during the cold weather. In the steamy season black spots of mould appeared within thirty-six hours. We became expert at using the various powders and bleaches to rid the walls of infection. The caustic cleaning powder stung my bare feet as I stood in the cubicle sweating freely as I scrubbed – and it wasn't even 8 a.m.

Craig had still not returned from Australia. His shelf pile of paper, magazines, dictionary and pencil case was pilfered by the residents of the tea room. I made off with his ruler, which would be particularly useful for doing the *Shinkoku Book* – the public diary kept of every class we took. There was no word from Craig. Perhaps he'd chickened out. Stealing his stuff meant he was now unofficially dead, never to return.

We had changed partners. There was no choice in the matter. I was partnered with Little Nick, 'the Armenian'. I thought it would be 'good for my aikido'. Little did I know I would regret the day I lost R'em for the rest of the course.

Little Nick was short and powerfully built. He had unblinking black eyes, unshining killer's eyes. He was nineteen years old and as hard as nails in a fight, but when he went back to the gaijin house where he lodged he longed fervently for his mother's cooking and slept twelve hours a day in prolonged homesick depression. He had recently recruited the 'fat brothers' – two fat Canadian boys on holiday in Japan. He ordered them around and forced them to break into a nearby school pool with him to go swimming each night.

Obsessed by aikido since he had seen Kancho Sensei on a Canadian tour in 1990, Little Nick idolized Mustard, who returned the compliment. 'Nick will pass me,' said Mustard, over a lager at Paul's birthday party. 'No!' I protested. I was beginning to learn the sly art of brownnosing, but I needed more practice. No one could surpass Mad Dog in this field. When watching a teacher demonstrate his head would loll stupidly on one side and he would bark hoarse laughter at the sheer impossibility of it all. Sometimes he would slap his thigh just to emphasize how advanced the teacher was and how slow he was. When training with me he was full of kind and patronizing advice.

After one class my dogi was dripping wet, unwearable. Only R'em wore the same dogi for three classes and several days running. The teachers complained of our collective stink. R'em's dogi was a suspicious greying colour. In the line up for *shinkoku*, the daily parade at full attention with bows and shouted commands made outside the dojo office, we pointed the group finger at R'em. His face was full of injured pride and protest – he genuinely did not know he stank to high heaven. I gave him another dogi, a collector's piece rescued from the dogi chuck-out box, an absolutely original Jacques Payet dogi top and trousers, complete with 'Payet' embroidered in katakana script on both. Payet was considered the equal of Mustard, but his opposite – he practised an ultra-soft, but still very powerful, technique. He had recently gone back to France after ten years in Japan. A short man, unassuming, he was one of the few foreigners to have mastered Chida's super-subtle style of aikido. I was sad to give up my souvenir, but it was necessary as a way of maintaining harmony in the dojo.

There was a new visitor to the tea room – Dolores the penniless. She had learnt aikido in Spain and come to Japan to emulate her teacher. At first it was good to have a new, and female, face in the dojo. The excitement wore off when it became obvious that Dolores was one of those girls that never paid.

The high heat of summer brought even more girls than usual out in their mini-skirts. Tokyo at that time must have been the mini-skirt capital of the world. What Japanese maidens lack in the way of imposing breasts they make up for in presentably skinny legs. Often you'd see a young girl in a mini-skirt walking with the pigeon-toed shuffle necessary for walking in a kimono. But these girls may never have worn kimonos in their lives. Certainly the knock-kneeded shape of some of their legs makes the pigeon walk easier. I only ever saw one Japanese girl with the sheer-straight legs of an African or a Swede. I followed her across several blocks wanting to fix for ever this abnormality in my memory.

In the dojo the heat presented other problems. Adam and Danny had both been close to collapse through heat exhaustion. Danny started panting like a dog and this turned into hyperventilation of a dangerous sort, the lesson ending just as his strength finally gave out. Adam went bright red and had to be dragged through the technique by Will after he fell repeatedly to the floor in utter fatigue.

Ben passed out twice and was revived, only to pass out a third time. He told me that the warning sign before you collapse from heat exhaustion is that your mouth goes all tingly. Adam confirmed this. Ben was hauled to his feet by Aga, but not before he was reprimanded by the soft-spoken Chida. '*Usagi tobi*, Ben,' said Chida. When Ben appeared not to understand, Chida said in English, 'Rabbit jumps.' Ben managed one lap of the dojo before collapsing again. It was unusually harsh treatment for Chida to dish out, but in this lesson we were being observed by a group of police officials.

After the lesson we force-fed Ben liquid and stood him under a cool shower. In an unusual show of concern Chida came into the locker room to see if Ben was all right. He told Ben to mix salt with his water each day. It was the only time that Chida ever visited the locker room. After Chida had gone Kikuchi, the *uchi-deshi*, exclaimed: 'Yoshinkan aikido is kamikaze!'

I learnt to exert no more force than was necessary, trying to float through the basic movements to minimize exertion. In between classes I was drinking two or three litres of liquid and not pissing a drop of it out.

At night there was sometimes a thundery drizzle, but it dried up all too soon. The rainy season had simply decided not to arrive.

We had progressed through the basic techniques and had now entered the month of *suwari waza*. *Suwari* means seated techniques, and they are all performed from a kneeling position. All pivot movements are made on the knee and this quickly rubs the skin off that delicate part of the body. Chris informed me that it was impossible to grow calluses on the knees. I countered with the example of wolf children found in Bangladesh with huge knee and palm calluses from never having learnt to walk. Many Westerners held that *suwari* training was a similar and unnecessary retrogression. After all, when was the last time you had a punch up whilst kneeling down?

The dojo magazine contained a story about a previous graduate of the police course who, as a Japanese police detective, had been forced to enter a house full of suspected gunmen. He had evaded being shot by coming in speedily on his knees. He was reported as being grateful for all the knee-walking practice given him at the Yoshinkan dojo. Less obscure justification was that since it was very hard indeed to do techniques on your knees, then if you mastered them there, doing them standing up would be no problem at all. Movement of the hips is central to deploying power in aikido. *Suwari waza*, we were told, would help to build hip power.

The price to pay was the skin on your kneecaps. In the first hour of pivoting practice I wore palm-sized patches of skin off both knees. I was given conflicting advice about how to speed up their healing. Paul recommended rubbing in alcohol. R'em said do nothing. Ben suggested antiseptic cream. I tried all three and nothing worked – the knees started to weep with pus in a couple of days. No matter how much they healed at night, the next day's practice wore them raw again, and having run out of skin I was soon down to raw flesh. Each turn became a major act of will. It was like having nails driven into the kneecap. It was nasty to experience and nasty to contemplate and each evening I tried to work out a new method of protection.

Kneepads became a big issue, in fact they became *the* issue – whether to wear them or not. None of the teachers wore pads. All of the riot police did, some of them sporting outsize volleyball pads that they constantly adjusted beneath their dogi trousers. Wearing pads was considered wimp behaviour, since pads got in the way of fast techniques. It was rather like the argument about wearing helmets in cycle racing – the experts didn't do it so any serious aspirant shouldn't either.

Paul told me that after a month of abuse the knee flesh started to heal from behind. At first it tries to heal from the sides, as in a conventional wound, but since the scab is broken each day this inevitably fails. 'The body works this out,' said Paul, 'and then it heals up from underneath the wound. And then you'll never have trouble again.'

A month of agony in order to refute current medical beliefs about the necessity of rest for adequate healing – this was what Paul was suggesting. Stephan and Darren backed him up. They were the real tough guys.

Adam and Will had been wearing kneepads since the beginning of the course. They favoured rubber tubes of wetsuit material, but when you sat in *seiza* it cut off the circulation to the feet. Aga, at first boastful about not wearing pads, was soon in a pair. Mad Dog and Little Nick followed, and then everyone was wearing them. Danny was the last to succumb, but his SAS spirit finally deserted him in the two pools of blood that were his constant companion whenever he knelt down. I spent thousands of yen on kneepads. I tried every kind with the avidity of a man searching for religious solace. I cut the backs out of pads, customizing them to fit my own, increasingly knobbly knees. In the end I discarded pads in favour of bandages and sticking plaster, since the backs of the pads were doing more damage to the back of my legs than they were worth.

Fixing my bandages became a lengthy ritual that was eating into my shower-cleaning time, but I didn't want to fix the bandages when I first arrived at the dojo because by the time of the first lesson they would be all sweaty and the skin soft enough to just peel off. I ended up hiding in a toilet cubicle just before the lesson, so I wouldn't be noticed conspicuously not cleaning the showers, which at any moment threatened to be overgrown with lurgy. 'We're undermanned here,' I told Adam. 'We need an extra hand.' Adam did the locker tops and the hoovering. I did the mirror and the four shower cubicles. Since Craig had gone we were definitely shorthanded – though those on the dojo-cleaning detail did far less work than us. But I found a sense of peace in the simple ritual of scrub and polish. Finding a new place where dirt accumulated always cheered me up. I discovered a line of dust on every vent on every locker. I made an ambitious plan to work my way through the entire locker room polishing every vent before the course ended. It was something satisfying that required no skill and earned me no harsh punishment. 'We're going to be the meanest motherfucking janitors in the world after this,' Adam said for about the fiftieth time. The joke was wearing thin.

We checked the thermometer each day. It was always 38 to 40 degrees with 75 per cent humidity. The newspapers announced it was the hottest summer since 1963. There was air-conditioning in the dojo but it was never switched on. 'Good training,' said Paul.

Out on the mats Little Nick had scant respect for an old codger like me. Old! I was only thirty, but to his nineteen-year-old eyes I was the same generation as his uncles and aunts, a real oldster. Stamina, I found, was not a major problem. I believe stamina increases as you get older, up to a point. Despite the heat I was fortunate never to have any trouble breathing in the airless superheated atmosphere of the dojo. Neither did Little Nick, and though he complained that he 'didn't like not being able to breathe', I guessed he was just being modest.

Age was less of an issue than my technical inability. We were forced to learn a new technique every other day and I was slower to pick things up than the others. Paul put it differently: 'You learn things fast, but you don't seem to remember them, you just go back to the way you were doing them before.'

None of the senshusei wore trousers any more. We all wore shorts or cut-offs. Trousers were too painful against the weeping sores on our knees. Sitting on trains I watched the people opposite become fascinated by the repulsive open wounds on each knee. Let them guess what caused it, I used to think.

Mustard's mother had died and he had returned from Canada. It was good to see him, but the pleasure wore off after about a day. He glanced at my knees and said, 'Those are the worst knees since Tim Joyce's.' Tim Joyce's knees were famous, indeed they had become a byword for senshusei misery. Joyce had missed the early part of the previous year's course because of a visa problem. He had been thrown in at the deep end without a chance to acclimatize and his knees had suffered. They had not properly healed for nine months.

I invited Ben back to Fuji Heights after training one Saturday. I turned the fan on my suppurating knees to get them to dry up before the evening. Even when dry I didn't want to bend them too much or else they would crack and dribbles of yellow pus would congregate around my ankles. Ben helped himself to some Wild Turkey whiskey from Kancho's fishtank though he assured me he didn't like strong liquor. I had a few shots myself and began to feel a lot better. In minutes my head lolled forward and we were both asleep at the table. When I awoke it was dark. I looked outside through the open kitchen window at the bike-filled yard outside Fuji Heights. I could hear the insects, cicadas chirruping in a nearby cedar. Not as loud as autumn insects but loud enough to be foreign, different from England. It was still ludicrously warm, the intimate warm of the Japanese summer night, which somehow feels welcoming. There is no breeze on such nights. It's an indoors kind of darkness, as if the whole night sky is an invisible glass dome and you are walking through a hothouse garden. And somehow the illusion is maintained by the stars, which on these nights look much closer than they ought, as if they are lights in the roof of the glass dome you can reach out and touch. There is very little scent in Japan, but the night air is palpable, you feel it moulding around your body. The only odour is the odour of humidity, an ozone of damp that pleasantly putrefies everything.

Miraculously it was still early, no later than eight. I felt rejuvenated and full of calm energy. I woke Ben and insisted that we head into the city to seek some kind of adventure, or indeed anything sufficiently distracting to take my mind off the prox-imity of Tuesday, the looming resumption of methodical torture. Why didn't I just give it up? It was obviously doing me no good at all. This was the line my thoughts always took and when they got to that point I would remind myself again that I was doing what I wanted to do, I was doing what I had chosen to do. This

151

alone made me luckier than nine-tenths of the population. And a little hardship, a little discomfort – it would go eventually. Always deal with what pain is and never with what it means.

Another quick shot of whiskey and we headed for the station. The course was forgotten, only the night counted.

The train had that rainy-season smell, a damp air-conditioned cool, faintly ammoniac from the people sweating freely into the carriage cloth. Ben and I had a whole bench seat to ourselves. No one would sit next to us, not unless the train became freakishly crowded. It was something that I accepted easily in Japan – that Japanese people would be irrationally nervous and not want to sit next to me on a train. Sometimes I had people get up on me during a trip, get up and stand in a crowded gangway rather than sit next to a foreigner. Of course the ones that got up always moved down the train, faking as if to get off, but they never did. I developed a sixth sense for knowing if someone was moving away from me for a legitimate or simply prejudiced reason. It bothered Chris enough to make him talk about it in aggrieved tones. He suggested we fought back with a t-shirt campaign. On the t-shirt it would say 'Glad to be Gai' as in gaijin.

There were times when I revelled in the fact that I was inspiring people to move away. I could see how blacks could easily get into intimidating whites rather than being annoyed by discrimination. If someone is irrationally afraid of you it is hard not to play on that fear.

The train rounded the slow curve into Ikebukuro station and we ran through the crowd to the Yamanote Line connection. 'It's too hot to run,' called Ben, but he carried on running out of a natural sense of competition, or wanting to keep up.

We squeezed on to the train south next to a hard-looking beautiful Japanese girl with peroxide blond hair, white plastic dress and white plastic thigh boots with five-inch platforms.

'She's looking white,' Ben said.

'How do you *wash* a plastic dress?' I said.

152

'Under the cold tap,' replied Ben. 'Come on,' he said, pulling me off the train, 'this is our stop.'

We were heading for an *izakaya*, a huge open-plan beer hall where hysterical groups of salarymen, office ladies and university students sat around drinking *dai-jokkis* of foaming lager. A *dai-jokki* is about a litre of beer, except the top third is all foam, so it's more like a pint. Ben kept asking them to cut the foam off. For a phlegmatic seven-foot Australian he was getting skittish, almost excited.

'I'm not paying for foam,' he told the waitress. She came back with the first full *dai* I'd ever seen. I tried it too. Then the manager came over and told us, '*Dai-jokki* style is to have big foam head.' We were back on the foam.

Soon Patrick arrived, with 'the party'. We were celebrating the launch of a new language school where Patrick worked. He had brought most of his students to the *izakaya*. They were all female.

'Be a *bit* careful,' he said. 'This is my bread and butter.'

I looked at the girls. Temporarily my view was impaired as Ben threw some foam on to my glasses. He was demonstrating his dislike of foam to the girls. They tittered dutifully at the seven-foot baby. With vision impairment I made out a tall one, a short one, a fat one, a thin one, no, make that two thin ones, a normal one, a beautiful one and a very beautiful one.

I wiped my spectacles. Kirin beer must be full of chemicals – already a hard scum had dried on to my lenses.

I talked to Patrick. He told me he had completed his lavatorial beer-can shrine. 'Yep,' he said, 'every wall is covered. One thousand four hundred and seventy-seven cans. I count them while I'm on the bog. It's a kind of meditation.' Was he joking? He gave me his sidelong unwavering look as he exhaled Marlboro smoke.

'What next?' I said. 'The kitchen?'

'The wife won't allow that,' he answered, with complete

seriousness. 'She drew the line at the toilet door. "No cans past here," she said.'

I wondered where Patrick's mysterious cool came from. Maybe it was his deadpan voice. Or his unflinching eyes. Or the drink.

Patrick was still sceptical about aikido. He was tall, maybe six one or two, and believed he could handle himself in a punch-up. 'But it's not about punch-ups,' I protested. 'So what is it about?' he countered, half amused.

I did my latest painful locks on him and found his body even stiffer than mine – apparently I had learnt something in all my weeks of training. I showed him some nifty elbow pins and jabs to the jaw. He still wasn't convinced. The problem with demonstrating aikido is that if the other person doesn't know aikido they'll get hurt. I explained that to Patrick and he nodded slowly. I could tell he didn't really believe me.

Somehow the boy Ben seemed to be taking control. In the drunken swirl he towered like a maypole around which we skipped our merry way. He was calling for a change of venue. Two of the girls were hanging on to his arms and staring imploringly up at him. He shouted across to me: 'The Rolling Stone!'

Built as a *venue d'hommage* to that illustrious British rock group, though 97 per cent of Japanese believe them to be American (just as an astonishing 68 per cent believe Rolls Royce cars are German), the 'Stone' was, in reality, a seedy little flea pit full of frenzied drinkers and dancers served by grumpy gay-biker staff. The disc jockey sat behind a chicken-wire screen in a wooden hutch where he span endless heavy rock tunes. Certain nights were Stones songs only, but these were not the most popular nights. It was the only place in Japan where I saw a 'no fighting' sign.

The Stone was known to foreigners but it was not dominated by them, not in the way the big clubs in Roppongi were. Roppongi, with its wide main strip and teeming discos, was the prime pick-up location in Tokyo. The Stone wasn't like that, dominated as it was by the shifting street gangs that hung around the Kabuki-cho district. In fact the Stone was in the heart of the area that sixty years earlier Kancho Sensei had prowled looking for a fight with the gangs of that time. Was such a consideration at the back of Ben's mind? Or mine? Or was it just coincidence that we were hunting for action, or something, in that same seedy area?

Kancho's most notable street brawl, and the origin of his precise '70 per cent of a street fight is *atemi*' (hitting), actually happened about three blocks from the Rolling Stone, an area still notorious for its pimps, prostitutes, gangsters, low life, transvestites, queens, queers, rent boys and salarymen.

But Shioda was no salaryman, no bespectacled geek, eager to be drunk and to spend his salary on salacious waftings of vice. He was a hard bastard in search of victims to beat up, scientifically of course.

The master Ueshiba counselled the students strongly: 'On no account go looking for fights.' But like good students everywhere they totally ignored him.

Shioda and a fellow disciple selected a street gang lounging on a corner in the Kabuki-cho district. They sauntered through the gang, no doubt knocking into shoulders in time-honoured fight-starting fashion.

A gang member confronted Shioda: 'We're members of such and such a gang – you better watch out?'

Shioda replied: 'We're member's of the Aiki-gang – and you better watch out.'

Not waiting for a reply, Shioda had already realized he wasn't talking to the gang leader, who he supposed would be the hardest nut to crack amongst them. Out of the corner of his eye he saw one man taller than the rest, tough looking and taking an amused interest in the proceedings. Giving no warning, Shioda marched up to him and gave him an almighty punch in the solar plexus. It wasn't exactly sporting, but it gave rise to another one of the founder's favorite dicta: 'In a fight against many, always make the first blow count against the strongest man.'

The strongest man doubled over in pain and the fight was on. Confused by their leader's early downfall, the gang were soon felled by the viciously able Shioda, the most deadly goldfish any of them had ever encountered.

As he tells the story in his autobiography we are left with an image of Shioda and his co-student rubbing their hands together with glee as they realize that aikido actually works, that all the hard training had not been in vain.

In England, people who like fighting can find what they are looking for in pubs or at football matches. In Japan, there is not really the same 'rumble culture'. Since the 1960s, motorcycle gangs, or *bosozoku*, have become known as the preserve of youths looking for violence. Two years previously a Western journalist had been killed whilst photographing such a gang, but this was, all agreed, a most unusual event. The movie *Black Rain*, starring Michael Douglas, portrayed a particularly well organized and venomous bike gang. The ones I had met with and the ones that R'em rode with were much more passive. They had more in common with North Circular Ace Café racers of the 1950s than Hell's Angels.

People recognized the *bosozoku* as recruitment centres for the *yakuza* proper. In Kabuki-cho the *yakuza* were on open parade. Wearing punch perms and driving big black Mercedes Benzs they looked more like trouble than the average Japanese law-abiding citizens. Gangs that followed a music style were usually harmless, even if, for fashion's sake, they carried a buck knife or a switch blade. In Harajuku, next to Yoyogi park, where rock 'n' roll dancers gathered on a Sunday afternoon with quiffs and pointy boots and genuine oil-stained '50s Levi's at $300 a pair, there was little sense of menace – it was harmless posing at its most innocuous.

Next to Harajuku was Shibuya, with its huddled quarter of pink neon-lit love hotels. The place was tame enough, but its

Senta-gai, literally 'central street', was a little rougher. There were odd stabbings and beatings which made the place off limits to the more strait-laced Japanese. The gangs that hung around there, composed mainly of misfits and runaways, were still physically unintimidating and those killed were usually lone university students, the most defenceless prey to venture out at night.

The rock 'n' rollers of Kabuki-cho, who hung about the tiny bars and dark alleys, were different again. Vain and narcissistic, Patrick called them the apache queens. Many of them had dreadlocks, their straight Japanese hair treated with chemicals to make it mat. Older than the Shibuya mob, around twenty-five to thirty, some of them were distinctly rough looking. The 'no fighting' sign in the Stone was directed at them. They were professional street people, with the patina of streetwise cool that adheres to even the more feeble physical specimens, who have no respectable job, live by night and enjoy the *frisson* of violence promised by late bars and venues.

What would Kancho have made of such streetwise yobbos? One to one, not very much at all. But if the gang descended, and you had the misfortune to stumble and fall, you could expect no fair play. A good kicking if you were lucky, a vicious stabbing if you weren't.

I had seen students in Shibuya openly laughing at a man on crutches making his painful way up Senta-gai. To gain a bigger laugh, a young lad of no more than twenty kicked one of the crutches away. I bellowed a string of English obscenities and the cripple lurched away without a look backwards. But the students were, until my outburst, which stunned them momentarily, laughing and joking at the cripple's misfortune. And this was a mixed group, all at a respectable university, boys and girls from 'decent' families. The Japanese, like no other race I have encountered, have a great capacity for distancing themselves from the vanquished underdog.

With zero trepidation our drunken party descended on the

Stone. Patrick ordered a bottle of spirits and plenty of soda. He had forgotten his earlier fears about unruly conduct in front of his students. We had now coalesced into a tight-knit group of revellers. This happens in Japan better than anywhere else. Actually, one of the thin ones was still holding back, she excused herself with the usual 'my train is leaving soon' and the party reached critical mass with no freeloaders.

The DJ hunched behind his chicken wire and seemed to be playing endlessly the Red Hot Chili Peppers' 'Give it Away'. The sweaty pit in the centre of the Stone erupted into a frenzy of dancing. Such single-minded, utterly serious, manic, crazed dancing I had never before seen. Without a scrap of irony or humour at indulging in such a ludicrous activity, it was repressed humanity in search of total release. The flashing lights on sweaty faces spoke of a writhing purgatory, an endless disco where you are condemned to dance as if your life depended on it, until God made up his mind that you had expiated your sins on earth. I sipped gin and soda and sat back mesmerized. It was far too dangerous to join in for more than a dance or two. You risked being sucked into a head-banging frenzy. I might even lose my spectacles again – something that had happened on a previous visit to the Stone. Wanged away from my face during a frenzied foot stomper, I had foolishly got down on my hands and knees, pawing the wet and butt-strewn floor for my precious glasses. It had been a big mistake. The crowds surged over me. I was almost trampled to death. In a panic I hauled myself up the front of a girl pounding in front of me. She hardly noticed such attention and when I discovered my specs snagged in her lacy blouse I gave thanks and left the dancefloor never to return.

The gin and soda worked its slow and insidious effect. The merely beautiful girl had revealed a set of teeth that doubled and trebled before my eyes. They seemed braced, stayed and metali-cized far back into her smiling mouth. How could so many teeth fit into one mouth? It was beyond me. She was telling me about a TV commercial for apple juice she had appeared in. I kept waiting for another glimpse of her teeth. She was the first person I had met who had kept their milk teeth into their early twenties, had grown them alongside their adult teeth. It was like something out of Greek mythology. I turned to the normal-looking one, whose dedicated face under the sublime and artificial lighting of the Stone now appeared quite beautiful. Her teeth were small and perfect. She was quite entranced by the madness of the place. It was too loud to talk except for witty, or witless, soundbites. I sat her on my knee and she squirmed a bit with embarrassment.

Then all hell broke loose. Some kind of altercation on the dancefloor between an apache and a kid dressed in exact imitation of Sid Vicious had escalated into a slapping match. They pushed and slapped each other like schoolgirls. Then the apache, in his leather vest, fell heavily to the ground with a beer glass in his hand, which somehow broke before it hit the floor. A spurt of blood sprayed on to the cuff of my shirt. The girl who had been cut started to scream a mad falsetto scream which brought no one to her aid, rather it kept people away, as a stuck pig keeps away those intent on killing it. The guy on the floor was, meanwhile, being given a very thorough kicking by an assortment of male, and female, aggressors. Demure, and I would have thought, quite ordinary Japanese girls were laying into the man on the floor with great vigour and fanatical enjoyment. These girls wore stilettos and boots and did not know the man on the ground. They didn't know the Sid lookalike either. Instinctively they had decided to lay into the fallen man, an underdog. It was one of the most shocking things I had ever seen.

Somehow the apache was dragged by his friends to his feet. The cut girl was seen to by one of the gay-biker bar tenders. The chicken-hutted DJ called for order and then put the Red Hot Chili Peppers on for the fifth time.

'Did you see that?' I said to Patrick.

He nodded, staring at me somewhat fixedly.

'Hey! Where's Ben?' Unnoticed, Ben had slipped away. One of the girls had gone too.

'Maybe in the toilets,' said Patrick. 'There's a hell of a queue.'

'With a girl?' The question went unanswered. More activity was taking place around the door of the club, but it was hard to see. Patrick stood up to get a better look. His head nearly touched the roof of the sweaty basement dive. People turned and stared at his sudden height.

'What's going on?' I said.

'Can't see. Some kind of trouble, though.'

'Forget it,' I said. 'It's none of our business.' A phrase I'd heard so often in Japan, but now, as I parroted it, it felt false, not my words at all. Patrick sat down. I swigged some more gin and soda. The ice had all melted, leaving a bucket a quarter full of water. Patrick glugged at the water. The girl shifted uneasily but prettily on my knee. Her name was Sara, which is a rare name in Japan, though it is a Japanese name. She was nineteen and had just graduated from high school. She told me she worked in a supermarket where the customers sometimes made her cry.

There was a heavy banging at the door, which opened into the club down a stairway from outside. There was some kind of altercation at the door, but it was still too crowded to see properly. The music stopped and there was an announcement over the PA. Could everyone stay in the club for the time being, the DJ said, since there was trouble in the street outside. The doors were being locked, which was probably against every fire regulation written, but the Stone was the kind of club doomed to end in showy fireworks, possibly an arson attack during a Bo Diddley retrospective, or a homemade handgrenade lobbed by a disaffected founder member of the Japanese Red Army.

After the announcement and before the music started again there was an eerie, sweaty, almost-silence, when all we could hear was a heavy thump-thump-thump on the club doors. From where I was sitting, across the dance pit from the entrance, I

160

could see the doors flexing and shuddering under the pounding. Eventually it faded away. The Red Hot Chili Peppers were on again. I returned to my gin and meltwater. Sara, the ex-high-school girl, had left my knee. I was now talking to the moon-faced Taeko, who had a tight curly perm. She told me she had just quit being a dog beautician.

'Why?' I asked.

'At first I loved dogs, that is why I learned to cut their hair. But day after day cutting dogs' hair and clipping dogs' nails, I began to hate dogs. Also the owner made me sleep at night in the pet store with all the dogs.' She gave me a wan smile.

'You slept with the dogs!'

'It was very smelly, but after a while you do not notice the bad smell. But I began to hate dogs and I didn't want that so I quit.'

'Come to think of it,' I said carelessly, 'you do look a little like a dog, maybe a St Bernard or something.'

Taeko looked at me with great seriousness and said in English: 'Do you say that because I'm . . . chubby?'

'No. No. Not at all. Not at all.'

Where was Ben? There was a renewed surge of banging, a cracking sound and the door flew open. Two foreign men, one blond and one dark, came tumbling in through the doorway like time travellers who'd just landed in another century. They went to the bar trying to look as if everyone's eyes were not on them, but they were not wholly successful in this, despite the loud music taking up the slack and dissolving crowd attention.

'Let's find out what's going on,' said Patrick. 'Coming?' he insisted.

'All right,' I said. I wondered if he was going to try and prove something to me.

The blond man, who was short and young – I guessed no more than twenty-two or twenty-three – was shaking with fear. It was the first time I had seen someone whose eyes were wide with fear. He looked from side to side and around him as he talked.

'There's hundreds of them out there,' he said.

'Who? What happened?'

'They think that I was kicking one of their gang when he was on the floor. But I wasn't. I was here with my girlfriend.'

The girlfriend seemed to have vanished.

'I saw that,' I said. 'That guy being kicked was kicked solely by Japanese nationals, girls mainly, from what I could gather.'

'But they don't think so. And they're out there waiting. How can I get home? They took me outside and that's why we were banging on the door to get back in.'

He lit a Marlboro cigarette with shaking hands.

'They're waiting out there for me. They want to get me. There's about twenty or thirty of them.'

He was young, with a squarish head, short, medium build – but all the fight had gone out of him. The dark haired man with him was older, an American. He was smoking too.

'It was hairy out there,' he said.

'What do you want to do?' said Patrick to me. I didn't like the way he was involving me, despite all the watery gin I had consumed.

As we talked there was a crowd surge emanating from the entrance. The blond Australian was instantly surrounded by dreadlocked, leather-jacketed Japanese. The apache gang were back in force. We were all surrounded in a swirling mass of figures. I tried to break through to the Australian who was being hustled towards the door. 'What's going on?' I shouted. Members of the gang were pressing up behind me. I turned to Patrick: 'Move away, let them go, get out of the way!' This was knife country, the worst possible situation to be in if people have knives. 'Always fight with your back to the wall,' Chris used to say. We were surrounded in a dark club by anonymous thugs. It would be very easy for someone to stick you and get away. What with all the crowds and the frenzied dancing they probably wouldn't find your body until they were clearing up the next day. Patrick was trying to talk to about five people at once. I pulled him by the shoulder and we broke free of the crowd around the Australian. We saw his helpless face, pale and scared, disappearing out of the door in a wave of gang members. Then he was gone and the door was slammed shut. The club seemed suddenly empty and peaceful, but the door, massive and shut, stared back like a reproach.

Back at the table we explained what had happened. The girls said: 'It's frightening.' No one had any suggestions.

'What's going to happen to him out there?' I asked Patrick.

'Probably get the shit kicked out of him.'

'We can't be sure about that, though, can we?'

'No.'

'We had to let them take him,' I said, feeling a lot less *laissez-faire* than I sounded. 'We had to let them take him. We couldn't do anything. There was a real chance of being stabbed in that mayhem.'

Patrick lit another Marlboro and calmly sipped his gin.

'What are we going to do?' I said. I looked around the club. There were about four or five foreigners dotted around the place. 'We could enlist support. Form a gaijin posse.'

Patrick looked around and then looked at me. I knew what he was thinking. I'd been training every day for five months. What had I been training for? What? This. This is what it came down to.

'I'm not too happy about this,' I said.

'Come on,' said Patrick. 'He's out there on his own. We've got to do something.'

We went over to the American, the guy who'd forced his way back into the club with the frightened Australian.

'We're thinking of going out to give your friend a hand,' I said.

The American looked nervous. 'He's not my friend, no. I

mean, I just met him when we were out there. I don't really know him at all.'

'Will you give us a hand?' asked Patrick, leaning over him.

The American glanced up quickly. 'No, I mean, I don't know the guy. Really I don't. I'm sorry.'

We went over to a table where two foreign men were talking and drinking beer. They looked about my age or a bit older. I repeated the request. One, who was English, replied. He had a drawl and sounded drunk: 'I don't give a shit, right. I come here to have a quiet drink and really I don't give a shit.' He looked at his friend, who wore teardrop-shaped glasses, for support. The friend looked away.

'It's none of our fucking business,' continued the Englishman. 'I saw those guys. They're fucking trouble.' He took an awkward swig from his beer bottle. 'And I just don't give a shit.'

I turned away. 'We're wasting our time,' I said.

'It's just us then,' said Patrick.

'Looks like it.'

I opened the big wooden nightclub door with a feeling of grave misgiving which was, at that moment, suddenly overtaken by an extraordinary sense of curiosity. No fear at all, just extreme curiosity. What would we meet at the top of the stairs? What would we do?

Up the stairs we went and emerged in the crowded lamp-lit street outside. The gang and its shadows surrounded our Australian friend. His face was blotched with pink and he was being pushed back and forth, taunted, a prelude to pushing him to the floor and working him over with the boot.

We sailed through the twenty or thirty who were around the frightened face. I realized, as if for the first time, how tall Patrick was, tall and relaxed in the English teacher's uniform of shirt and suit trousers.

The leader of the gang, the main protagonist, whose hand was jabbing the unresisting Australian backwards, had dreadlocks and wore the wooly hat of a Rastaman. He seemed aggrieved.

With no plan or conference Patrick touched the Japanese Rasta on the shoulder, causing an upward interest from the man who was, I guessed, somewhere under thirty. He had a few loose strands sprouting from his chin, like a female athlete on steroids.

At the self-same moment, in an unrehearsed ballet of diversion, I put my arm around the shaking shoulders of the Aussie. 'Time to go home,' I said, in a voice which memory conveys to me as several tones deeper than my usual speech. 'But they won't let me,' he blabbed. Patrick, with heaven-sent inspiration that only the seriously cool can ever seem to muster, indicated by eye the red, yellow and green Jamaican lapel badge on the Jap-Rasta's beaten leather waistcoat. 'You like reggae,' he stated in his preternaturally slow English. 'I like reggae too.' The Rastalike looked wary at the cool Englishman soliliquizing. 'I like reggae,' Patrick repeated, 'and reggae is about peace.'

Anywhere else in the world this line would have probably earned him a punch in the face. But Japan is different. Peace is a strong word in Japan.

Everything was now in freeze-frame and I heard no more for I was walking, slower than slow, restrainedly slow and definitely NOT RUNNING with the Australian shoulder under my brotherly arm, walking towards a taxi rank some forty yards away, where our road T-junctioned into a bigger road. There was the usual nightclub queue of thousands, waiting for a rare taxi, standing behind a pole stuck in a bucket of concrete. The night was black and my ears, neck and the back of my head were burning. I was desperate to look back, to see if Patrick's spell was broken, if the apache horde had been released and were about to fall upon me with buck knives and straight razors. But I did not look back. I was Orpheus escaping Orpheus as he should have been.

A taxi appeared in slow motion as we closed on the front of the queue. Amidst multiple protests of those waiting I grabbed open the door, stopping the legitimate line servers from entering, bellowing now at the little Aussie to get in and go. Magically, the girlfriend appeared again, from where I have no idea. Leggy and grateful she thanked me eight times before, on slamming the door, I allowed myself to holler: 'Go, Go, Go.' Really, it was too exciting. The bickering taxi queue did not exist.

I walked back, thoughtful, to the distant height of Patrick, now standing off to one side in deep conversation with the leader. I stood on the threshold of their conversation. Nothing should be rushed, I knew that much.

'I sorry. I very sorry. Thank you. I sorry,' said the leader, who had been miraculously converted by the calming influence of Patrick. The Jap had switched, switched sincerely.

'I sorry,' he repeated, 'I sorry. Very sorry.'

We talked in a threesome, general and apologetic conversation for as long as I could stand, Patrick's fatherly hand on the Rasta's arm, firm friends they had become, the gang dissolved, the night empty and clean again, before heading back into the haven of the club. I had no idea what time it was.

Beer, from Patrick's new mate, arrived at our table and periodically the leader of the once warring but now peaceful gang came over to repeat his tirade of self-accusatory apology. It was a relationship that had, I felt, limited possibilities.

'Tell the girls what happened,' I said to Patrick, but Patrick's version of the story needed me as a prompt, which confused the narrative. I could tell the episode did not mean as much to him as it did to me. In a few months, I guessed, he'd probably need reminding that the thing had actually happened. He was like that.

There was a noise in the nightclub, like the call to the muster stations on a cross-channel ferry, a bonging noise which signified the night was over. We struggled out into the pre-dawn gloom, a misty traipsing that ended in the twenty-four-hour donut and coffee shop. I put my head down for grateful kip, in amongst the wrappers on my tray. When I awoke everyone had gone except for Sara.

'Have you got school, I mean work, today?' I asked.

'No,' she said.

'We should go to the park and eat our donuts there,' I said.

On the way to the station we met the Sid Vicious lookalike who'd started it all. Silly little cocksure twerp. I greeted him like a longlost brother and engaged him in matey conversation. He asked for a donut. 'Buy your own,' I said, 'these are for me.' I said it laughing and at the same time wondering why I was talking to this Japanese boy punk.

Yoyogi park was empty except for the joggers appearing like gravel-crunching wraiths out of the mist. We sat on a trestle picnic bench with a table. I took it upon myself to kiss Sara. We kissed for a satisfyingly long time, coming up periodically for breaths. When we finished the donut-eating and the kissing we started back for the station.

'Why did you kiss me?' she asked.

'I just felt like it.'

This sounded insubstantial.

'I felt it was the right thing to do. In the park, this morning. This misty morning.'

'Someone who kisses a lot in Japan we say *kissama*,' she said, with a straight face.

There is stray poultry wandering in Yoyogi park, and this diverted my attention for a while.

'Let's go to a hotel and take all our clothes off,' I said, adventurously.

'Perhaps after some time,' she said, smiling. 'But not now.'

We walked on in silence. At the subway entrance I said goodbye to Sara. She told me she'd call me.

I turned and walked down the back streets of Harajuku towards Shibuya. The tiny streets were full of marvels that morning. A woodworking shop where the sun caught the hurrying motes of dust in a single beam from the skylight. A cat with a bell that tinkled as it ran away. A coffee machine that played a silly tune as I waited for the can to drop. A 100 yen

167

coin on the floor, which gave me just enough money to buy a morning paper. Marvels.

Ben came around the next day. He was bashful about having left with a girl. He was romantic about women and didn't want me to think he was sex mad or anything. I told him about my adventure, and all through it he kept wanting me to say how I'd broken this guy's jaw, or kneed that guy in the face. 'That's not the point,' I said. 'Patrick showed me it was all about relaxation. Relaxed but aware – that's got to be the key.'

It was Sunday night. My knees were still in a rotten condition. The idea of voluntarily putting my whole weight on to the two open wounds on each kneecap was disheartening, to say the least. It was the first time I had seriously considered giving up the course. I had become obsessed about not giving up, but things were looking grim, not rosy at all. And early morning special summer 'hardship' training was coming up soon too. The adventure of the night before had been a distraction. This was reality, and I wasn't sure how much more I could take. I swigged from the Wild Turkey bottle in order to forget about it. Ben reached forward for the bottle.

'You don't even like whiskey,' I said.

'I do,' he said cagily. Ben had a backpacker's instinct for grabbing anything that looked as if it was going for free.

'When it's gone it's gone,' I said sententiously. 'And then we'll only have our pain to share. Here, give it back.'

Sara had not called, but perhaps I had confused the message. The warmth of the whiskey was beginning to make itself felt.

'Do you know how much this stuff *costs*?' I asked Ben.

The telephone rang.

It was not Sara. It was Paul. A strange, delirious feeling came over me.

Paul spoke with official decorum. 'Got a bit of bad news. Kancho Sensei has died. He passed away early this morning. Not that we weren't expecting it sooner or later, but it's still a shock.'

'Yes.' I infused my voice with concern. 'How awful, I mean, what a terrible thing.'

'Yes, well, these things happen. The dojo will be closed, of course, for a week. Senshusei are expected to attend the funeral on Thursday.'

I commiserated some more and rang off. I punched the sky once in jubilation. Then I checked that the phone receiver was properly crutched.

'Yes!' I shouted. 'Yes! Yes! Yes!'

'He's dead, isn't he?' said Ben.

'Yes! Yes! Yes!'

'How many days' holiday?'

'One whole magic . . . week! Yes!'

We grabbed each other and did a victory dance around the kitchen floor.

'Time for some more whiskey.'

'Not whiskey – get champagne!'

Punch-Up at a Funeral

'Ther are three things that concern the loyal servant. The Master's will, his own vitality and the condition of his death.'

From the seventeenth-century Samurai manual *Hagakure*

I passed Kancho's lamppost on the way to the station. Perhaps in years to come a plaque should be fixed to it to celebrate the life of a great martial artist. Though he travelled widely in his life he was born, in 1916, in this, the same area where he died seventy-nine years later. His father was a wealthy doctor and built a judo dojo at their house for local people to practise in. It was called the Yoshinkan dojo, which meant 'the place of cultivating spirit'.

Kancho liked the family touch, so when he set up his own dojo and started to teach police and civilians the deadly arts he knew, he continued using the Yoshinkan name. For nearly four decades he had taught, and now that he was dead no one really knew who would take over the mantle of master. Kancho had left no clear orders, so a power struggle was lining up, principally between Chida Sensei and Kancho's son, Shioda junior. At the funeral I knew that the top teachers would present a unified front to the world, but afterwards it was rumoured the dojo might be split into two factions.

It was a hot day for a funeral: '34° C' flashed the neon digital thermometer on a tower building next to the station, and it was still only 9.00 a.m. My regulation black suit was wool, and already harboured pints of perspiration in the soggy lining of the underarms. I was sweating so much I decided it would be pointless to take my jacket off – why reveal my discomfort?

170

From the station to the funeral shrine schoolboys in traditional long black coats with Prussian collars and armbands stood every few yards to direct the constant stream of mourners. The foreign senshusei got into a huddle in front of the Shinto shrine to await instructions. The shrine was a huge gravelled area filled with pagoda-style outbuildings and one big ornate wooden building where the final respects were to be paid. There was money to be paid too; for the senshusei it was computed at two thousand yen each, higher earners would be expected to pay more. The midget disciple, Fujitomi, swamped in an outsize black suit, directed us to a cluster of white tents where the money was being collected. The cops had been drafted in to be funeral ushers. They wore their suits and were under orders from Oyamada. The foreign senshusei were without duties; when push came to shove they didn't want a bunch of gaijin messing things up. In Japan misunderstandings are feared more than anything; excluding foreigners is not done out of dislike, it is done out of a pathological fear of a misunderstanding developing, and an overactive imagination about the consequences of such a misunderstanding.

I calculated that a funeral was at least cheaper than a wedding. A guest at a Japanese wedding is expected to part with five thousand yen, minimum, and if you have any pretensions to being a close friend it is more likely to be twenty or thirty thousand – two or three hundred dollars. Being invited to a wedding in Japan is, like everything there, an apparent delight with a nasty sting in the tail. There's a word in Japanese that covers all such onerous social obligations, especially those designed to be for pleasure that end up a pain, like drinking with the boss after work or having to buy chocolates for colleagues on Valentine's Day. The word is *mendokusai*, the most useful word in Japanese studies you can learn. It's a word that encapsulates a cultural concept.

Paul was deputed to organize the foreign senshusei. He was, I noticed, wearing a tatty brown suit and had a black eye. Everyone noticed the eye but no one got more out of him than 'bicycle accident' – Paul was too brisk for that. Other foreign instructors turned up. They all wore grotty ill-fitting suits. What was going on? The Japanese, to a man, were clad in perfect funeral black. The foreign senshusei too, were smartly attired. R'em was wearing my dark blue suit again. Adam had no jacket, but he was able to borrow one for when we filed past the coffin, in the manner for deceased world leaders and tyrants everywhere.

We were summoned by Stumpy to be addressed by Paul.

'We've got a bit of trouble,' said Paul. 'Her.' He gestured with a nod towards Dolores, who was standing outside the entrance to the shrine.

Dolores had, it transpired, a serious crush on Don Fernando Sensei, a top Spanish teacher. She had become obsessed by him, and coming to Japan had been a brief gap in her staunch dedication to staying by his side. Now he had come to Japan for the funeral and she could renew her assault, for this is what it was. When Don Fernando had arrived at the dojo two days before she had sidled through the crowd and refused to shift from his side, even when he went into conference with the Japanese teachers. It was all very embarrassing by the Japanese standards that even foreigners adopted when dealing with the Yoshinkan dojo. The next day, at the private funeral, she had got wind of the event and burst out of a hedge to hijack the unsuspecting Fernando. Paul put *san kajo* on her (a standard police arrest lock) and marched her away. As he told us this I got the impression he really enjoyed doing it, which was odd, because it all seemed a little sad to me.

We were detailed to guard the neatly bearded Fernando 'in case she tries anything'. Paul demonstrated he'd lost none of his police expertise. In pairs we were assigned twenty-minute slots, each man forming the two corners of a triangle base, behind which was Fernando and in front of which was Dolores, who would be ideally kept located at a nominal third point of the triangle. Ten hulking men in dark suits protecting a top martial artist from a ninety-pound girl with amorous delusions.

'Is it worth it?' said Adam.

'It's good training,' said Paul. 'It really is.'

The temperature was now up to 36 degrees in the shade, except there wasn't any, so we stood sweltering in the broad sunlight waiting for our turn on 'Fernando protection duty'. The line of over a thousand mourners stretched five deep all round the shrine area. At Tesshu's funeral there had been over five thousand, but Kancho's certainly wasn't under-attended. It took two hours for the line to pass through the shrine building, where each person clapped their hands in front of the dead man's coffin and laid a *sasaki* sprig on an altar. The business inside the shrine was over very quickly. It had been like queuing two hours for a forty-second ride on the ghost train. It had all the characteristics of Japanese public life – torture disguised as celebration, a huge wait, entertainment massively disproportionate to waiting time and discomfort endured. Everything formal in Japan follows this format. If it doesn't people suspect that the event hasn't really happened.

That someone had to be guarded seemed bizarrely appropriate. At Tesshu's funeral one of his most loyal students had to be taken into custody. Tesshu's followers feared that he might commit *seppuku* out of respect for his dead teacher. Would anyone drive a short sword into their guts for Kancho's sake? Maybe once, before the war, but not now. The only honourable form of suicide now in Japan is *karoshi*, death through overwork – often stomach cancer, appropriately enough. *Karoshi*, not *harakiri*, is how loyalty is measured these days.

Finally, we saw Kancho's coffin being carried by the Japanese teachers and loaded into a Japanese hearse. Japanese hearses are quite the best hearses I have ever seen. I so liked them I wanted to get one secondhand and ship it back to England as an example of Oriental splendour and excess. The modern Japanese hearse is a monstrous copper pagoda on wheels, a black estate car, which instead of an estate back has a highly ornate, steep-roofed version of a shrine. It looks like something out of *The Wacky Races*. My last almost-glance of Kancho was of his coffin being manhandled into the back of one before it trundled him off to the crematorium. Almost all Japanese are cremated – there isn't enough land to bury people, as they did in the past.

Suddenly there was a flurry of activity as Stumpy moved like a bodyguard to block the nimble Dolores as she made a break for the black mourners' minibus. Don Fernando was getting on board with all the other top teachers for the final ride to the crematorium. He looked away, embarrassed by the scene, as Stumpy frogmarched Dolores through the pressing crowd.

The story of Paul's face gradually came out. Stephan gave away most of the story to Ben, and Darren supplied the rest. And it was connected to the teachers' state of dress.

At the smaller Buddhist ceremony the day before, only family and aikido teachers had attended. After the ceremony the foreign teachers had gone drinking in Roppongi. Some of the teachers had trained together years ago in Japan and flown in specially: Payet was there, David Rubens from England, Don Fernando and others. Robert Mustard and Fernando had sensibly gone home early, when Roland 'the Terminator' had taken against a bartender in a Roppongi club. Swinging a punch the barman went down, but not before the chief bouncer had been called. A former member of the French Foreign Legion the head bouncer then made a big mistake: he laid a hand on somebody's shoulder – whose, no one was ever quite sure, but it was undoubtedly a bad error. Not one of the foreign teachers was less than third-dan black belt. They were all supremely tough, aggressive and drunk. It was apparently the first trouble the ex-Legionnaire had been forced to contend with – he was quite new to the job. His mishandling of the situation also led to his sacking, but not before he'd been taken out by Roland. Darren finished it off by choking him out and then stood on his neck wagging a drunken finger: 'Just don't move a fucking inch.' Then all hell broke loose and the foreigners dished out several more beatings before going downstairs and starting another fight there. 'Was there any aikido?' asked Ben. 'Not that I saw,' said Stephan Otto, imitating the slow swing of a novice's haymaker punch. 'It was just brawling.' Darren disagreed: 'Aikido training came in when I choked him out. I was able to relax my full weight down on to his neck.' Payet, deemed too lethal for such an encounter, had been shifted by Stephan into a corner on the grounds of respect for his seniority. In reality Otto reported Payet's assassin's eyes searching the place for a chance to test his deadly skill.

They moved on to another bar but word had already spread through the neighbourhood. 'Oh no,' the doorman had pleaded, 'not the black-tie gang!' Still dressed for the funeral in their dark suits and black ties, the unruly gang were set for another punch-up when the police arrived.

The Roppongi police are used to mad foreigners – drunken sailors and marines out for a good time – they wade in with batons first if there is the slightest sign of resistance.

Rubens then took charge in what looked like a desperate situation – criminal damage, GBH, ABH, possibly even a light custodial sentence. Rubens's Japanese was very good and he started to run through every Japanese cop's name he could think of – he had to find a connection to the grim-faced officers about to incarcerate them. The people Rubens had trained with back in 1986 would have been promoted from street-response duties by now, the people he knew would be at home at four in the morning on a sticky summer night. Eventually he convinced the police, though the teachers had to apologize profusely to the stern-faced officers. In Japan, anyone over third-degree black belt must register his hands with the police. None of these guys was registered, and if they were teachers, as they claimed, they were setting a very bad example, weren't they? The disgraced aikido brass nodded their bowed heads in unison and prayed they would be let off. The newspapers would love the story: FOREIGN AIKIDO MASTERS IN FIGHT THE NIGHT OF CELEBRATED FOUNDER'S

FUNERAL. On second thoughts the Japanese press are so hogtied by management and ownership interests, any wartime buddies of Kancho in the publishing business could easily quash bad publicity.

Their suits tattered and dirty, the drunken teachers were apparent by the clothes they were wearing at this second funeral ceremony. Without exception they looked a shabby lot, squinting in the bright sunlight, some with shaving cuts and bruises. No wonder Paul had been anxious to deflect interest in the previous night's exertions.

I plucked up the courage to speak to Jacques 'the assassin' Payet, using my brief ownership of one of his dogis as a conversational gambit. Short and wiry, Payet was very special, even among the Japanese teachers. He had spent ten years in Japan, the last five as one of Kancho's closest friends. Because of the strict hierarchy it was impossible for a Japanese younger than Kancho to be on equal terms with him. Because Payet was a foreigner he had managed this. It caused resentment amongst the Japanese, but as Kancho welcomed his friendship Payet didn't care.

'For five years I tried to be a Japanese and then I went back to France. I did some teaching and then I realized I was only teaching what I had been taught. I was only teaching hints and tips that I had learnt, and gradually I was running out of things to say. I realized that I did not know aikido. So I go back to Japan and this time I say I am not a Japanese I am a foreigner. OK, what is the advantage of being a foreigner? I can ignore all the ritual of Japanese society and go straight to Kancho, so this is what I did.

'I look at Kancho and I say to myself: How can this tiny little man, who must be getting weaker physically each year, who only drinks tea and watches television in his office and reads the newspaper, and smokes, how can he get stronger at aikido each year? How is this possible? Because, I assure you, it is true – he was stronger at seventy-three than he was at seventy, and this

176

continued until he got cancer. One day I saw a *shoji* screen fall on to Kancho and he fell over. He fell over from the force of a paper screen, so I understand that he has some secret which is quite different from normal ideas of physical power. So I try to find this secret.'

'So what's the secret?' I asked.

'It is three things that all connect to each other and reinforce each other. As words they are nothing, but if you can understand them then you can do aikido. And it does not take a lifetime. Ueshiba only studied for a few years; Kancho maybe five years, allowing for breaks. What they understood are balance, centre and confidence. When you know where your centre is then you have balance. After that you get confidence, which again helps balance. Aikido techniques are only there to build these things. I have fought against karate experts. I could not use *shihonage* or *kotegaeshi* – so I have to improvise, but I succeed because I use balance, centre and confidence.'

Payet smiled a self-deprecating smile. I noticed he had huge forearms, despite his slight build. He made it all sound so simple.

'First, keep adjusting your centre, move it back and forwards until you find it. A traditional Japanese dance teacher watched a video of mine and told me my weight was thrown too far back. That was a great help to me.'

'What was Kancho like?' I asked.

'He was actually a very simple man, with simple tastes. He did not care if you were a foreigner or a Japanese. Sometimes I think he hated the way he became trapped by the organization he created. He needed students but also he despised slavishness in students; but that is the Japanese way. He was a kind of rebel himself. He liked beer very much. Sometimes he would call me away from a lesson and say, "Come on, Jacques, let's drink beer in my office. You say you can't do *tai no henko*? I can't do *tai no henko* either, and I invented it!" When he became ill I felt very sorry for him. He seemed like a lonely old man who had made something he could not control. That is why I left Japan and return to France. I had learnt everything he had to teach me.'

Payet shook my hand instead of the usual bow. 'Remember,' he said, 'we are not Japanese.'

Paul's Swiss girlfriend Eva was comforting Dolores after her abortive break for the mourners' minibus. It had been the final straw for Dolores, who had broken down into tears. From her garbled English I gathered that things were not so simple – Don Fernando, she claimed, had actually been having an affair with her. He had wanted to finish things but Dolores thought otherwise. 'Men,' snapped Eva, 'you're all cowards, aren't you.'

Back at Fuji Heights there was still no message from Sara. I went to the supermarket where she worked and queued up at the checkout with a bag of unwanted oranges. She smiled when she saw me. 'What do you want?' she asked. 'You,' I said. She agreed to meet me in a few days after she finished work, but only for a few hours. Her father was very strict, she said. It didn't sound promising.

The week's reprieve did the trick with my knees. Bright pink flesh had replaced the weeping sores. For once, as I entered the dojo, I felt elated and didn't have to will myself into a 'tough' frame of mind.

There was a new member of the shower detail – Craig, who had finally got a cultural visa, had flown back from Australia. He was fat and flabby and three months behind everyone else, but he was back. He said nothing about the pilfering of his locker. During lessons he was taken on one side by a *sewanin* and beaten, driven, insulted and bellowed at to try to rush him up to our level. His main trouble was that he could not do the basic movements without stumbling. We had been practising them every day for months. With candour he told us he had spent his time back in Australia playing football and drinking beer. Judging by his gut, less of the former than the latter.

Craig scrubbed extra hard in the mouldy showers, giving

Adam and me a nice break. He was cowed and subservient and eager to be accepted into the team.

Craig's back soon became a mass of yellowish-purple bruises as he was forced by Darren to do endless breakfalls. Craig's howls of anguish punctuated the steamy summer silence of our own training. We had long ago learnt that shouting just wastes energy, however much it hurts. Craig, though, was not convinced, and he bellowed like an animal caught in a steel trap. His knees, too, were soon a red and mushy pulp, no worse than mine, perhaps a little better, but not nice at all.

After one particularly punishing session with Darren, where each fall had required two yells from Craig (one to psyche himself up to do it and another caused by the pain of doing it), Craig sat in the changing room in a very glum posture, a slump of imminent defeat. I tried to get him to see the bright side of his torture – it would soon be over, we'd all been through it, how he was improving fast; the usual brew of half truths we dredge up for conventional encouragement. In words reminiscent of Danny after the toe incident, he said, sorrowfully, 'Don't be surprised if you don't see me tomorrow, lads.'

Had they broken him? If he went, our unique record – the first course with no quitters – would be broken. At the same time *schadenfreude* was also there, the undoubted rush of energy you get when you pass others who fail.

My own new misfortune was to be back at the hands of Little Nick, the Armenian Hotspur. He was becoming increasingly arrogant and moody and just plain difficult to deal with. He didn't like being in Japan and he didn't like training with me. And he worshipped Mustard. And, of course, he was the apple of Mustard's eye. Oh, these were trying times indeed.

'You're a man and he's a boy,' said Wild West Will. 'You've just got to show him who's boss.'

Chris was more sceptical. 'The only way to deal with Little Nick is distance. But you're his partner and there is no distance, so you can't really do anything.'

Little Nick's faults were only the faults of a nineteen-year-old delinquent who had come from a rich home, dosed as a kid on ritalin, an American drug prescribed for hyperactive children, and then spoilt rotten – his mother going specially to Hollywood to buy the latest fashions he demanded.

Ben, who was the same age as Little Nick, used to complain, 'When I was fourteen I had a second-hand judo suit that was too small. When he was fourteen his parents paid for a year of tap-dancing lessons.'

'Who paid for your judo lessons?'

'They were free. No one pays for judo in Australia. But tap dancing – that's really expensive.'

I had nothing against Little Nick's tap-dancing skills; indeed, he seemed to be putting them to good use at the Baseball Café in Tokyo Dome, where he had a job as a dancer.

'What do you dance to?' I asked, during one of our rare moments of communication.

'Oh, Village People, "YMCA", stuff like that.'

'Village People!' I could hardly contain my glee. 'When are you next on? I've got to see this!'

But the Armenian remained coy about the exact times he was on stage, shaking his stuff, and before we had a chance to get up there and check him out he'd been sacked for breaking the arm of one of the waiters.

'Actually, I resigned,' he said, modestly. 'After I did the guy I figured they wouldn't want me back. Plus they're all assholes there anyway.'

He showed me how he'd beaten up his co-worker using a sequence of moves in a combination of *nikajo* and *hijishime* to take him down.

'His arm made a real noise so I think I broke it,' he said. 'His face was messed up too after I'd kneed him a few times.'

'At least you used aikido,' I said, lamely.

'Yeah,' he said. 'Apart from the knee, that wasn't aikido, that was me.'

In the tea room Little Nick told Robert Mustard, 'I did something, but I don't know if I should tell you . . .'

Mustard didn't look up from the paper he was reading.

'So you got in a fight, did you?'

'How did you know?'

Mustard shrugged. Then he said: 'Did you win?'

'Yes.'

'That's OK, then.'

But one day Nick went too far. We were doing a technique that required a stomach punch that was blocked. Done over and over again, people become careless at blocking. To exploit such carelessness would be acceptable by a teacher, or even a fellow student, but not if it leads to injury – these were my thoughts, anyway.

Little Nick evaded my block with deliberate malice and landed a hard punch on a rib, which was suddenly painful. I was so annoyed that I punched him back in the kidney and told him to back off. Suddenly contrite he offered his hand to make up and forget. I grudgingly shook. But I did not forget. I couldn't. The little jerk had, with his well-aimed sharp punch, put me in considerable pain. A broken rib? Surely not, and embarrassing to admit, since technically I should have blocked him.

I described the symptoms to Darren.

'Sounds like you're having a heart attack to me,' he said.

Sato, the bald masseur, was summoned by Mustard. Sato checked me over and shook his head. 'Maybe the rib is broken,' he said. But he was adamant that I should go to the doctor and get it checked. Mustard was very decent, so decent I felt bad for exaggerating the pain. Then I corrected myself: it is bad, it really hurts. But at the back of my mind, I thought, This injury is only as bad as Armenian Nick. When he goes, it goes; of that I can be sure. Mustard went to punch me playfully in the stomach. He indicated some university students. 'Do you want to train with the girls?' 'No!' I said, with feeling. '*Yosh!*' He punched me again. Good for you, son, he was saying. He would have made a great dad. A while later we were talking again. He said: 'Sometimes I'm brushing my teeth in the morning and I get some terrible pain in my chest and I think I must be having a coronary, but then I think, I can't be, because I'm still brushing my teeth.' Had he picked up intuitively on my own hypochondria? Mustard was like that – a combination of what seemed like obtuseness mixed with incredible intuition. He had nothing to hide and he did not care to hide himself.

To earn more injury time I would have to visit a hospital and get some medical evidence of my injury: X-rays to flourish in front of a suspicious sensei's eyes, or a chit signed by a bonesetter. The problem was that I had no medical insurance, which was related to my complicated semi-legal status in Japan. Ben, however, had a medical insurance card. He lent it to me. Only as I entered the Catholic Hospital in Ochiai, staffed by pleasant Japanese nuns, did I realize that I would have to pass for nineteen years old. I was thirty. I had grey hairs showing on my shaved head. I filled in the registration form, slyly copying Ben's birthdate, which I didn't know – another flaw in the plan. The nun gave my card a startled look and then looked at me again. 'You are nineteen?' she asked. 'Yes,' I said airily. She accepted my lie, questioning it only by another look at the medical card for a misprint. I quickly had an excuse lined up – I came from a family with a history of a dreadful wasting disease that aged you prematurely; it had only been discovered recently and diagnosed. The nun simply let it go. In Japan an outright lie is seldom questioned – it is too confrontational to do so, but people may hold a different opinion behind their backs. On the surface they will pretend to agree. I was also a foreigner, considered a somewhat lower form of human being by most Japanese. If I looked a little odd that was just part of the general inexplicable oddness of gaijin.

But as I waited, in full sight of the reception desk, I tried to act as I remembered Ben acted. He was usually slumped forward asleep. But with me that would be interpreted as adding years not subtracting them. My greying hair had already caused me to be mistaken for a forty-seven-year-old Japanese sensei from behind when I was hailed by a student in the street, much to their embarrassment when I turned around. No, falling asleep was the wrong strategy. I started instead to bob my head up and down in restless imitation of a kid listening to rap music on a Walkman. I touched my hair a lot too – something I've noticed a lot of teenagers do, and maybe I did too when I was that age.

The doctor agreed to see me. I hoped very strongly he would speak only Japanese. I would then limit my own capability, and as little communication as possible about my age would take place.

It was good. He addressed me in Japanese. I stumbled out a satisfactory answer. He packed me off to X-ray after a cursory examination.

Down in X-ray a laughing Japanese lad extinguished his cigarette in the corridor and beckoned me over to the machine. He flicked lead shields about my body in a most casual manner. After this, I thought, I'll be sterile at only nineteen, at the height of my sexual powers.

The doctor called me in for a discussion about the X-rays. The lungs looked completely black. 'Don't worry,' he said, 'this means nothing'.

The rib was not broken. It had just been tweaked a little. Rest for a month, he said. A month! I'd be lucky to get three days for this scrape, maybe a week if I could re-interpret the injury into more impressive jargon. It was then that I came up with the terms 'rib separation' and 'detached intercostal muscles'. People had shoulder separations so why not rib separations? It sounded nasty – ribs forced apart in agonizing . . . well, agony.

The doctor gave me a showy elasticated corset to wear around my chest – perfect, I now had visual evidence of my traumatic wound. I enthusiastically paid the fifty-dollar bill.

Then the doctor took off his half-moon specs and started to speak a rusty, but perfect English. Fear flooded through me – in the guise of wanting to practise his college English he would unmask this anti-social scrounger.

'Where from?' he said.

'Australia, Melbourne.'

He beamed. 'I went to Melbourne last year, for my holidays!'

'Must have been nice,' I struggled to convey a blasé lack of interest in a deeply unconvincing Australian accent, a Crocodile Dundee twang that threatened to spiral into Pakistani at any moment.

'I liked Australia very much, and Melbourne too.'

'Did you go to the Ned Kelly museum?' This was the only thing I knew about Melbourne.

'No,' he said. 'It was closed.'

'Really?' I said, 'Well, I've been here for years – I've lost touch. Well, not years, months – it just seems like years sometimes . . .' Christ, I was digging my own grave. 'Did you go to the Opera House?'

He looked puzzled. 'In Sydney?'

'No, in Melbourne. The Melbourne Opera House. It's very old and grand. Much more interesting than the one in . . . Sydney. You should visit the next time you go.'

'Yes, I will,' he said, glancing at my paper.

I had to distract him. 'Do you get many Australians in here?'

'No, we don't,' he said. 'You're the first I've treated.'

'How interesting,' I said. Then I remembered to look at my watch. Being Japanese he had to take the hint.

'I've got to go,' I said, and moved to the door.

'One more thing,' he said.

This is it, I thought.

'Don't forget this.' He handed me the offending medical card. 'This is very important,' he mock chided me.

I stormed out of the hospital, running like a nineteen-year-old hooligan. I felt better already. Chest corset or no chest corset.

Ben, I was beginning to realize, was one of life's imitators, like those moths that imitate birds, or insects that look like sticks, or flies that pretend to be wasps. I was injured and so, by God, would he be. Not that this went through his rational external processing unit, but it happened all right, once his imitative subconscious had got to work.

The next day, during my third class of *seiza*, Ben was thrown and landed awkwardly on his neck. Shioda junior was the teacher and he expressed little interest in the incident. Ben joined me at the sideline, the familiar tears running down his unabashed face. This was embarrassing for Shioda, so he instructed Will, who was training with Ben, to take him to the hospital. I watched all this in mute agony. If I called out I would suffer rebuke. A sharp remark from Stumpy perhaps, nothing too bad. Was it worth it, should I warn Ben to find a different hospital? No, he surely was not that stupid.

He was.

Later that day when I was back at Fuji Heights putting my feet up and scanning the newspaper for a good movie I received a phonecall from the hospital. Being of a suspicious nature I pretended that I was out and would take a message. Not only had Ben blown my cover, he'd actually been stupid enough to give my phone number to the nuns. I was livid.

A little while later Will called. He advised me to call the hospital. It was he who had advised Ben to hand over my name and number. Such law abiding cretins.

'Did Ben really think that they would have forgotten the only prematurely ageing Australian ever to visit their hospital, twenty-four hours after the event?'

'He seemed to think it would be OK,' said Will.

'Great. Terrific. Well, there's no way I'm calling that hospital.'

'It should be OK. We explained it was a simple misunderstanding.'

'A simple misunderstanding! It's obvious fraud! I spoke in an Australian accent. I gave his birthdate. I answered dumb questions about Melbourne! This is not a simple misunderstanding.'

'I find it's usually best to come clean about these things.'

'You do, do you? How about sticking to coming clean about your own misdemeanours rather than concentrating on other people's?'

It was a low shot. Will was an honourable man. When his girlfriend became pregnant I advised him to think seriously about abortion. Instead, he married the girl, and things, as it happened, were turning out pretty well for them. The baby was due in a month.

I would not be calling the hospital, neither would I be answering the phone. Actually, it might be a bonus. I could wait until we were next cut off for non-payment and then never get us reconnected. A money-saving solution.

Ben, for all his height and affectation of cool, was still the seven-foot baby. I would not be calling the hospital and neither would I be getting injured again. It would be far too expensive. I simply couldn't afford to be ill. Strangely, this thought calmed me down. There could be no more cop-outs in the future, I had burned my boats on the illness excuse front.

Despite his moaning and wan warnings of not reappearing, Craig was surviving, and losing weight. As he lost weight, the training became easier. He was tough, too; able to take a beating without suffering any serious damage. Like a lot of people who do excessive contact sports, he looked a lot older than his twenty-two years. He told me of his spartan life as we cleaned the endless mould off the shower walls. He lived in a room in a rented house: 'But I'd live alone any day if I could afford it.' He worked every night and weekends in a Mexican restaurant as a waiter. He had no girlfriend ('not enough time') and no friends as far as I could make out. He was a prickly chap, difficult to get to know, but he was no slacker. He was the most assiduous scrubber of shower mould in the dojo.

I asked Frank how I should play my first proper date with Sara. 'Make all the decisions and pay for everything,' was his advice. I met Sara outside the supermarket after she finished work. 'Let's go to J's Bar,' she said, taking my hand. J's Bar had two huge speakers at one end and was walled with records. On a pedestal stood a record player. They only played R & B at J's but they played it very loud. The sleeve of the album being played was displayed behind the bar. Sara wasn't hungry and only drank a coffee. I drank a beer. Somehow she managed to pay without me noticing. Things weren't going according to plan. 'Let's go for a walk,' she said.

We strolled through a small park by the railway tracks in Shibuya. Sara put my hand and hers into my coat pocket. We sat down on a park bench. For some reason I couldn't stop smiling. Hey, I was enjoying life again. It was simple. Sara had no worries, so now I had no worries. I looked up at the few stars I could see through the lamp-lit haze. The Great Bear, the Pole Star and, twisting around, Orion's belt, the most visible constellation in Japan's night sky. Looking at stars always makes me feel good. Sara looked at her watch. 'I've got ten minutes,' she announced. After ten minutes of concentrated snogging, she left, running for her train. 'I'll call you soon, tomorrow, or the next day!' Somehow, this time I knew she would.

The Bad Guys Have Hairstyles

*'No true Samurai should wash his hair, in case at that
moment he is surprised from behind.'*
From the seventeenth-century Samurai manual *Hagakure*

Little Kancho, our pet goldfish, was having problems. As if he
knew his namesake had passed away, Little Kancho was getting
weaker and weaker each day. The other two fish were fine,
healthier, if anything, than when they arrived.

'It's lack of oxygen,' said Fat Frank. 'Those other two are
taking all the oxygen and leaving none for Little Kancho.'

'It's not what they're breathing, it's what they're drinking,' I
said. 'That filthy water – you should clean the tank more often.'

'Why don't *you* clean the tank?' Chris added. 'Or at least do
the washing up?' Eventually Ben cleaned the tank, but Little
Kancho didn't perk up, so I rigged a balloon so that it would
slowly deflate into the tank, thus adding extra oxygen to the
water.

'Nice idea,' said Chris, 'but it won't work.'

'Why not?'

'I've been watching Kancho since we got him. He always
swims with a slight keel to the left. The other two are perfectly
upright in the water. The keeling has just got worse. I think he
was sick before we got him. Terminal case.'

Ben came round and stuck his face close to the fish tank.
'Come on, Kancho, don't die! Please don't die!'

I could sympathize with Little Kancho's suffering. Every time
I breathed, a strange clicking sound, like something coming
unstuck, was audible coming from my chest. I was coughing up

yellow phlegm too. Every day in my diary for that time starts 'nadir day' or 'it can't get worse than this' or 'reached absolute bottom today'. I was beginning to formulate the watchword that kept me going: 'It can always get worse, however bad it is, it can always get worse and usually does. But remember, this too will pass.'

R'em, too, was close to breaking point. The cause was the new photograph of Kancho Sensei that now hung below the shrine shelf. R'em announced that he could no longer bow to the shrine because in orthodox Judaism you do not bow down before human images. But bowing to the shrine was a considerable part of daily ritual in the dojo. It was done in full view of everyone six times a day. Was R'em proposing to give up the course because of his religion? Chris, who had got to know R'em through Ben and me, argued the theological toss with him. The argument usually went something like:

Chris: 'You bow to your partner after training. That's OK, isn't it?'

R'em: 'Yes, that's OK.'

Chris: 'The reason that it is acceptable is that bowing in Japanese culture is like shaking hands. That's its meaning.'

R'em: 'But I cannot shake hands with photo!'

Chris: 'But it's the same.'

R'em: 'Photo is different.'

Chris: 'Bowing to the photograph in Japan has no meaning if you do not believe it.'

R'em: 'I cannot stop my belief! No bow!'

But R'em solved the problem, or at least found a temporary solution. He started to bow slightly off centre, not quite at the shrine. 'I bow at the wall,' he said, proudly. It was such a slight movement that no teacher noticed, but it saved his conscience.

One photo was conspicuous in its absence from the dojo: 'Iron' Mike Tyson's. The dojo had remained loyal to Mike all through his rape trial. And even when the guilty verdict came through it stayed up. All through the appeal Iron Mike beamed

189

down on his Japanese friends, but when the final appeal was quashed, the photograph had to come down. In Japan, the ghastly truth is that rape only carries a two-year sentence, and when an Iranian student raped six Japanese girls he became something of a national celebrity. He had enticed the girls into his apartment by telling them he could cook great pasta sauce. *Brutus* magazine, a bizarre cross between *Hello!* and *Loaded*, actually published the recipe, perversely giving it aphrodisiac status. The dojo had slightly more taste. I knew Tyson's picture would not be rehung, even after he was released from prison.

Keiko, a new addition to the dojo, was only too pleased to bow down before the shrine. After lessons I saw her prostrated for five minutes at a time in front of the unsmiling photograph of Kancho.

Keiko, like Dolores, who had now been banned from the dojo, had become absolutely obsessed by aikido. Male aikidoka tended to hide their obsession better, submerge it in endless training and practice in front of the mirror, whereas women obsessionals sometimes feminized their obsession. For Dolores it was infatuation with Fernando Sensei and for Keiko it was the love of Kancho.

Some of the teachers at the dojo had married their favourite students and some had married the dojo office girl. This was expected, she was picked by Kancho solely on her merits as a potential partner for one of his junior teachers. Chida and Takeno had married office girls, Ando and Nakano had married students. With his slicked back hair and bark of a voice Nakano gave a good impression of being a thug. We never saw him in the morning because he was training to be a chiropractor. His general demeanour, I felt, would work against him in his newly chosen field.

The monasterial life of a modern *uchi-deshi* (dojo disciple) gave little time or opportunity for meeting women. The cops were more normal, most of them having girlfriends they could meet on their rare days off.

In Tesshu's day things were more relaxed. He claimed: 'In my twenties and thirties I was obsessed with the nature of sexual passion. I slept with thousands of women, hoping to bridge the gap between man and woman, self and other.'

Tesshu's wife was not sympathetic to her husband's loftily inspired pursuit of sex. Brandishing a dagger she swore she'd kill herself and the children if he didn't stop sleeping around. He stopped.

Ueshiba, the founder of modern aikido, and Kancho's teacher, also had many mistresses. He used to encourage his young disciples to build their sexual *ki* by masturbating in front of paper *shoji* screens. 'If one of you can punch a hole through a *shoji* with just your ejaculation, then you'll be a real martial artist!'

Keiko was of indeterminate age, late twenties, early thirties; the age most Japanese women are expected to get anxious about marriage. In the middle of one lesson she ignored the teacher completely and started sweeping out the corner of the dojo. In a culture where you learn by watching and copying, Keiko was a radical individualist. Not even a crazy foreigner would dare to initiate their own cleaning programme in the middle of a lesson. One of the disciples rushed over and hustled her out of the class. Though she didn't pick up her broom again I could detect a certain nervousness amongst the teaching staff whenever she turned up for future lessons.

All this madness at the dojo was about to be transferred for a few days to the countryside. It was *gasshoku* time. The annual *gasshoku*, dojo summer training camp, has no exact parallel in the West. The whole dojo attends, including Riot Police, children, young mothers and foreign senshusei. The top sensei at the camp, in recent years Nakano Sensei, is like the big father presiding over a huge extended happy family. The sensei, *uchideshi* and *sewanin* run things, and the Riot Police administer their wishes. It was, of course, compulsory for the foreign senshusei to attend. The consensus was that this was no bad thing – girls would also be in attendance, and training was rumoured to be softer than usual. We would also be training with regular students which, compared to our strict and grim regimen, was like a holiday anyway.

Assisting Nakano was a slyfaced fifth-dan, a non-professional aikidoka, who was there to administer the proceedings, Fujitomi, the diminutive *uchi-deshi*, and Stumpy, the *sewanin* – plus Sakano Sensei, who, at fourth-dan, was the highest-ranking woman in the dojo, and the only female teacher.

Compared to other styles of aikido, Yoshinkan was heavily male oriented, though from time to time there were female disciples. This was a long tradition in Japan, one of Kancho's fellow students in the 1920s being a woman. Not as strong as men, women usually mastered correct form more quickly, since the commonest beginner's mistake is to try and use force instead of technique. The much feared Takeno's top student was a woman. Behind her back men would concede that while she looked good there was no power in her throws. Women who were built like men were often just as good as men, but women who weren't had to use speed and perfect form to shift their bulkier counterparts. Japanese women tend to dislike bloody noses and chipped teeth and are content to remain as technically proficient martial artists rather than risk disfigurement in the quest to become an outstanding fighter. Because women were treated equally in the dojo I could see that it wasn't an unpleasant place to train. The women aikidoka, mostly young high-school and university students, were keen and many of them had decided to attend the summer camp.

As we got on the bus, and naturally the police and the senshusei grabbed the back seats, I noticed that Keiko, with her fixed, mad and impassive smile, was also coming. How welcoming of the aikido family, I thought: this is real care in the community. The reality was that in Japan people rely on you excluding yourself. Many Japanese are familiar with the English term 'to be sent to Coventry' – they instantly recognize this

192

practice, since they will create such an unpleasant atmosphere that you will eventually be forced to do a Captain Oates and sacrifice yourself if you are not wanted. (Incidentally, Oates' grand and heroic gesture is interpreted as purely normal by most Japanese – they assume that he was forced out of the tent by unstated group consensus, which is what would happen in Japan.)

The bus ground on through Tokyo and into Chiba. We passed a garbage incineration plant, and a fulsome young woman employed as a 'hostess' by the bus company told us exactly how much garbage they incinerated each day. We admired respectfully 'Gomi' Island, which is made out of garbage and sits in Tokyo Bay. We drove over the Rainbow suspension bridge and we were told its exact length in metres, and how it was 327 metres shorter than the Bay Bridge in Yokohama. Bridges seem to epitomize romance in Japan – on any Saturday night you will see rows of Toyotas and Nissans parked with their flashers on along the length of the Bay Bridge, while lovestruck couples stare into the murky waters hundreds of metres beneath. No one is engaged in the act of sex, love hotels are for that, they are simply savouring the inexplicable romance of the situation, marred slightly in Western eyes by the presence of so many others.

At the *budo* shrine in Kashima, Ibaraki prefecture, which is set in a miniature forest, huge pines and cedars dominating the wooden pagoda-esque shrine buildings, we threw money into the grating at the shrine altar and then looked for a place to buy soft drinks. Knick-knack shops selling lucky slivers of wood and *budo* impedimenta were all around the entrance to the shrine. As we boarded the bus I saw that Keiko had bought a traditional wooden sword wrapped for sale purposes in clear plastic. The irrepressible Hal, the university student, commented, 'It's shrink-wrapped – but that doesn't mean you can eat it,' and she gave him a stern look. But it was an odd thing for a woman to buy;

despite there being a female martial tradition in Japan, you rarely see evidence of it.

We pulled into the site where the training camp would be held.

'Shit,' said Ben, 'it's like an army barracks.'

'I told you,' said Will, though he hadn't. 'What did you expect?'

'I had an image of log cabins around an open dojo, mats in the open air, that kind of thing,' I said.

'It's a four-storey concrete barracks,' said Ben, with disappointment.

The dojo was better. A short walk from the barracks it was a huge wooden structure with massive doors at either end which were open, giving a sufficiently airy feeling. You could smell the sea air if you concentrated hard; the sea was within walking distance, but in which direction no one knew.

When Aga saw the steps up to the dojo he whooped with glee. He and Little Nick had brought their rollerblades with them and saw the ten steps up to the dojo, which ran along its full length of a hundred and fifty metres, as prime skating ground. What a fool Aga was! A dojo is a place of religious significance. Rollerblading around it was bound to antagonize the Japanese, but neither he, nor his new protégé, Little Nick, seemed to care. They quickly put on their lycra shorts and blades and started desecrating the dojo area.

We were assigned to rooms. I was in with Sakuma and Hal and a couple of cops, the only other foreigner was Will. After his earlier humiliations Sakuma had slowly improved. He had dramatically lost weight, and most importantly he hadn't given up, even when the kickings and beatings were at their height. Sakuma had earned respect the hard way. Instead of ignoring him the cops called him Kuma, or Kumachan, meaning bear, and there was something teddybear-like about him. He adopted me as his *sempai* and insisted on running errands for me, pouring drinks and making seating space for me. In return, I suppose, I had been encouraging and not bullied him when he started the course. This is the *kohai–sempai* relationship – both sides benefiting from a relationship which, to a Westerner, looks like one party dominating another, with the other extracting little from such an arrangement. A true *sempai* has to be like a good elder brother. He will be deserted if he abuses the relationship too much.

Will and I were glad to be the only foreigners in our room, as far away from the other senshusei as possible. We spent eight hours a day five days a week together. I'd seen them crying, laughing, screaming and showering. I'd cleaned up their shit in the toilet. We'd all pummelled and thrown each other to exhaustion and then sat around in the tea room insulting anyone and everyone. The last thing I wanted to do was to have to keep up the group pretence in the bunkhouse.

With the police and the Japanese senshusei it was different. We trained with them every day, but they had their own rest room and a natural distance had grown up between us.

The camp was strictly timetabled and we all had copies of the timetable. When we weren't training, having a communal bath, eating or attending group meetings, we were ordered to return to our rooms. There was a very controlled feeling about the whole thing – Japan as a Communist country is not hard to imagine, perhaps without Kancho and the strikebreakers he organized in the 1950s it would have become so. As a leading martial artist with conservative connections, Kancho used the university martial-arts club as a recruiting ground for strikebreakers. Though he successfully defeated the Communists' control of such giant concerns as Nihon Kokan Steel, I never heard the subject discussed at the dojo. Had his actions been less successful, and Japan succumbed to a Communist takeover, it would have made no difference to the feel of the training camp.

The day started at 6.00 a.m. with the wake-up call: a cop knocking on every door to wake the inhabitants up. At 6.15 we all stood to attention as the Rising Sun was hauled up the flagpole. Then we bowed en masse. What would Colonel H. Twigger make of his grandson bowing to the false god of the yellow peril?

One of the children was selected each day to raise the flag. Slyface took the ceremony, Nakano not appearing before breakfast. ('Conserving his *ki*,' as Ben put it – i.e., exercising his right as leader to have a lie-in.) Selecting a child to raise the flag and lower it in the evening was very cunning. It combined indoctrination (of the kid concerned) with making the whole thing a relaxed 'family' affair. Rather like the camp, which was essentially militaristic, but presented as a family get-together. I had seen an animated propaganda film from World War II. In it the Japanese hero pilots of the Pacific are chipmunks and rabbits. The enemy are debauched humans, drunks and villains fighting against the 'pure' world of cuddly disneyfied animals. Japanese fascism has a family feel, which is why it converted so efficiently to capitalism – the family unit as consumer and saver rather than sacrificer. If an adult raised the flag people might protest that things were too serious. There might also be problems of insubordination, people refusing to bow to the flag once it was raised. But if a kid raises the flag, we're on his side, we know he's nervous and we don't want to see him fail. Moreover, we take as sincere his matter-of-fact handling of the flag – if it drops in the dust by accident we know this has no ironic overtones at all, it is merely an accident.

At 6.30 a.m. we did radio exercises, exercising in rows to the hysterically lively presenter and old-fashioned musical accompaniment of the radio. Again a child and an adult led the class – Slyface made human by the addition of a kid at his side. It's a technique of manipulation that has a name in Japanese: 'man calling with his daughter' – when a man visits his boss he takes his youngest child with him to humanize the visit, which is usually a demand for a pay rise or a holiday.

I knew Hal would take the piss out of the radio exercises but I wondered how he would do it. Sure enough he did them with total commitment and seriousness – the perfect pisstake, since it was obvious no one in their right mind could be anything more than half hearted about such idiocy. To take them seriously and perform them well served the double function of announcing your individuality without dragging the group down.

After exercise came an unappetizing breakfast. I could never get used to a bowl of dishwater fishy soup and a bowl of over-cooked rice sprinkled with dry sprats and seaweed for breakfast. The only palatable bit was the seaweed. But if you're hungry, anything will do.

Lunch and dinner were not much better, composed of traditional institutional Japanese food, basically junk food, which is universally, in my experience, terrible – over-cooked and yet cold or luke warm, bland, lacking in fibre and only edible if bolted fast. All those who profess a love of institutional Japanese food are bolters, sucking down fast such delicacies as: noodles floating in thin soup, curry rice with cold curry, pus burgers that rupture and spray you with fine opaque liquid when you puncture their outer skin, greasy spring rolls, cold mashed potato with a sprinkling of chilli pepper on top (why?), micro-salads of very little imagination and a dressing that is indistinguishable from odourless and tasteless semen; little sausages that closely resemble excrement. And always accompanying everything: white rice – sticky with very little nutritional value. A part of Japanese culture that was emphasized by the nationalist movement of the 1930s, white rice symbolizes the sticky mess that the Japanese periodically manage to get themselves into.

It is interesting to note that Yamanashi prefecture, which has the highest life expectancy on the main Japanese island of Honshu, used wheat and not rice as a staple. Country Japanese cooking is not overly rice based, because white rice was, until the twentieth century, a great luxury. It was used as a 'king's shilling' to persuade country boys to join the 1904 army that defeated the Russians. A war in which more Japanese died of vitamin B deficiency than from bullet wounds. It was known by Ogai, the surgeon general at the time, that white rice was a deficient diet,

197

but this information was suppressed in order to help with recruitment.

Japanese people express pleasure when you admit a polite dislike of their junk food. It confirms yet again their difference from other cultures. But my guess is that deep down they know their food is mostly disgusting and tasteless; promoting it as something exotic and different is just putting a brave face on things. People with really excellent cooking don't go on and on about their marvellous cuisine – they just get on with it and eat. The Japanese obsession with their food is a cover for a deep embarrassment about its adequacy.

Before dinner Ben and R'em came into our room. They passed on the unsurprising news that rollerblading had been banned. The room was walled with heavy bunks, with a thin futon mattress and cover on each bunk. We sat on the bunks chatting. Everyone was more expansive, more willing to talk about their past life, which previously was deemed hardly to exist. The course created this odd atmosphere that real life began with the first day of senshusei training. Before that was an ethereal other world that no one cared about. It was a bit like going to an English public school.

Perhaps because of this easy atmosphere Will asked R'em outright: 'So how many men have you actually killed?' In the odd world of martial arts it carries considerable kudos to have actually dispatched people from this earth. R'em, smiling, gave us an account of his confirmed kills: two 'terrorists' he dropped with rifle fire near the Jordanian border; a Palestinian (I guessed there might be more than one) who had died after a severe beating.

'Maybe you think I'm a crazy, but it's not like that. Another Israeli would understand.' He grinned his round-spectacled grin, looking not at all like a killer.

He complained of all the red tape in the army, said it was one reason he left. 'You kill one man – there are a thousand forms to fill in. That is the crazy.'

In the Lebanon they had been ordered not to beat women. 'But what can you do? A woman spits in your face because her son is dead. She tries to tear your hair out. And all your men are watching. You have to beat her. So I say to my men – only beat behind buildings, off the main street.

'But in Gaza I was afraid all the time. Even when you sleep there is a small piece of fear deep inside your stomach. I never lose that fear until I leave.' R'em grinned quizzically. 'You think I'm crazy.' He looked at Ben, who was Jewish but not Israeli. 'Another Israeli would understand.'

The group leader came and announced it was dinnertime.

'Heavy stuff,' said Will, as we trooped down to the mess hall. 'Aga and those army guys are just playing at soldiers. R'em's actually done it.'

'He is a bit crazy, though,' I said.

'What's crazy?' said Will. 'He's more normal than those other freaks we train with.'

After dinner we held the group meeting, which was an excuse for drinking beer. In Japanese fashion everyone had to make a speech, which meant we had to listen to about forty speeches, finishing up with Nakano Sensei. 'He looks like a killer whale, doesn't he?' said Little Nick, and he was right. With his tiny eyes staring out of a big hard face, Nakano did resemble a killer whale. He was not a big man but he gave that impression. There was something coarse and brutal about him.

When it came to my turn I decided to make a humorous speech, despite Nakano's injunction that the speeches should be about what aikido meant to us.

'In England,' I said, standing up, 'we have a form of *budo* ... it's called cricket.' Nakano laughed and others joined in too. 'And about cricket we say, "It doesn't matter whether you win or lose, it's how you play the game." Aikido too is about playing the game, or should be. But there is one distressing way in which aikido and cricket are different: in cricket you can wear huge bloody knee pads.'

Sato made a speech saying how much he hated aikido. This was a conceit designed to show how much of a grip aikido had on his life. Nakano took up the theme in his own speech where he reminded us that Kancho had said, 'Aikido, you take to the grave, because if you give up and stop practising, you lose it.'

Mercifully the speeches were usually short, and soon we were all drinking bottles of Kirin beer. Will opened up and started talking about his previous life. He had gone to college later in life than most, at twenty-four, and before that he had done a variety of jobs, working for airlines in the Northwest of America, before going to Alaska to work on a fishing boat. Somehow the conversation got around to nationalities and race.

Will said to R'em: 'Are you a whiteman?'

'What you mean?' said R'em.

'What colour do you consider yourself?'

People started to make noises, as if to say, 'R'em's white, he's all right,' but Will persisted.

R'em couldn't understand the question at first, but when he did he went into a long and detailed explanation. Yes, he said, in Israel Yemenis are considered the blacks, and some of them are very dark skinned, but compared to them R'em was white. 'You're more Mediterranean,' I said, ever the peacemaker. 'Like Italian or Greek,' said R'em.

Then Danny started up. 'The first black I saw was an old Abo woman getting out of a taxi in Alice. Man, I did not want to get in there after her. They're just so different from us.'

He continued in a similar vein about Vietnamese pissing on loo seats and other racial offences he found unacceptable. But Danny was a village boy – Aga was his friend, and Aga was Chinese-Portuguese; Danny also had a sixteen-year-old Japanese girlfriend. His racism was theoretical. When he got to know people he adjusted himself to their differences and treated them normally.

After his success at spotting Nakano's resemblance to a killer whale, Little Nick tried to link the other teachers to animals and fish. Chino was a hammerhead shark and Oyamada was a big seal; Mustard was a lion and Chida was a cheetah. Disagreement turned to hostile barracking after he described himself as a mountain lion. 'But seriously, guys,' he persisted, 'haven't you noticed how all the bad guys look like fish and all the good guys look like cats?'

We carried on drinking until the killer whale told us it was time to go to bed.

The same routine was repeated the next day, except we did some morning and afternoon training. That night we were crowded into someone's room drinking with the cops when Nakano's voice was heard outside in the corridor. In a fantastic display of acrobatics the cops piled into two futon cupboards in seconds. It was real slapstick comedy. Then Nakano came in and looked suspicious and told us to go to bed, but he didn't notice the cops hiding. The cops reappeared to much all-round mirth. Except from R'em, who for once couldn't see the joke. 'Why can't they act like men? They are like women or children the way they fear Nakano.'

Some time before breakfast the following day Hal stormed in and announced that Keiko was 'threatening the children with her wooden sword'. I found this hard to believe so I went down to the lobby and saw Keiko sitting very grumpily with the wooden sword, still in its polythene cover, next to her. The fact that it was still wrapped in plastic made the sight of her more pathetic and touching. I carried on walking towards the dojo and met Slyface and the dwarfish Fujitomi coming back to the barracks. Suddenly Keiko rushed past me and brandished her sword at Slyface. Fujitomi did nothing; Slyface looked petrified. So much for aikido sword training. Keiko took several swipes at Slyface and connected with his knee. Then she belted off towards the dojo. Slyface sent Fujitomi after her and Fujitomi sprinted away. Then it was time for breakfast and Fujitomi did not appear to say the Shinto-style 'grace', so Sakano said it instead.

After breakfast R'em got his camera and we went in search of

Fujitomi and Keiko. The tiny *uchi-deshi* was trying, unsuccessfully, to manhandle her out of the dojo. She was staging a sit-down protest in the middle of a kendo class and, being heavier than Fujitomi, he would have had to employ considerable force to make her leave. Fujitomi saw us and waved his hand as if telling us to clear off. So we did. It was obviously very shameful for the dojo that all this was going on. Later, Fujitomi told me he had actually been beckoning me and had wanted me to intervene, but I had forgotten that the Japanese gesture for 'come on' is the same as the Western one for 'go away'.

That day we trained with Nakano while the cops made a tourist visit to another shrine. They had voted not to train, but the foreign senshusei, anxious to show willing and keen to be taught by tough guy Nakano, had opted to suffer. Throughout the lesson Nakano was distracted, constantly going over to the window to look out into the courtyard. He demonstrated his electrifying *kotegaeshi* on Danny, who beamed incomprehension at its speed and sudden force. Then he returned to his window vigil. Half an hour before the lesson's end he cut things short and excused himself. He told us he had to go and deal with Keiko, who was still running around causing trouble.

A two-man cop guard was put on her door twenty-four hours a day from then on. She couldn't even go to the loo without an escort from the Riot Police. That night two of the cops kept watch over Keiko while we had a firework display. Deemed too dangerous for Keiko, she was kept indoors. No one knew or cared why Keiko had gone mad. 'She's just *hen-na*, strange, that's all,' said Hal. The fireworks were great fun and, as usual in Japan, far superior to Western fireworks. Safety was very lax too. Kids would run up to me and beg me to light rockets and Roman candles with the glowing butt of my cigarette. With a semblance of precaution I obliged. There were a few near misses – rockets that tipped up on the ground and shot sideways at head height, whizzbangs that failed to explode mid-air but did so when prodded on the ground.

Safety-conscious Mad Dog and Danny were appalled at the relaxed gaiety of the occasion. There was no centralized control of firework ignition. Instead it was free enterprise all round, with the best fireworks tending to be set off by a group of the police and the older staff. This was fireworks pre-nanny society, when everyone accepted the best way to set off a medium-size rocket was to launch it from your hand. Mad Dog stood with his arms folded like a disgusted health and safety official. 'This shouldn't be allowed,' he repeated to everyone who passed him.

We continued the party after the fireworks. Then there was an announcement: Keiko's brother had arrived to take her home. Everyone cheered. The cops and the senshusei got excited and took their shirts off for a photo. This annoyed Nakano and he rebuked us, especially the foreigners because we should be more respectable than the police, as we were destined to be teachers and should therefore be looking to set a good example. This was a blind. What Nakano wanted to do was criticize the group en masse for being 'difficult', and rebuke the early foolishness and palpable rudeness of Little Nick and Aga rollerblading down the dojo steps, which had set the scene for many minor but, to the Japanese mind, serious infringements of sobriety and regularity. For these Nakano wanted to punish us, but his explosion over the shirts was not understood as covering this multitude of sins; rather, it was read as over-reaction, an injustice. Little Nick, still with a touching faith in the supposed fairness of adults, went into the biggest decline. He just couldn't square the superb quality of Nakano's aikido with the fact that the man was a grumpy prejudiced bastard.

The party, somewhat muted, continued in another room. Sherlock and I planned a sea-fishing trip later in the summer. Elfman massaged my shoulders and Elfman's brother spoke his only English, memorized when he was fourteen. He repeated it many times, so I remember it clearly: 'Taro wanted to play baseball but he was easily disappointed . . .' Here he forgot what came next and burst into hysterical laughter. Sherlock took me on one side and told me 'his secret'. In Japan, when you get to know someone, the process of progressively revealing personal information is dramatized. There is the everyday stuff and then 'the secret'. One woman, who I taught for over a year, eventually told me, 'I have a secret. You know I said I live with my brother? In fact he's my husband – I'm married, but I hate him!'

Sherlock's face was bright red from drink and his eyes had almost closed up. He leant towards me and muttered: 'I have a secret . . . I am not Japanese!'

I started to laugh but he regarded me with an unsmiling face. He was serious. 'My father is a Japanese. My mother is Korean. Sometimes I hate the Japanese. What do you think?'

'Sometimes I hate them too,' I said.

'Good, isn't it?' said Sherlock, taking another swig from his bottle.

I enjoyed being with the police. They were easy going and good natured, even when drunk. Before one drinking session the foreign senshusei had bought a lot of beer themselves. Mad Dog administered the payment for it and Stumpy, being a *sewanin*, was allowed to break bounds to buy it. He also bought cigarettes, which were doled out to a line of us as he lounged on his bunk taking his time. It was uncomfortably close to a prison movie. But Mad Dog said in loud English, when the cops came into the room, 'No one drinks who hasn't paid.' The cops understood or half understood, but what you couldn't miss was the heavy-handed unwelcoming tone of Mad Dog's voice. In Japan people always pay their share because they would be ashamed not to. But they pay afterwards; to break up a party for an impromptu round of debt collecting is just not the done thing. But Mad Dog didn't know this – he'd only been voted into the job because of his heroic meanness with money, and no one else wanted to do it. (His meanness was legendary – he'd got married on Friday the 13th because receptions were discounted on that day.) So the cops were made to feel uncomfortable and left at the first opportunity on the pretext of 'rescuing Sato' from Nakano's room, where another staff drinking party was going on.

By the end of the camp, riding the bus back, a quite unnecessary 'us and them' had developed. Will and Ben had been told they were 'good foreigners' (pliant, quiet, friendly) whereas Little Nick and Aga were 'bad foreigners' – *urusai*, which means noisy, but in Japan being 'noisy' is the equivalent to being 'a bloody pain', and is not tolerated.

When we left the bus at the dojo, people barely said goodbye to each other. I realized that bringing people together does not reduce prejudice. It may, in fact, substantiate and increase it. What we lack in information about another culture we have to make up for in tolerance. The alternative is confrontation. And unfortunately, in many ways, confrontation certainly makes life a lot more interesting. And though individual friendships persisted, general relations between the cops and the foreigners never really improved in the months after the camp. A certain professional cool hovered over our joint training, the knowledge, perhaps, that we were never going to be real buddies, whatever high hopes we may have entertained at the beginning of the course. There was no energy left over for emotional sightseeing, it was too late now, the course already half over for the cops, better to get on, get it all over with as quickly and easily as possible.

One memory stuck in my mind from the bus trip back. We stopped at a restaurant for lunch. Outside the restaurant was a Mild Seven cigarette machine. Slowly walking up the side of this vending machine was a huge praying mantis, at least six inches in length. Cops, foreigners and Japanese gathered in the humid afternoon heat to just stare at the thing. The mantis stopped moving and extended its praying front claws, as if doing a stretching exercise. We whispered, afraid, perhaps, that it could hear us. Nakano walked past and was beckoned over. He too fell silent in a watching reverie. Time slowed down, the praying mantis became immobile. Nakano's all right, I thought, taking pity for a moment on his silly, almost womanish slicked back hair-do. The watching continued. How would it end? As if hearing me, Nakano, as quick as a flash, snatched at the mantis, making as if to throw the insect at one of the girls. The girl shrieked, the mantis fled, and Nakano's booming raucous laughter filled for a brief moment the airless parking lot.

There was no real break in senshusei training throughout the summer. The high school was different, with its eight-week summer break. On my first Monday back Mr Wada told me he was getting married.

'Congratulations!' I said.

He looked pleased and told me his fiancée was a teacher at this very school.

'Who?'

'She is the sports teacher.'

'Great,' I said. The sports teacher was the most attractive teacher in the school. Then I remembered he'd told me his girlfriend worked in an office. He obviously hadn't trusted me, or rather, in Japan, if you tell something to someone it means you want that news spread. He'd told me she worked in an office so that if I told others they wouldn't suspect it was really the sports teacher.

'She used to be a student here too,' he said. 'My student.'

'Really? Did she like you then?' I asked.

'Yes,' he said, unashamedly.

'She came to this school, then she left and went to college and then she came back as a teacher,' he said.

'Amazing,' I said.

I looked at Mr Wada's impassive face, his wet lips. Was he lonely? I remembered another teacher telling me Mr Wada was

206

an only child. Even with his new wife I had a feeling he would still be alone.

It was now September and we were preparing for the second test. Five months in, six months to go. This would be the last test before the black-belt exam.

Three months after the black belt was the final course graduation test, which was meant to be even harder than the black-belt exam. But right now the only important thing about the next test, for me, was the promise of a change of partner. I was prepared to take anyone; no one could be worse than Little Nick. My chest clicked and my lungs rattled, providing a constant reminder of working with the boy Armenian.

R'em shaved his head completely bald for the approaching test. Chida Sensei, amused, asked why. 'Every day I shave my head and then I think of aikido and how I must train harder,' said R'em. 'It's the wrong way round,' said Chida. 'Instead of fantasizing about training hard and in reality cutting hair, you should be fantasizing about cutting hair and in reality train harder.'

Will and I had started a routine which would continue throughout the course. After training we went to a coffee shop which served good coffee. The quality of coffee was important to Will, who came from Seattle and considered sitting and talking over a coffee one of the finer pleasures of life. For me, too, the coffee-shop sessions quickly became the one thing I could look forward to each day.

Will's child had been born, a daughter, and his wife was staying at home with her parents, looking after the infant. Will was brisk about the whole thing: 'I don't expect you guys to have any sympathy or interest in the kid – I certainly didn't until it happened to me.' This kind of tolerance characterized Will. Although a non-smoker, he had no gripe with smokers and never complained about the fumes.

There was something old fashioned about him, perhaps

207

because he had been brought up by elderly foster parents rather than his own family, who all lived on welfare and whom he affectionately despised. 'I don't care if it's right or wrong, it just plain irritates me. That's why I connect to Adam. I know where he's from, his family are wasters like mine.'

Will was a natural athlete and had been a successful high-school basketball player, but he'd burned out on the competitive aggression of college sports. Though he believed Mustard disliked him (Will needed to be liked, but he was proud, and I think this made him lonely at times), he was tipped, after the invincible brat Nicky, as one of the best at aikido.

I'd seen Will close to tears after a Shioda session where we had performed endless high flips over a line of outstretched arms. He had, at that time, a trapped nerve in his back and every landing sent a wave of severe pain through his body. And though he found even breathing painful, he didn't complain. He just kept it all to himself and toughed it out. Once, when Ben cracked a joke, and we were all outside the front of the dojo laughing, Will said, 'Don't make me laugh, man – it hurts too much.'

When his back was better Will sometimes used to chide me about how little sympathy people showed him when he was hurt. 'But you never asked!' I said. 'We didn't know it was that bad.' 'No one should have to ask for sympathy,' he replied. 'But that doesn't mean you can't receive it gratefully.'

Mad Dog and Adam were Will's favourite targets for sarcasm. When Mad Dog was lecturing the tea room on his tedious lifeplans: 'Anna Marie and I plan to have two children,' Will responded, quick as a flash: 'Two point three – isn't that the average?'

It was at this time that I entered the 'Winston Smith' phase of my life. Many foreign men go through this necessary phase, occasioned by going out with a Japanese girl who has the common misfortune to still be living at home. Sara, as a recent high-school graduate ('University?' I asked. 'No way,' she said, and outlined her plans for visiting India, home of Sai Baba, her current favourite guru, and England, the birth place of Brian Jones) was, quite naturally, still living at home. She wouldn't even give me her phone number. All meetings were arranged at the meeting before, so we engaged on a precarious chain of liaisons, all of which, she assured me, her father would be furious to find out about. I took to scouting parks and riverbanks for secluded spots. Good place for a snog, I'd mentally note, and then see a cardboard shelter and realize some homeless person had beaten me to claiming this rare privacy. And it was rare. Pursuers of feral sex are well catered for in London or Paris, New York or Singapore. Not so in Tokyo. Vacant lots do not exist. Parks lack bushes of any substance, trees of any width, grass of any height. A further bane to the amorous couple's search for privacy is the constant likelihood of *nozoki*, or Peeping Toms. The *nozoki* is an accepted part of Japanese culture. Old seventeenth-century prints feature lewd scenes of sexual abandon viewed by a third party through a convenient knot hole. The modern equivalent has high-powered Nikon binoculars with zoom lenses. Hiding behind trees at night, engaged in some rudimentary subterfuge by the bins in a park, or pretending to fish in a stretch of empty river, the *nozoki* ensures no tract of virgin turf remains without surveillance. If there is a key to the Japanese character it can be found in the spirit of *nozoki*.

Sara would press herself deeper into a pile of leaves as heavy footfalls signified the approach of someone, possibly a Peeping Tom. Her anxiety conveyed itself to me and, like my alter ego, Winston Smith of Orwell's *1984*, I planned ever more cunning ways to evade the thought police (i.e., the public at large and especially the *nozoki*, who would have been soundly beaten up in England for such brazen snooping). In Japan they had furtive lovers running scared. I was not about to make a stand, or even a sit-down protest, and regular visits to love hotels were too expensive to contemplate.

The best places were fenced-off thickets in public woods. These were strictly no entry; all other Japanese were too timid to trespass so openly in places reserved for conservation or ornament. I worked out a list of such venues, and the times that they were safest and most accessible. My favourite garment was a light mackintosh, an excellent groundsheet, though grubby and disreputable from in-the-field use. From time to time I could negotiate time off alone in Fuji Heights, but it was difficult since I had to arrange meetings a week in advance and the others led more unpredictable lives. Plus there were no quid pro quos and plenty of piss taking, so much of the latter that seeking out an undiscovered bower in a municipal park was almost preferable. It was a strange life, certain permutations made worse by the tender sores on my knees.

In our favourite coffee shop Will and I bitched about the others on the course and especially the teachers we didn't like. Chino, we agreed, was a brute; Nakano a narcissistic brute. Mustard was unstable, Shioda a sadist, Paul too gung-ho and Stephan too out of it. We approved of Darren. 'He does blue-collar aikido,' said Will. 'Not great to look at but it really is strong.'

'They expect everything from us,' said Will, after one session, 'but all we wanted was a chance, a chance to see if we could become good at this thing. But they don't recognize that. They're down on us the whole time, trying to make life as unpleasant as possible.'

'Right,' I assented. When Will got going it was good to let him run with the ball.

'And right now aikido is not the most important thing in my life. I've got a wife and a child and I'd quit tomorrow if my wife asked me to.'

This was dangerous talk. It was considered bad form, and worse luck, to talk about quitting. After Adam was singled out by Chino and berated in rude Japanese for being so weak and told, rhetorically, to go home, the nervous American mentioned, with trepidation, that he could still get a black belt doing the *kenshu* classes (intensive regular classes – tougher than average but nothing like senshusei) like Chris and Fat Frank. This had been downed on immediately by all senshusei who heard him. There was an unstated rule that talk of giving up was infectious and a very bad thing. The greatest of all our obsessions was the belief that to quit was the worst possible thing. 'It's all right for you guys,' said Adam. 'You didn't understand Chino – my wife's father is *yakuza* and I know that kind of talk, the guy hates me.' Again this was shouted down as an irrelevance, but all of us harboured the belief that certain teachers had it in for us.

Sara thought martial arts were pretty silly. To a trendy young Japanese aikido was about as sexy as doing rugby in England. (Rugby in Japan was a different matter and was most definitely fashionable.) Actually, aikido was even more archaic than rugby, it was like a cross between morris dancing and rugby, a bizarre mix of ultra-traditionalism, silly clothes and violence. Foreigners doing aikido were intrinsically funny. If Sara had taken up the bagpipes and gone to Scotland to join a bagpipe band, she would have returned the cultural compliment perfectly. I could then have made endless fun of her. Instead she preferred the Rolling Stones, and with a nihilism common to youth, thought Brian Jones the sexiest of them all. At least my only competition was a corpse, but she made up for it by fuelling her teenybopper mind with rare, and surprisingly lewd, Stones videos that she collected with avidity. I see now that all this behaviour was really very healthy, a reaction to the stultifying conditions of living under the tyranny of a traditional Japanese father. She was also practical, saving every penny she earned in a part-time supermarket job for her escape to England.

I paid for most things, but it was never expensive. When you're eighteen you don't have expensive tastes – at least Sara didn't. Drinking in bars bored her; she much preferred roughing it in a park and dodging the beady-eyed prowlers.

When I wore my senshusei 'team jacket', which was modelled on a baseball jacket, she collapsed with laughter. OK, it's funny, I thought, but it's not *that* funny. Baseball jackets and short hair

211

were what all the uncool jocks at high school wore. To be going out with one who was thirty and foreign was too funny for words.

The jackets had been Aga's idea. They were black faux silk with our names embroidered on them, and in big writing on the back: YOSHINKAN AIKIDO – INSTRUCTORS' COURSE. They cost $200, which was excessive, and somehow everyone felt railroaded into buying them by the business-minded Aga. Rumours flew that we had subsidized his jacket by allowing him to get a group order, but the rumours were never substantiated. Later Aga would moot the idea of team t-shirts, to which Will and I organized opposition. The t-shirt was to be modelled on a special-forces shirt that Aga owned, and which said: 'No fear, No excuses, No regrets.' ('And no poofters,' Danny added.) Even Mustard thought the slogans were ghastly and self aggrandizing. Aga pushed on and in the end settled for a t-shirt which said the same as our jackets. In a definite display of poor team spirit Will and I asked for plain shirts with only the Yoshinkan Eagle symbol ('Looks more like a demented chicken,' said Chris) and a few words in Japanese *kanji* script. Even this innocuous item was laughed at by Sara. Her own preference was for vaguely sixties flower gear, afghan coats, beaten-up old bags and her grand-father's war-issue jackboots.

When the time came for the second test I did not cut my hair. It was a bad omen. Haircuts were a definite part of being a senshusei. While R'em went again for the complete bald shave, others kept it short but not razored. It was definitely 'harder' to have a real close No. 1 buzz cut. With that peculiar narcissism of the locker room haircuts were admired, criticized, primped and preened. By not cutting my hair for the test I was, in a small way, splitting away from the programme. And though Little Nick tried hard to be a good partner for the test, my heart wasn't in it. We had to perform seven techniques chosen at random from the fifty or sixty we had learnt. Though I made no grave errors, Chida's comment was that I was not making a connection to my partner, I was holding back too much. How that man saw everything! Along with Ben and Adam I received a grade 2 pass, everyone else passed at grade 1 level. Danny was complimented on his *kamae*, which was high praise indeed.

I was beginning to see that Danny's approach suited the structure of the course. He just did what people told him. He did not rely on his own feelings about things. For a long time he complained 'that nothing worked'. But instead of altering and prematurely personalizing his style he persisted practising perfect form. In the end this was paying off. Aga was the opposite, and had his own way of doing everything. It was not hard to see that his aikido could only progress so far in this way.

Sakuma and Dopey were still the worst performers but they had caught up considerably. The main difference was now between Sato, Hal and the international senshusei on the one hand, and the cops on the other. Technically we looked the same but the civilian senshusei tried much harder to make their aikido effective.

After the test I shaved my head. Time for a new start. I waited expectantly for the new partner list. More odd and unnecessary mystification surrounded who actually decided who was partnering whom. We were never told. Japan is an information-poor country. If people can withhold information from you they will.

We ran to our old spots and the new partners were announced – I was with Mad Dog, and this would be until the black-belt test in December. Things could be worse. He was co-operative and grown-up enough not to bring his personal problems to the dojo. We weren't equals in any sense – he already had a black belt – but I was faster and lighter than him, although he still had his mad-dogness, his bite-it-off-and-chew-it-to-the-boneness.

In the middle of September we had one more hurdle: The All Japan Yoshinkan Aikido Demonstration. Demonstrations have been an integral part of Yoshinkan aikido since Kancho's triumphant success in 1954 at a huge demonstration of *budo* sponsored by the Japanese Life Extension Association. Like many groups involved in things suspected as militaristic they had concocted a name that the 'stupid' Americans would not take exception to.

Similarly, local *kempeitai* groups, the Japanese wartime equivalent of the KGB, were not disbanded – they were simply reformed as neighbourhood watch associations.

The 1954 demonstration was a huge affair, with over 15,000 spectators. Because of a US ban no one had seen martial arts for nearly ten years, and the whole event, I feel, was staged as a show of Japanese pride, despite the humiliations of wartime defeat.

Kancho participated in this show and, according to most sources, was awarded the grand prize, making him the most outstanding martial artist in Japan. Other sources claim that there was no overall top award and claims for Kancho's supremacy are based on the fact that the firebrigade band burst out into spontaneous musical applause no fewer than three times during his performance. They did this for no other person, which perhaps accounts for the story of first prize.

Having achieved such fame because of the 1954 demonstration he found little difficulty in attracting wealthy sponsors, who put up the money to found the first Yoshinkan aikido dojo.

Kancho's teacher, Ueshiba, had been less keen on demonstrations. In the 1930s he was asked to demonstrate at the Imperial Palace. At first Ueshiba had refused, saying that he could only show real aikido to the Emperor, and real aikido always resulted in the death of your opponent. Was the Emperor ordering him to kill someone? Come on, be a sport, the palace message came back; surely you can demonstrate something that isn't lethal? Reluctantly the Master Ueshiba rose from his futon. He was, at the time, suffering from his periodic liver trouble sustained as a young man after drinking eight gallons of sea water for a bet. Once in the royal presence Ueshiba staged a massive recovery. His first disciple attacked him on command and Ueshiba restrained himself but still managed to break his arm. The second disciple, who was the young Kancho, lasted the rest of the forty-minute demonstration. He wrote later that he spent a week in bed recovering from the experience.

Our demonstration was to be held in the Nakano Police Stadium. Instead of royalty our audience would be businessmen, government ministers and university and high-school clubs from all over Japan. We would march on with the police, kneel while they did their display, do ours, and then march off together. Everything was synchronized and everyone did the same technique at the same time. Our display started with a punch, one of those punches from the hip that snap the canvas of the jacket as the fist reverses back and forward. Mad Dog countered this by moving into me and throwing me to the ground. I rolled right over backwards and stood up in one graceful move. There was then a medley of wrist grabs and throws before the grand finale, when I dropped straight to my knees, bringing the Mad Dog down with me. As he lay on the ground I got to chop him across the temple, which he blocked as I gave a deafening warrior's shout, a *kiai*, desperately hoping I was shouting in time with everyone else.

Paul was always best at drilling us. He was careful and systematic, breaking down the display and concentrating only on the parts that were a problem. He forgot his usual method of breaking any rhythm that occurred during practice. This time he seemed totally bound up in getting us to perform as well as possible and the lessons passed quickly. The Japanese teachers were more casual and less inventive. With them we practised the whole thing, all the way through, again and again. It was a two-minute display and we did it hundreds of times. It involved being thrown twice and landing the same way each time. Pretty soon this resulted in the aikido equivalent of a repetitive strain injury (i.e., the dreaded knobbies reappeared with a vengeance.) My left hip bone was surrounded by permanently swollen tissue. A direct hit on a knobbie produced a searing pain throughout the body, a unique pain I might add, which made standing up after sustaining such a landing a major act of will power. Once,

Adam lay on the floor after a knobbie landing. 'Old woman,' said Chida, and moved on.

We complained about our knobbies to Reynaldo, a Venezuelan male model, who had been one of the few foreigners to actually fail the police course without dropping out first. He still hung around, two years after his course had ended, picking up highly paid modelling jobs and dabbling in martial arts. His aikido was not bad but the teachers found his attitude of Latino insouciance intolerable.

There was a lizard-like quality about Reynaldo, even when he was trying to be sympathetic. 'Oh that's bad, maan, real bad – you remember what I said – if you done hit the mat, the mat hits you. You recall that?'

We agreed that he had said something along these lines.

'Like on my course, maan, there were people wearing towels and shit down there to pro-tect themselves. You understand what I'm saying?'

We understood.

Reynaldo looked at his Cartier. 'Hey! Enough shooting the shit with you guys. I gotta be elsewhere. Yo, maan!' He high-fived Adam on the way out.

Reynaldo's advice to hit the mat harder was correct advice but not much use to the arch knobbie sufferer. Alon, an Israeli from a previous year's course, had been so badly affected that he could hardly walk properly or sleep. He'd taken a course of acupuncture and the problem had disappeared.

Ben had moved into Fuji Heights. We were all running short of cash so it made sense to further reduce our quality of life by sharing the rent between four. His huge bulk was immediately noticeable. All four of us slept in the same six-mat room on mattresses, which we rolled up by day. Ben's head touched one wall and his feet touched the other. It was fortunate he liked to sleep curled up in a foetal position. Even so, we were constantly tripping over his size 13 feet. One day he came home with a pair of sneakers that actually fitted him. It was the only time in

Tokyo he was able to buy something that wasn't too small. His only other footwear was a pair of massive Dr Martens boots which took up the whole space under the table. I started to nurture an irrational grudge – what the hell was he so big for? Where was the evolutionary advantage? He ate a lot too. I began to fantasize about lopping his feet off below the knee – that would probably ease the food and the accommodation problem.

Every day Ben and I now cycled together to the dojo, though Ben had been tempted by the offer of a small motorcycle, a Honda 90, which Stephan the Bavarian was selling for $200.

'I strongly counsel you not to buy a motorbike,' said Chris.

'You're mad if you buy that moped,' I said.

'Why?' said Ben, defiant.

'A) because you've never ridden one before, and Tokyo is a traffic nightmare with no regard for motorbike riders. B) because everyone I know who has ridden a bike has had some sort of accident, and C) you're careless and accident prone anyway.'

'No I'm not,' Ben resisted.

'You are. Take your neck, for example.' Ben had, after the earlier hospital fiasco continually re-injured his neck. He simply did not seem to be able to take care of himself and protect himself from injury.

'OK. I hear what you're saying.'

The next day Ben bought the moped.

But he wasn't the only person riding a small motorcycle. Adam had a scooter which he had hand-painted. On one side, in huge white letters, it said: 'Mobile Cancer Unit', with a picture of a large smoking cigarette. On the back, in equally large writing, it said: 'Beware – Alcoholic on board'. The dojo weren't happy about the Cancer Unit being parked in front of the building every day, so Adam arranged a feeble sort of cover that obscured the lettering to some extent.

Adam had suffered a stream of minor injuries which allowed him a day's respite here and there ever since his fainting in the

217

first week. Understandably no one took these at all seriously. One day he came in with a cut hand and a 'strained pelvis'.

'What happened?' said Stumpy, at the morning meeting where he always rounded up with: 'Any thoughts, questions, comments, verbals?'

'I got drunk,' said Adam. This was a bad start. Self-inflicted injuries outside the dojo were considered worthless. 'And I fell down the stairs. I was holding a glass. Look, I cut myself.'

'Fake! fake! fake!' we all chanted. Initial sympathy had hardened into cynicism.

'Oh sure, guys, sure. I threw myself down the stairs on purpose,' said the aggrieved Adam.

'Next?' said Stumpy, wanting to get through the injured list as quickly as possible.

Later on the Cancer Unit also became an accessory in one of Adam's injuries. He came in limping and moaning one morning. I think it was the quality of his playacting which annoyed people more than his self pity.

'What now?' said Will.

'I crashed the bike,' said Adam, with some drama.

This was repeated to Stumpy at the meeting.

'He's faking,' we chorused, as Stumpy heard the details.

'Oh right, guys, sure I'm faking – like I really want a bruised toe.'

R'em, whose English was usually too poor to understand swift repartee, caught the details for the first time: 'A bruised *toe?*' he said, incredulously.

But it wasn't all over-acting. For one day I have a single diary entry that rings ominously of what was going on. 'Tuesday 20th August. Today Craig cried from pain.'

As the demonstration loomed we had to learn how to march. This was fine for the police and the army boys but I had never marched before in my life. I found it delightfully easy compared to the rigorous complexity of simultaneous aikido. I even started to stamp my feet a bit as we marched endlessly around the dojo, trying to get a more military sound. 'Stop stamping your feet,' said Ando Sensei. 'You're not wearing boots!'

Around and around we wheeled and marched and ran at the double. It was reassuring to be inside a comparatively big group rather than the lonely isolation of solo or pair work. Yes, I thought, now I understand the lure of the army, being at one with a marching horde, responding perfectly to barked commands – and no technical difficulty! The marching was the best thing about the whole run up to the demo.

It was at this time that my breakfall flip came in for heavy criticism. It was too close to the ground and too hurried, not nearly relaxed enough. Mustard ordered me to flip again and again, but I think I got worse not better. Partly it was being injured and partly it was having a wrong mental image about what flipping entailed. The Japanese were less uptight about it. Ando took me back to basics and explained that I had to perfect the basic roll before I could grasp the perfect flip. 'Every time it must be the same,' he said. In his lessons, which were so thoughtful and so well structured, I felt I really improved. He would stand there, shake his head and work out what you were doing wrong, then bend you into the right shape so you could feel for yourself how it should be. With Robert Mustard all I did was irritate him. 'I'm going to beat the snot out of you!' he snarled. It was the first time I realized he probably didn't like a 'snotty' English accent. Too bad, I thought. At heart he was impatient, a disease that affects all foreigners who study in Japan, it seems. It is as if they know their time is limited so they try too hard. 'Each day is just another day of training,' said Chida Sensei. 'It is not day 3 or day 103.' But that is how we thought about it, and when the group diary was filled in the writer would call out the day with triumph: 'Day 100 – only 187 training days to go!'

I knew something was wrong. Ben had left the house before me but when I arrived at the dojo he was not there. He was riding the ominous moped. I went to get changed and Ben limped in. Blood seeped through one of his sneakers. He was, predictably, crying.

'Guess what?' he sobbed.

'You had an accident.'

'A car ran over my foot!'

'I'm not surprised, they're big enough.' Then I relented a little. 'How bad is it? Anything broken?'

Ben shook his head. Then Darren arrived and was surprisingly sympathetic. Ben's sneaker was removed and his foot looked like an ugly, bruised mess, but nothing appeared to be broken. He went off for the regulation X-ray and earned himself two days' rest in *seiza*. Oyamada thought he was in *seiza* as a punishment for some minor infringement and kicked him as he went past during a lesson. Later he found out Ben was injured and doing *mitori geiko*, watching practice. He didn't apologize – martial artists never apologize, and only rarely explain – but he did express concern for Big Foot's disaster.

We crowed over poor Ben when he got home.

'I knew this would happen!' I said.

'OK, OK,' said Ben, beaten.

'Do you think it will be better before the demo?' he asked.

'It won't,' said Chris, 'but you will be.' There was a week and a half to go. Ben bandaged his foot and soldiered on with the training. He never rode the moped again.

We did one complete run through the day before the demo, and it went perfectly. It seemed like a miracle, compared to our raggedy-assed efforts of three weeks before. And what's more, just the addition of being in time seemed to make our display significant, like a ballet or a piece of theatre. Six synchronized *kiais*, signalling the end of a fantastic display of flipping and punching. This alone ensured it would not be perfect on the day. Either my flips had improved or the teachers had given up correcting me. There was a silence in the dojo after our run

220

through and I knew it stood for applause. We were as ready as we'd ever be.

On the day of the demonstration we turned up in our lousy jackets and got changed into our dogis. In typical Yoshinkan fashion we'd been ordered to assemble four hours before the event, which started after lunch. We helped university students lay out the mats under megaphoned instruction from Ando and Chida. Chida Sensei, one of the world's greatest aikidoka, helping college kids to lay out tatami mats – it was a humility I would never expect to see in the West.

As we lined up to march on, the feeling of nervousness grew incredibly. It was much worse than for a test. Stumpy went around giving last-minute advice: 'It doesn't matter if you feel nervous, it's how you use that feeling that counts.' It was a quick homily, a trademark phrase, but it calmed me – for about a minute.

We stood on the huge mat in the middle of the covered stadium. Aikido enthusiasts from all over Japan crowded into the seats that rose up on every side. There was indiscriminate cheering, stadium noise and then silence. We waited for the command to begin.

I thought: I won't make a mistake *because I can't afford to*. Then I heard the order to start. It was as if the sound had taken a long time to reach me. My opening punch felt like slow motion, then Mad Dog battered into me and we were running at faster than normal speed. I recall a swirl of white-clothed bodies and then, like a jump cut, my hand was shaking above my head and ready to chop down. Should I go now or wait? The collective finishing cry filtered through just as my hand came down. I was fractionally late but shouted all the same.

Our timing was satisfactory, but there was no group magic this time. I had glimpsed perfection and this wasn't it, but everyone congratulated us. As we watched the video afterwards Mad Dog said: 'The good thing is you can't see our mistake.'

Both of us had made minor errors, but no one, not even the video, had noticed them.

Would the great Takeno select Robert Mustard as his *uke*, demonstration partner? Once, a few years ago, Takeno didn't choose Mustard but gave no reason. Perhaps he wanted to stop Mustard from being complacent. The previous year he had and I had seen a display of aikido the ferocity of which I'd never seen subsequently. Mustard attacked Takeno with what looked like full commitment – 'Ninety-five per cent commitment,' he later said. 'The five per cent I hold back stops me from being killed' – and was smashed repeatedly to the ground with uncompromising force.

Takeno had run the police course for twenty years before finally falling out with Kancho over a forgotten umbrella. Takeno had been Kancho's most faithful pupil and it was whispered darkly that Takeno would even have committed *seppuku* for him. But after a dojo meeting Kancho's umbrella had been left behind. Kancho groused, 'None of you love me, none of you even care for me – you only think about yourselves!' It was too much for Takeno, who had given his life to serving the founder. He went back to his native Yamanashi prefecture in a huff and started his own dojo.

Takeno's dojo won most of the prizes at the all Japan demonstration. Everyone knew he'd had students practising three months in advance, whereas our dojo usually allowed a couple of weeks. It was part of the difference in style between the two greats, Takeno and Chida. Chida was ultra-relaxed and had perfected an aikido which was undramatic to watch but utterly stripped down, without a move wasted. To feel it was to experience a strangely irresistible power. Takeno had followed a path to develop an explosive aikido, incredibly fast and powerful and very scary to be on the receiving end of. To be his *uke* required considerable courage, since it was difficult to breakfall out of his version of the 'helicopter', which left you flying halfway across the dojo and hitting the mat at an awkward angle.

Mustard clearly believed Takeno was the greatest, and though never openly disrespectful to Chida Sensei, everyone knew Mustard held Takeno in the higher regard.

Mustard and Takeno sat at a table talking. It seemed that this year Takeno would be demonstrating with his own students. While it wasn't Robert Mustard's right to be offended, Takeno invited him down to Yamanashi to give a demonstration the following month – this would offset any bad feeling generated by rejection as *uke*, a most coveted role, indicative of the teacher's high regard. Even a man with a 'hard bastard' reputation like Takeno was careful of feelings in Japan.

Towards the end of the day the top teachers all gave demonstrations of *jiyu waza* – freestyle attacks with knife, sword or bare hands, all of which the teacher disposes of in a more or less stylized way. Sometimes it's as direct as a palm smash to the chin, other moves involve balletic pivots and steps in order to throw *uke* safely but dramatically.

Ando performed his characteristically high-speed aikido, and I saw Chida do *ogi*, secret techniques, for the first time in a demonstration. He ordered two assistants to hoist him into the air, each assistant firmly holding one arm so that Chida was apparently helpless, two or three feet off the ground. It was like watching Houdini escape. For a moment nothing happened and then Chida jumped to the ground while at the same time the two assistants flipped up into the air. Chida's secret power was to send his centre of gravity down to his feet *without* moving. At the same time he changed, minutely, his arm position, which broke the assistants' double-handed grip. It was all done so smoothly that before they knew what had happened both assistants had been flipped over.

He then did *jiyu waza* with the first person to hand, who happened to be Mike Kimeda. Kimeda was too slow for Chida and limped off with a cracked ankle bone.

When it was the belligerent, highly coiffured Nakano's turn to display, he chose as *uke* the mild-mannered and utterly likeable Kikuchi, one of the *uchi-deshi* disciples. At twenty-eight he was one of the oldest *uchi-deshi*, but also the most approachable. His aikido was good, certainly as good as the midget Fujitomi, but not up to the natural genius of 'rubber man' Yoji, the youngest disciple. Certainly what happened next was not explicable in terms of anything except raw brutality.

Unlike karate matches and boxing bouts, an aikido demonstration is completely one sided. The *uke* is there simply to allow the master to show how good he is. This doesn't mean the *uke* should dive instead of waiting to be thrown properly, but it does mean that a certain level of co-operation is required. At the highest level – Mustard's or Takeno's – whatever the *uke* does will result in his downfall. In fact, Mustard was now at the stage where he found stiff and uncooperative *ukes* easier to deal with. Unfortunately a stiff *uke* is more likely to be hurt. A soft, slippery *uke* like Yoji can easily protect himself, bouncing and rolling out of trouble like a rubber snake. The *uke* co-operates to the extent that he makes an attack. Some teachers didn't care what kind of attack was made, they were ready for anything. Others, no less good, but anxious to show some particular aspect of aikido, will demand a certain style of attack – a side strike, a front punch and so on.

What Kikuchi did was to mishear the command from Nakano. He struck from the front when Nakano wanted a strike from the side, a chop aimed at the temple. Nakano easily blocked the wrong strike, immobilized Kikuchi and then dumped him heavily on to the back of his neck, giving him no time to break his fall. Kikuchi tried to get up, stumbled, and fell to his knees – he was clearly knocked out. Another *deshi* ran on to take his place, and Kikuchi was dragged to the side.

It had been nasty to watch. Kikuchi had been punished in a brutal way when he had put his trust in his teacher. The *uke* knows that every time he attacks the teacher with commitment he will be thrown. This is the trust side of aikido. As Mustard said: 'If you don't trust the teacher, don't be his *uke*.' It wasn't so easy for the *uchi-deshi*, they had to do what they were told. They had bought into the whole system, and if one teacher had it in for them then they were in for a hard time.

I could list the things that made up the seamy, unacceptable side of Japanese *budo*: Sakuma being repeatedly kicked up the arse after every attempt to do a technique, Ben's round of 'rabbit jumps' after he'd passed out in the heat, Fujitomi's harsh treatment of Danny, causing him a permanent knee injury, and now the pointless knockout of Kikuchi.

There were other injuries at the demo – one Japanese broke his shoulder and was led off with blood and bone ends showing through his pyjamas. And as well as 'Spike' Kimeda's cracked bone, there were other breaks and strains all round. But these were honest injuries, obtained without malice, accidents and not prison-camp-style punishments.

When we got back from the demonstration Chris had some more bad news: Little Kancho had finally keeled over and died. We buried him inside a big *sake* bottle, a fitting end for a great teacher. Ben had suggested pickling him for posterity, but we were all against it, on the grounds of space. With touching reverence the bottle was laid to rest in one of the big black plastic bins outside Fuji Heights.

How to Commit the Perfect Murder

'When one has made a decision to kill a person it will not do to think about going at it in a long roundabout way. One's heart may slacken, or one may miss his chance. The Way of the Samurai is immediacy, to dash in headlong.'

From the seventeenth-century Samurai manual *Hagakure*

October – November

I had to face I'd lost control of the class. There were only twenty girls in the class but I'd lost it. There were four girls who didn't like me. They claimed not to speak a word of English. When I spoke Japanese they laughed and said they couldn't understand what I was saying. These four infected the rest and that was how any authority I'd had began to slip away.

My method of teaching English, if it could be called a method, had always relied on the students liking me and this, together with their natural desire to get good grades, had resulted in a form of discipline. Sometimes they got a little rowdy, but nothing I couldn't handle. I always tried to make the lessons as interesting as possible – quirky and amusing, I liked to think – the kind of lesson I'd like to take. I wanted to stretch their imaginations, get them thinking, give them the freedom they were denied by more traditional teachers. Suddenly this had all unravelled. No one was interested in my 'interesting' lessons. I wasn't popular. Even the girls that had liked me in the beginning had somehow turned against me as I lost my temper in the desperate fight to control the class.

I shouted, I raved. Exploiting their ignorance of English I took to openly swearing, and pretty soon I got to hate going to the school. I was only grateful that the leader of the four girls, seventeen-year-old Naoko, was not that attractive. If she had been it would have been the last straw.

Once I saw Naoko fondling her own breasts, as if weighing them for size.

'That won't make them grow any bigger,' I said, petulantly.

I started walking a different way to the school so I didn't have to mingle with the hordes of sailor-suit-clad girls going the same way.

It was getting ridiculous. What would Chida Sensei do? Or Shioda? Or Robert Mustard? One phrase of Will's stuck in my mind: 'We can't live in fear.' And I was living in fear of a teenage girl. I asked Mr Wada what I ought to do.

'You can force Naoko to leave your class,' he said.

'What happens then?'

'Then she will fail the English course.'

'Is that a big problem?'

'If she fails the course she will have to leave the school.'

This, I knew, was a big deal. If a girl is thrown out of a Japanese high school in her second or third year she will find it difficult to get into another school, if not impossible. She would not graduate with her friends, and in Japan your high-school friends are sometimes the only real friends you make. This is what I told myself. I think now I should have failed her and let her face the consequences, the irate parents, the lowly paid job, an eternal bitterness towards the English race. Everyone wanted me to do it. I felt like Martin Sheen in *Apocalypse Now*, where he has orders to kill Marlon Brando but he keeps putting it off. 'Everyone wanted me to do it,' says Sheen. 'Even the jungle wanted him dead.'

While I couldn't count on the playing fields and the tennis courts wanting to be rid of Naoko, the entire staff had problems with the girl. Mr Wada was the spokesman for all those whose wrath she had raised.

'Many teachers have problems with this girl,' he said. 'Ever since she was in junior high school she has been a problem.'

'She's just so ... insolent,' I said, and launched into yet another tale of her refusal to work.

'Perhaps she should go,' said Mr Wada. I detected that this was the decision he wanted me to make.

'What would you do?' I asked.

'I have never taught this girl,' he said, looking directly at me.

It was obvious I was to be the fall guy. Everyone wanted her out, but because it was a private school no one wanted to take the responsibility when the parents inevitably complained. I was the gaijin. I was expendable. If there was any complaint they could heap it on me and say, 'He's only a foreigner, he doesn't understand Japan. It's terrible, I know, but he is the teacher, so I'm afraid Naoko cannot return to our school.'

The more I thought about it the more I believed that everyone had been waiting for years for an opportunity to get rid of this girl. But I couldn't decide what to do because in a bizarre way I sympathized with Naoko. We were in the same position. Except I was being persecuted by Robert Mustard in a traditional Japanese dojo.

At the beginning we were often threatened with being thrown off the course. Now we felt we'd earned our place. Mustard didn't think so. He kept up an atmosphere of insecurity. A momentary lapse would result in a sweeping denigration of all efforts. I felt like the guy in the joke, indignant at being stopped for disobeying a red traffic light: 'Come on, officer, what about all the green lights I obeyed? Surely that counts for something?!' With Mustard it most definitely didn't.

For the first time, his standard comment, 'If you don't like it, go home,' was being personally directed, and mostly at me. I kept an account of whom he said it to, and I was ahead in this game. I was being singled out for special treatment. At times it seemed like a childish psychological war. He would taunt me, and Adam sometimes: 'You're frightened. Come on, if you're

228

frightened stay home.' It was disconcerting and, more to the point, it didn't work. I became increasingly resentful at being insulted. At the same time I knew I'd signed my rights away on this course; the Japanese way was to give the teacher a complete free hand, hence the odd death that occurs in high schools where a teacher's punishment routine can get carried away.

In the previous month two children had been locked in a steel tank for eight hours as a punishment for lying – they died of heat exhaustion and oxygen starvation. This was an odd excess that came along with the Japanese way of doing things, but none of the Japanese sensei was as deeply personal as Mustard. I tried to be reasonable about it to Will.

'He probably had a hard childhood. Maybe his father was very demanding.'

'Great,' said Will, 'now we have to psychoanalyse our teachers!'

We were sitting on the beaten-up chairs at the back of the locker room next to the dogi chuck-out box. A couple of times my belt had ended up mysteriously in that box. I suspected sabotage.

The locker room had become an alternative to the tea room. Essentially, the course had split into two factions: Will, Ben, R'em and myself; and on the other side, Mad Dog, Little Nick, Aga and Craig, with Danny and Adam floating between the two. It wasn't completely fixed – after all, I had to work out every day with Mad Dog, spend several hours locked in a sweaty embrace with the guy – but broadly that was the division. As Will said, 'War either makes you a monk or a maniac – we're the monks.' What did he mean? At heart I think he meant that if you are treated badly you either choose to pass it on as you received it, or you go the other way and try to make it easy on those who come after you. Will was a confirmed monk, and at this stage good enough at aikido to be able to progress without really hurting his partner. But I was beginning to suspect that progress in aikido came when you were indifferent to your partner's fate and did the technique as hard as possible – why else would all the teachers, even Ando the Merciful, go through a 'killer' phase?

Currently it was Chino who was still dishing out the most dojo injuries. The bald Sato, who before the course had trained a lot with Chino, was known as 'Chino's little brother'. He had suffered considerably at Chino's hands. His collarbone had been broken by Chino's *nikajo* lock. Chino had given him five or six other breaks and bone separations. 'How can you like the guy?' I asked Sato. 'After all the pain he's given you?' Sato gave me a wry look. 'I like his aikido very much, but do I like him? I suppose so, but I have not forgotten the injuries he has given me. I have not forgotten.'

Back in the changing room Will had moved on to the general topic of brain damage. (We had briefly considered and then dismissed the idea that Mustard was brain damaged, and this was why he was behaving oddly.) 'Down in Mexico I met a few guys that boxed for over ten years and they are, I would say, most definitely brain damaged. In Japan it's worse, I've met guys who have only been pro for two years and they're already brain damaged – eye focus gone, hands shaking, balance impaired.'

'Why's that?' I asked.

'It's the general dimensions of the skull. If you take your wrist or your ankle, that gives the best indication of bone thickness. Now the average Japanese has very thin wrists, and I guess this translates into a thin skull.'

I ventured that maybe that is why the Japanese are obsessed with building up skull strength – Ueshiba used to repeatedly bang his head against trees in Hokkaido to strengthen his head-butting power.

At first it was just a macabre joke. I started to consider ways of killing Mustard, or crippling him in some way. Then the fantasies became increasingly detailed and realistic. I realized it was actually quite difficult to kill someone, when you really work it out. I discussed this with Will:

'I saw him in the shower today and I thought if I had a baseball bat I could lay into him through the curtain and he wouldn't know what had hit him.'

Will was sceptical. 'He's one hard son of a bitch. With him you have to kill him, because if you don't he'll get you – and you make one mistake, you're dogmeat for sure.'

'You're right. It would have to be a gun.'

'But even then, have you the guts to pull the trigger, staring into those eyes, man? One shot is all you got because if he isn't dead after one shot, you sure will be.'

He was right. The eyes – the only real way to tell a serious martial artist: remorseless, pitiless eyes, without a flicker of warmth.

Ben's advice was to send a parcel bomb. 'But what if Carol opened it?' I asked. 'OK, put a bomb inside his cigarette pack – he's always hiding those from Carol. That should put him out of action for a while.' 'It's too risky,' I said. 'What if he offered a cigarette to Mad Dog?' 'Two birds with one stone,' smirked Ben.

These conversations were almost serious. I'd like to think that it wasn't Mustard's invincibility as fighter that stopped him from being wasted; I'd like to think my sanity prevailed, but I couldn't be sure about that. Not 100 per cent sure.

A student asked Tesshu, 'It's difficult to kill someone, isn't it?'

'Not at all,' he replied. 'It's only difficult if you want to keep yourself alive.'

It wasn't just Naoko or planning murder at the dojo that was undermining my normal semblance of calm: I was in trouble about my visa. This was critical. If I lost my job or was kicked out of Japan I would effectively be flunking the course. It had happened in previous years, and no one remembered that you went for a bureaucratic rather than a 'real' reason. There was only finishing and failure. Nothing in between.

I had a working visa which I'd got renewed just before I'd given up full-time work. Now it was time to get it renewed again. But now I only worked one day a week, and to qualify for a work visa you had to work at least twenty hours a week. The company employing me, on a sub-contract basis with the high school, was intransigent despite my pleas. I had been myopically banking on them doing me a favour and fiddling the books a little. They'd done this for another teacher I knew. But I had fallen out of favour with the new manager, a 'career English teacher' from Iowa, when I led a successful revolt against his brainchild, a report system of intricate complexity and zero utility. I wasn't fired, but the little freak was getting his revenge – they would not sponsor me for another working visa.

I asked Nonaka Sensei to petition the owner of the company, a smooth, smiling Japanese property developer who had about as much compassion as a photocopier.

'I have spoken to Mr Harigata,' she told me. 'But he is not an honourable man. From now on I call him "bi-section".'

'You mean "two-faced"?'

'So, so, so. He likes to talk very much, but he will not help you.'

There were other choices – a cultural visa or a tourist visa. If I got a tourist visa I would have to quit my job, and live how? A cultural visa, remembering Craig's delays, looked too tricky a proposition. I didn't want things to backfire and have to leave at this critical stage of the senshusei course. There was one other option: a spouse visa. If I got married my troubles regarding work or continued residence to do aikido were over. My mind, clouded and strained by the psychological warfare at the dojo, leaped at the clear simplicity of getting an instant Japanese wife. Then I grew canny and wary. It couldn't just be any woman. Who knows what problems that might throw up. I immediately ruled out Sara. I actually liked her, she was my girlfriend, but she would, I guessed, have a hard time explaining such a thing to her parents, who didn't even know I existed. Plus I didn't want to confuse things – I didn't want a paper marriage turning by default and laziness into a real one. I explained all this to Sara

232

and asked for her advice. She was surprisingly clear on the subject. She thought the whole thing was a bad idea. I disregarded what I didn't want to hear and made a date with a girl I considered perfect for the job as my future ex-wife, figuring certain divorce would have to be part of the package. The girl I had in mind was nicknamed 'the Chinese Ghost' and had a knicker collection numbering hundreds of pairs of exotic underwear.

The Chinese Ghost, so called because of her fey, ghostly appearance, had been a secretary at a company I had previously worked for. Together we had worked on the publicity for a disastrous idea for a language course entitled '*Twin Peaks* English'. It was during the *Twin Peaks* TV series craze and we spent large amounts of the company's cash on a lifesize blow-up Kyle MacLachlan, artistic posters and other memorabilia ripped off from the programme. It was a complete disaster, despite the press conference with representatives of *Apple, Trendy, Cutie* and other likely magazines. A complete disaster which resulted in no students signing up and two enquiries from English teachers who had seen our fabulous window display and wondered if we had any jobs going . . .

Twin Peaks English precipitated the bankruptcy of the company. Somehow this established a strong bond between the Chinese Ghost and myself. No sex was involved. The Ghost loved to talk about it but not to do it. She preferred getting drunk and reminiscing about her days in London as a free-living Japanese girl about town. Not that I hadn't tried an advance or two in the past but she really was not interested and our relationship settled down to an easy and convivial equilibrium of going out to risqué nightspots and eyeing up the respective action. Totally self-contained, nothing seemed to shock the Chinese Ghost, but since starting the senshusei course I had seen her only once, my system no longer up to the long-winded drinking sprees she was able to endure. She was only twenty-six but, as befitting a ghost, she seemed ageless.

I knew she wanted to live in London. Apart from Japanese food she seemed to find Japan parochial and tedious. Her father had recently died after a long cancerous illness and I believed this released her from the obligation of staying in Tokyo. I'd even talked to her before about Japanese girls paying up to $10,000 to get married to a foreigner. I was offering to do it for free. I trusted her. She had no claims on me. It was a perfect situation.

We met in One Lucky, my favorite 'gaijin bar', after a hike through the pouring rain, made more uncomfortable because the Ghost was very, very short and her umbrella only came up to my chin. It kept sliding underneath my own umbrella, ceaselessly dumping water on to my shoulder and arm. Inside One Lucky it was warm and cozy and the Japanese owner, Masuta-san, befezzed, was doing his double-spread crossword. He was happy to see me and exclaimed about the shortness of my hair. We sat in a corner seat and my wet clothes steamed.

You know you've lost almost before you've started if you bring up a difficult subject with a Japanese and they head you off at the first opportunity. You can't put it down to obtuseness, or preoccupation – you never have to spell things out to a Japanese. If they pretend to not follow something then it means they aren't interested. I tried valiantly, explaining my case in general terms, seeing if it raised a flicker of interest from the Ghost. Not a chance. In the end I had to be uncomfortably blunt.

'So, I was thinking, as I said, that the only solution was marriage . . .'

No reply.

'So, er, do you want to get married? Think of that British passport, permanent residency in any of the thirteen EC countries . . .' I grinned, wanly.

The Ghost giggled appreciatively and shook her head, though she couldn't bring herself to say no. She kind of snorted and took a long drink of beer, then looked away.

The subject was dead. I had failed. Like my plans to murder Mustard, it was all unravelling in front of me. I had been living in Tokyo under the mistaken impression that any girl would jump at the chance of marriage. Wrong. The Ghost proved that. Now I was sunk. There was a week to go before my visa ran out. It was time to do some fast thinking.

We had now started doing *jiyu waza* (the freestyle attack training). Sometimes you are attacked by one person, sometimes by two or three, or, in Kancho and Ueshiba's case, five or six. The attack continues until the attacker is either knocked out, pinned to the ground or stopped by the teacher's command. The idea is for the thrower and the thrown to work together, since the more committed the attack the easier it is to deal with. It is supposed to be nice to look at; a continuous ballet of throws and attacks. As the attacker closes in and punches, you have to spin out of the way, foil his attack and throw him using something that bears at least a passing resemblance to an aikido technique. As you get better the throws become real aikido throws with power; but at first they are cosmetic, since all your effort is expended in not getting fouled up in the initial attack. After the throw, which the attacker flips out of, he bounces up and attacks again with another punch.

The thrower cannot use the same technique each time. Indeed, he won't want to, because the slight difference in angle and speed of each punch means a different technique is best suited to foiling that particular attack. Unfortunately you sometimes get 'stuck', using only one type of throw again and again. And like a needle stuck on a record, it's painful to observe. Planning a sequence of *jiyu waza* moves makes it look wooden; indeed, *jiyu waza* is closest to jazz, where pre-learned techniques are linked together freestyle.

This musical motif was explained by Stephan the powerlifter. He stood in front of the class and, like a heavy metal fan, imitated strumming a guitar. '*Jiyu waza* is like playing music, man; you just can't make a mistake and stop and say I'm sorry. You have to keep going, mistake or no mistake; you have to keep playing.'

Naturally, it is most exhausting for the one who attacks and is thrown, and after fifteen or so throws you are fighting for breath. As you get better and more relaxed it becomes easier. Unfortunately, with a body festering with minor injuries and huge demented knobbies it wasn't easy to stay relaxed.

I trained with Gimpy, whose weak bandaged wrists had recovered from their injury at the beginning of the course. He suddenly seemed confident and threw me all over the place. I guessed he must have already practised some throwing art like shorinji kempo, as for all his wimpiness he had brilliant timing. With Mad Dog it was more clunky. He insisted on dumping me over his hip, which was difficult to breakfall out of and often resulted in a crash-landing on a knobbie. After a few weeks of *jiyu waza* everyone was feeling decidedly beaten up.

Mustard's idea of *jiyu waza* training was to make each pair perform in front of the others. He was so much on my case that when I made one mistake at the beginning of a session, he barked, 'No good,' and ordered me off the floor. This happened again the next day. I wasn't even getting to do any training! But just as I felt this to be overwhelmingly unfair he did the same to Craig who, with tireless masochism, was fast becoming a Mustard pet. My frail grasp of objectivity was temporarily restored when I saw him treat one of his favourite students the same as me, the current dunce of the class. Mustard taught by that despised method of there always being an exemplar and a dunce in the class. Statistically it was Adam and I who were the usual dunce examples; Mad Dog and Little Nick the good examples.

It was 'good training', in Paul's sense, to be for once near the bottom of the class. For the first time I could empathize with the duffers at school, those who hadn't sailed through exams like me, those who really had to work and suffer no praise, only silence or criticism. It was 'good training' but it wasn't pleasant. And the duffers at school could exact revenge on the smart kids by beating them up. I couldn't even get that reward since they were all better at dishing it out than me! Being waspish in the tea room, or plotting the death of Mustard with Will was my only way to let off steam. It wasn't enough. I could feel things brewing to a head.

I decided to see Ken about the visa problem. Half Okinawan-Japanese, half Hawaiian-Japanese, but resident in San Francisco from the age of seventeen until two years previously, Ken was an ex-drug dealer who'd fled to Tokyo because things had become too hot in California. He was married to a very pleasant Japanese girl who ran her family's restaurant. Ken called her 'the bitch'. She understood no English but he enjoyed ordering her around using expletives: 'Get the tickets, bitch' . . . 'You drive, bitch' . . . 'Where's the money, bitch?' In reality she ruled the roost and Ken washed up in the restaurant, and was actually kind and considerate towards her. He'd solved his own visa problem by getting married. Then he discovered because of his Okinawan ancestry he didn't need a visa. Typical Ken. He went for teaching jobs but always failed by being too direct; he'd never learnt the middle-class way to lie. To questions like 'Why do you want to be an English teacher, Mr Hamada?' he'd answer, 'I speak English and I like girls. I notice you have a lot of girls around here.' Before one interview I had to tie his tie – he'd never worn one before.

Ken did aikido but he disliked taking tests. He just hated to be judged. He'd been doing aikido for some years now and was the most outstanding beginner in the whole dojo. He was also an aficionado of strange bars. His current favorite was Swamp Venus, a tiny bar with eight seats, run by the ex-lead singer of an all female rock group also called Swamp Venus. Ken liked to drink, and though he had no experience of successful visa acquisition, I thought he would be a good guy to air things with.

Swamp Venus was full of sci-fi memorabilia and souvenirs from the band's days on the road. The owner, who I guessed was thirty or less, banked on regulars and ex-fans to keep her in business. She had green hair and pierces and tattoos, but was a model of friendly politeness, in fact just like any other *mamasan* eager for custom.

Ken talked fast, very fast, a street patter littered with what I took to be old fashioned Californiaisms like 'cat'. Maybe they'd come back into fashion again.

'So what you gonna do, some cat's coming for you in the street, what dyo do?'

'Run?'

'No, no, no way, you're trained, they been training you. Brainwashing you. You are a killer. That's the whole point of this sicko macho course thing. It's kinda sick, isn't it? This Mustard guy – I mean, who is he? Who is he? He's a cat with a problem, that's what. His problem is power. He wants total control over you guys. He wants your hearts and minds. Hearts and minds. But the way he goes on about that Takeno dude, sounds like pure masochism to me. That guy enjoys being beaten up. It's not normal, man. The cat's crazy.'

'What about the visa?'

'Fuck the visa! That's what. Fuck the fuckin' visa.'

'Become illegal?'

'Whatever. The visa is just paper. Screw the paper. Screw it right up.' Ken fired off some Japanese at the smiling Swamp Venusian. Two cold Asahi beers appeared.

'You like this Asahi shit?'

'It's OK. Better than Sapporo.'

'The visa thing, man, it's a problem, but don't get married. Don't make that mistake. Look at me. I gotta go soon. This marriage stuff is crap.'

'Where will you go?'

'San Francisco.'

'What about your wife?'

'What about her? It's time to get back. Things aren't working out here.' He took a hurried sip. 'But watch out for that Mustard dude. He's one crazy cat.'

*

238

How I came to the decision to ignore Mustard, I don't know. I decided that since I had tried to follow his instructions to the letter and that had failed, then the opposite might have some effect. I also calculated that I had only two months until the black-belt test – I could surely weather his disapproval until then. And after the test? There would be three more months as a black belt before the course finished, but if he continued to harass me I'd quit the course and take the lesser prize of a black belt only.

The required 'oos' I gave him were mechanical and military, utterly insincere. There was a lot of tension between us, extraordinary, really, silly of course, but in the superheated environment where obsession was normal it did not seem out of place. He knew something was up, and at first he took to ignoring me back. Fine. I could at least practise on my own. He sensed this was what I wanted and he came back to start badgering me again. 'No good, do it again.' 'No good.' This was what I inured myself to hear again and again. Mad Dog was sometimes sympathetic, sometimes on Mustard's side. But mostly he was loyal. On one occasion I did some technique in front of the class, and when questioned for the mistake, Mad Dog said, 'Looked OK to me.' Apparently I was making some major error but no one could see it until it was pointed out, which didn't mean the error wasn't there, but it did mean the other senshusei, who sensed Mustard's mood, weren't going to hang me without a fair trial.

Three days before my visa expired I finally decided to ask Chris for advice. He always gave good advice, but if I asked him for advice I always felt I had to take it. You could never disregard Chris, and for this reason I tried to limit how often I went to him for a solution. But now I was desperate.

He was sitting at the computer in Fuji Heights facing a screen of indecipherable gibberish. After a virus infected our system Chris worked out what the gibberish meant and preferred beating the viral mix-up to getting the whole system cleaned out. The order to 'print' meant clicking on a bizarre window full of accented letters. It was Chris's way, living one step ahead of total disaster.

I asked him what I should do. He clicked on some more coded nonsense before answering. Then he said: 'I'm going to the 7-eleven. Do you want an ice cream?'

Chris was like Holmes, except that he needed ice cream instead of a pipe to solve problems. This was serious – definitely a Häagen-Daz-cappuccino-with-almonds-on-a-stick problem.

When he came back he had it all worked out.

'You fly out of the country. Go to Singapore or Seoul. Singapore is better, too many Iranians and other dodgy types are coming through Seoul. You fly back and get an ordinary tourist visa. Why not? All that business about marriage visas and cultural visas clouded the issue. You only need to re-enter Japan. That's all. Once you're here you can finish the course. No one at the dojo will be checking up on your visa at this stage. They won't know you're here as a tourist.'

'But a tourist visa is only for three months.'

'If you can't extend it, go illegal for the last two months of your stay. But you should be able to renew it. You haven't lots of renewal stamps cluttering up your passport. You should be fine.'

'What about the job?'

'Stall them if they ask to see the visa. But probably they won't. They know you've got problems, but tell them you're getting a cultural visa through the dojo. Tell them it takes months to process, which is why you can't show them your passport.'

It was so simple. My only problem might be on re-entering Japan. The immigration authorities were increasingly severe on people working illegally in the country. But for the first time in weeks I felt relaxed. Even if I was fired I'd find some way to survive. The important thing was to finish the senshusei course.

Two days before I was due to fly out Mustard came over and started to tell me where I was going wrong. I could hardly take in his words. I stared through him or around him and 'oosed' with a complete lack of connection to what he was saying. He stalked off in a huff. That morning we'd already been chastised by Paul for a lack of correct 'oosing'. It was all academic, I was beginning to split myself away from the programme. At the lesson's end Mustard gathered us around. When he was in a good mood he let us stand. Now he made us kneel. He ranted about the lack of respect.

'Especially from you.' He pointed and glowered at me. I said 'Ooos,' because that's what you're supposed to say when a teacher talks to you. It seemed to incense him more. 'If I don't get more respect from you I'm going to punch you in the face and kick you out of the dojo. You understand? Chida won't let me do that, but I'll do it anyway!' Then he dismissed us angrily.

No one wanted to talk to me in the locker room. I was definitely *persona non grata*. Will muttered to meet him at the usual coffee shop and left. Craig gave me a pained expression and said, 'If you just "oos" a little bit more . . . respectfully.'

'I know,' I said. 'I tried.'

'Yeah, I know,' then he patted me on the shoulder, which was a touching gesture I would not have expected from him.

In the coffee shop Will was more angry than I was.

'He has no right. No right to talk to you like that. If you'd walked out I would have been right behind you. I swear I was so mad at that guy. Jesus, what an asshole. He has no goddam right to say that stuff.'

'It's OK,' I said. 'I'm taking a few days off to get the visa. Things will cool down.'

'I'm talking basic human rights here. The guy . . . what an asshole.'

We berated Mustard for an hour or two behind his back and then I left feeling a bit better. I had warned Paul that my visa was due for renewal, so when I called him and asked for some days off to make the trip he, reasonable and professional as ever, confirmed that it would be no problem. It was odd that a stamp and a piece of paper was treated with such respect, commanded so much more attention than even the excuse of a serious injury. The visa trip was the ultimate 'Get out of jail free' card and this was my last chance to play it.

I bought a cheap ticket to Singapore and flew out a day later. I have never experienced such relief. Climbing higher and higher into the sky above Tokyo and then winging back across the mainland and over the blue Pacific, all the tensions of the previous days drained away. I ordered a couple of American beers and wrote in my diary: 'What is the value of freedom? To be able to breathe without difficulty.'

I relished my sudden and complete freedom in Singapore. No matter that there were $500 fines for urinating in lifts and chewing gum was banned, to me it was complete and utter freedom. I could do anything, go anywhere. I decided to make a trip into Malaysia to save money.

At Singapore railway station I bought a ticket to Johor Baharu. As the train pulled out and we were nominally in Malaysia, everyone on the train pulled out illegal packets of Wrigley, and started chewing happily. I caught a bus to Kuala Lumpur in Johor Baharu. An old lady occupied the entire back seat and defecated into a pinkish plastic bag as we drove along. The stench was appalling. Outside I could see the Malaysian country-side littered with similar pinkish plastic bags. For me it became the national colour of Malaysia. I didn't even mind the smell. I could only think: What have I been cooped up in a dingy dojo for so long for? Why had I voluntarily put myself in a Japanese prison? Why? I could think of no good answer. I'm never going back, I thought.

In Kuala Lumpur I stayed with a Malaysian friend from college. He was a successful lawyer and had a large house, complete with servants. Feasting off endless bowls of perfectly cooked rice, delicious curries, fresh fish, vegetables, mangoes and hot baked bread, the contrast with Fuji Heights was too embarrassing to mention. I was actually enjoying food for the first time in ages. In Japan I had adopted shove-it-down-your-face survival mentality to food, to fuel the body's machine. How wrong I was! Food must be savoured, enjoyed, considered and digested. In Japan I wasn't digesting food, I was processing it, and hardly doing that very efficiently.

I lazed around the luxury marble-floored house, drinking coffee brought by the maid, who babbled friendlily at me in Indonesian; so unlike the Japanese, who are embarrassed to speak to you if you don't understand. God, I feel at home here, I thought, drawing deeply on an English-made cigarette and looking out at the tropical afternoon rain beating down on the verandah. It was time to make a plan about what I should do next. Couldn't I just continue in Malaysia indefinitely? I went sailing and began to question the whole reasoning behind the senshusei course. Other people had such a good time! But if I quit now I'd lose everything. Everything would have been in vain.

Back in Singapore I walked around in a daze. I even absent mindedly brought out a pack of gum in a crowded shopping centre, before I felt a hundred censorious eyes upon me. I didn't want to get arrested for illicit gum chewing. I didn't even know the penalty. If it was a choice between a fine and a beating, I'd take the beating – it was what I was trained for.

I made a visit to Changi Gaol, which is close to the airport. Somehow it felt like the completion of unfinished business. As I stared up at the smooth architecture of the walls and watchtowers – the place is still in use as a civil prison – I wondered where Colonel H.'s cigarette case had been made. Unlike Dachau or Bergen-Belsen there is no perceptible grimness about Changi Gaol. The jungle encroaches too much, overhanging the road with foliage, pushing up against the concrete walls, a neutral, voracious growth that devours everything, even the suffering. If the jungle was left alone it would quickly swallow up Changi Gaol.

There was a museum and a few tatty reconstructions, but you could tell the Singaporeans wanted to forget the war. With so many Japanese on shopping trips it was probably a shrewd move. And though all high-school students know about Hiroshima, I never met a Japanese teenager with any knowledge of Changi or the death railway. In the guilt stakes the A bomb had obviously won.

There was a lifesize cardboard cut-out of General Yamashita, the Tiger of Malaya, in the museum. I had my photo taken standing next to him.

Kancho had passed through Singapore on his way to Borneo during the war. In his autobiography he wrote that the 'moral weakness' of Japan was evident in the way young officers surrounded themselves with every kind of luxury. 'Why, I, myself, even had a gramophone with a stylus and arm made entirely of gold ... This moral laxity was the reason Japan lost the war.'

I went to the Cockpit Hotel, Chris's favourite place for sitting on the balcony savouring the noise of the afternoon downpour. But it was now evening and the place was damp and chilly, though it wasn't raining. I drank two Singapore Slings, but they made me feel muzzy-headed and resentful.

I got a cab to the airport. Who was I kidding? And what would Colonel H. say if I allowed the Japs to get the better of me? I had to go back. I had to see the thing through to the bitter end.

On the plane I made up my mind. I would have to be a model senshusei. I would have to 'oos' louder than anyone else, take every throw to the maximum, submit to the madness in order to survive it. Being detached hadn't worked. You couldn't stand outside and calmly observe and still do the training every day.

I felt rested. My intense personal antipathy to Mustard had waned and I felt physically strong enough to at least get as far as the black-belt test. I could take as an example one of Tesshu's students, Hasegawa, who was so uncoordinated he never learnt,

244

in fifty years of training, to swing his sword straight. Nevertheless, he rose to be one of Tesshu's best students and was even able to give the master a run for his money during a practice duel. Hasegawa exemplified mind over matter and was fond of quoting: 'Unified in spirit – what cannot be accomplished?'

Survival

'Matters of great concern should be treated lightly. Matters of small concern should be taken seriously. Among one's affairs there should be only two or three matters of great concern. Private meditation on them allows them to be treated lightly in public.'

From the seventeenth-century Samurai manual *Hagakure*

I took a throw from Mustard and held on to the last minute, instead of letting go early to save myself. Mustard nodded acknowledgement.

When it was my turn to lead the warm-up exercises I shouted out the commands at top volume. Doing the basic exercises at the beginning of each class I found an extra reserve of energy I hadn't previously been aware of – the gung-ho factor. To draw on this energy I just had to shut down the part of my brain capable of making criticism. The next stage was to narrow my focus to only the next few minutes ahead.

The rest of the senshusei looked like tired old men. Perhaps I hadn't noticed before. I held my week of good living close to my chest, like a secret it's hard to keep. Knowing that there was life worth living outside the dojo would definitely help me survive the coming months.

My time in Malaysia had cleared up another problem. I'd come to a decision about naughty Naoko at the high school. After a lot of thought I decided I didn't want to do the Japanese teachers' dirty work. I would be magnanimous. But the lessons would have to change. I told Mr Wada that I would not ban Naoko from my classes.

'If it gets any worse I will,' I said. I noticed that Mr Wada was

246

wearing his glasses again. He seemed preoccupied. Nodding vaguely he stalked off to the teachers' room. If I failed with Naoko now I knew I could expect little sympathy from the Japanese staff. Whatever I did would have to work.

I asked Nonaka Sensei to sit in on one of my lessons. Less than five-feet-tall, she was an iron disciplinarian. I'd watched her classes – fifty girls all completely silent, until asked a question – it was a beautiful sight.

'How do you do it?' I asked.

'It is my classroom,' she said, 'not theirs. This is what I want. And children like a strict teacher. I have a reputation.' Her tiny black eyes glinted at me.

Reputation. I didn't dare think about mine. That was part of the problem, no doubt. I hadn't thought about my reputation until it was too late.

There was a stir amongst the girls as Nonaka Sensei took her seat at the back of the class. The girls, of course, behaved very well. Nonaka Sensei walked around quizzing the troublemakers imperiously in her sharp, persistent voice.

'They're not usually like this,' I said, at the end of the lesson.

Nonaka read from a scrap of paper her notes on what I should do.

'They don't understand what you are saying,' she said.

'Some of them do,' I protested.

'You must go more slowly. You must check they understand.'

'OK,' I said, easily beaten.

'Let them prepare for lessons in advance.'

'Right.'

'But I think you are too intelligent for them,' said Nonaka Sensei. 'These are very ordinary girls. You are a "cut above the rest",' she said, in her vibrant, idiosyncratic English. Her eyes shone with good humour. She had managed the difficult task of criticism by injecting this last, heavy load of flattery.

I thought about the aikido teachers. How little nonsense they stood for. In a rush of inspiration I consulted Tesshu's sword-

247

fighting manual. I paid particular attention to 'The Seven Ways to Attain Victory.'

'THE SEVEN WAYS TO ATTAIN VICTORY:
1. Suppressing the opponent's ki
2. Anticipating the attack
3. Responding to the attack
4. Holding down
5. Driving back
6. Overwhelming
7. Proper adjustment'

The next Monday I went in and handed out a sheet of 'rules'. I wrote some basic phrases on the board and we practised them again and again. I got the best student to translate them into Japanese for the rest of the class. Then we repeated them some more. And then some more. Then I tested them on the basic phrases. Then we repeated them again. Suddenly the lesson was over. It was all so easy.

My 'Aikido English' lessons mimicked the form of an aikido lesson. The first ten minutes or so would be repetition of the basic phrases, with particular emphasis on pronunciation. I developed catchphrases, that the girls were forced to repeat: 'Pronunciation is the most important thing'; 'If in doubt – guess'; 'Be happy to make a mistake'.

After the basic phrases I would take a micro-conversation. This was the equivalent of a 'technique'. The conversation was practised as a group, then as two groups, then in pairs. It was deeply mechanical. At the end of the lesson I would offer to answer questions. If there were none everyone repeated the basic phrases a few more times.

It was dull as ditchwater but it worked. There was simply no time for anyone to be distracted by Naoko. To counter the boredom I injected an unnatural amount of enthusiasm into the lesson. I could see I was developing a 'teacher's personality'. But it worked, and that was the main thing.

To gain more 'sucking up to Mustard points' I travelled with Chris to watch Mustard perform at a demonstration at Takeno's dojo, a two-hour train journey into the mountains from Tokyo. R'em was going too, with Ben riding on the back of his motorbike.

In the demonstration programme, the performing foreigners were described at the 'blue-eyed Samurai'. This was about as respectful as describing a bunch of Japanese competing at a Highland games as 'the slant-eyed expert caber-tossers'. But it served its purpose – the foreigners were flattered and the Japanese could laugh at its incongruity. Takeno took the microphone and introduced Mustard. He praised him lavishly as one of his most faithful students, but could not resist the jibe '. . . and he's living proof that how you look as you walk has no bearing on how strong your aikido is', which was a dig at Mustard's street walk, different from his haughty dojo walk, where he sort of hunkered down and looked slightly apelike and menacing.

Takeno beat up four or five students but reserved his real hard stuff for Mustard. You got the impression that Takeno was suffering from a huge excess of testosterone, as if he had to dominate all men totally, pound them into the mat, until, as Robert Mustard put it, 'even your eyebrows hurt'.

Mustard thanked us for attending. I was slowly worming my way back into the programme.

After the demo R'em offered to take Ben back on the motorbike. It was a borrowed bike, even huger than his usual machine – a 1100 cc Suzuki, and R'em was riding, of course, as fast as possible. I was surprised when Ben declined the lift. Maybe the trip on the way down had been too hair-raising and had brought back uncomfortable memories of the squashed foot incident on the moped.

That night we got a phonecall from a hospital near Takeno's dojo. It was R'em, sounding unusually weak and plaintive. He'd had a bad smash on the bike. No, nothing broken, but all the flesh was torn off one knee and he was badly shaken. The bike was a write-off. He would be in hospital for a few days and back training in a week, he said.

I told Ben. 'Hey, you must be lucky, after all – with your massive feet who knows what kind of catastrophe you'd have suffered on that bike.'

When R'em came back at the end of the week his knees were a curious dappled pink colour, like raw tongue. He had recovered his usual bravado and gave his account of the accident:

'The guy in the car pulled out. I see this and say he must see me but he hasn't. There is no time to brake. I'm going about a hundred so I go faster to get past. He goes faster too, so I know I'm going to hit. So my only choice is lie the bike down. And when I lie it down I'm flying along on my face like Superman, really, I'm like Superman.'

R'em had yet to tell the friend that his bike had been destroyed. It was something I wouldn't want to have to tell anyone either, but when I mentioned this to him he said, 'It's no problem.'

Adam, too, was feeling a little less than perky. He had taken a day off because of flu. The acting had been superb – he had stood and shook and whined and whimpered until he had been told to go home. That night he had made a miraculous recovery and had attended the yearly Yamanote Line Hallowe'en party. Every year for the past few years a certain train had been commandeered by foreigners, who gradually took up all the compartments, drinking and smoking and playing loud ghetto-blasters as the train whizzed round and round the circular Yamanote Line. A coded invite would appear in the English language *Tokyo Journal*, telling people what platform and when to board. The police did not intervene, and though the train was packed it was largely harmless fun. Mike 'Spike' Kimeda had been at the party and spied Adam on the party train.

The next day, after the first class, Adam had been given a wooden knife by Darren and told to attack. As Adam lunged, Darren palm-smashed him in the face and slammed him back into the mat. Groggily, Adam got up and attacked again. This time he was helicoptered across two mats to land like a bag of old meat. He attacked again, and again and was slammed even harder. The knife now wobbled in his hand and his sweaty pink face was creased with hurt. He tried to get a second's rest by lying panting on the floor, but Darren bellowed at him to get up and attack again. Predictably he was smashed back into the mat. It all looked pretty brutal. After it was over Darren went up to Adam and hissed into his face: 'Don't you *ever* lie to us again!' Adam crawled away, crumpled and exhausted. The day after when we'd finished sweeping, Adam said, 'I hope Darren won't want to teach me another lesson today, I'm feeling a bit bruised.' He said it without a shred of irony, not questioning at all the legitimacy of such rough treatment, only its frequency.

Back at Fuji Heights there was something horrible lurking in the lavatory. It was blackish green and looked suspiciously like an unwanted piece of intestine. No matter how many times I pulled the feeble flush it kept bobbing back up to the surface. I forced myself to take a closer look. It was a novelty condom. Fat Frank admitted the shameful truth. It was his and he would get rid of it straight away.

Frank had a new girlfriend, an Australian called Rebecca. She was a vegetarian and an expert cook, and dedicated to weaning Frank off such delicacies as his famous twelve-egg omelettes and two-pound steak burgers. Frank was the only person I knew who could rival Tesshu's ability to eat fifty hardboiled eggs. I knew he was serious when he told me his limit was about seventy, but only interspersed with ten oranges. Oranges were the secret to mega-eating, Frank told me.

The final training camp was optional. It would be the only

camp without any Japanese instructors. It was a curious invention – a camp for foreign senshusei only. Only Aga and Mad Dog wanted to go. Then I decided, in my push for acceptance, to sign up as well. That persuaded Will, and then slowly everyone came round and decided to go. No one told Craig of the reversal of interest – he had placed himself too much on the outside of things – and finally he was too late to get time off his work.

The camp was set for November in the mountainous area of Chichibu, a three-hour train journey from Tokyo. Chichibu is the inspiration for *The Mikado*'s Tittipoo, and coffee shops in town hand out matchbooks with an old illustration of an early Gilbert and Sullivan production on the back.

The camp was held in a rustic hotel with sports facilities (a basketball court) and a dojo for martial arts. Mountain ash trees that had shed their leaves dripped damp on to the hotel's wooden walls. There was a valley with a shallow, fast-running stream and mist hung there in the early evening. We all changed into kimonos and stamped around the place like Samurai.

The mats in the training hall were famous for being the hardest mats in Japan. When we arrived and pushed open the door, breathed out steam into the icy air and felt the rock-hard mats, there was trepidation from even the hardiest. This was knobbie-killer country, and if we were forced to do hours of *jiyu waza* we'd all be in predictable agony, a dull but necessary reflection for a committed survivor like myself. For that is what I had become, not a fighter, but a survivor, who'll fight when it's necessary but anxious mainly to take his turn and get the hell out alive. A fighter . . . well, a fighter is a purer thing, someone whose mind perfectly rules their body, who will not listen to their body, who are not concerned about their body because they have so much faith in their own abilities as a fighter.

A survivor, I reflected, was someone with an indecent amount of luck, just when they needed it. Luck, and not obvious skill, which is the fighter's domain – he is somehow less dependent on God's good will.

I looked at the iron mats and thought: OK, survive that.

A survivor's life is dependent on minutiae. Inmates of Auschwitz, if I may be permitted such an analogy, were considered lost, had given up the struggle for life, when they lost their footwear, their wooden clogs. Those most likely to survive took extravagant pains over packing their clogs with old newspaper for additional warmth and protection from blistering.

Footcare as a barometer of health, and by extension desire to survive, is mentioned too in Graves' *Goodbye to All That*. He states that trenchfoot was by no means endemic, and that to a considerable extent those who had 'given up' – succumbed to the neurasthenic torpor common when men 'break' in a stressful situation – were many times more likely to get a damaging case of foot rot than a man still struggling on and refusing to give up looking after himself. Perhaps the only difference is a few minutes drying out one's feet on a dampish cloth; it seems that the attention you concentrate on the affected part is the important thing, as if you are instructing your mind: 'I care about this part of my body, now get to work and heal it.'

Paul, too, subscribed to this theory. He advised us to 'pay attention to our bodies, give them the right sort of attention. Don't ignore your knees, massage the pain away.' Danny had followed this advice most carefully with the care of his incipient knobbies. He was the only guy not to have developed a really bad case of them. He told me that after taking such a harsh beating on his back he would massage the spots on his pelvic bone where the knobbies start to grow. He had, from the beginning, refused to allow them to develop. I had heard that they would and assuming the worst had suffered it. He had assumed nothing and been spared some of the agony.

Knowing when to tough it out and when to pay attention to minutiae, this was the 'survival line' we were learning to tread.

Without any Japanese teachers breathing down his neck, Mustard became a surprisingly playful and tolerant instructor. Only Adam and I 'failed' our mock black-belt test, but instead of scorn Mustard gave us helpful advice. Though I disliked the way mutual failure drew me closer to the weird world of Adam, it was good to know I wasn't failing alone. I could always recall the chilling words of Spike Kimeda: 'Just make sure you're not at the bottom, because when things start to crack, it's the man at the bottom who cracks first.'

The mats were hard, but it was becoming apparent that the teachers were going to be soft on us. It was icy cold, but they allowed us to run round and round the dojo as a way to warm up before the lesson.

Away from the eyes of the Japanese the errant foreigners could play. On the camp programme each morning it stated that we would jog for forty-five minutes, starting at 6.00 a.m. Jogging was cancelled each day in favour of lying in warm futons. The camp programme was printed for the benefit of the Japanese teachers, so that they would think we were out in the woods having a real hard time, when we weren't.

Paul had attended the Gracie jujitsu seminar just before the camp. He talked about it on the train to Chichibu and Ben became enthused about learning a new martial art. The Gracies were an ambitious family of jujitsuists from Brazil. The grandfather had visited Japan and learnt basic grappling techniques more or less similar to judo techniques. His surname was Gracie (originally Scottish) and he refined what he had learnt to invent Gracie jujitsu.

Something must have worked because the sons and grandsons of old man Gracie won every grappling contest they entered. They had hit on a good idea: since most fights end up on the floor, if you dominate on the floor, you will win. And since most 'fighters' concetrate on kicking and punching, which are nowhere near as crucial as wrestling skills, a skilled grappler will usually win. If a Gracie jujitsuist is placed against another grappler then the Gracie man will come out on top because he can also take and give punches – something a sport grappler is unused to. Gracie jujitsu is to the nineties what kung fu was to the seventies. For several years Royce Gracie, a kind of Bruce Lee figure, had defeated kickboxers, shootfighters, pro-boxers and kung-fu fighters to win the title at the Ultimate Fighting Challenge, an annual tournament that took place in an oddly makeshift octagonal ring, which instead of ropes had a high chicken-wire fence admitting of no escape. There were no rounds and a fight ended only with submission or a knockout. There were no rules, and no gloves, but eye gouging and testicle punching were punished by $1000 fines.

At the seminar the Gracie brothers had taken on all comers and defeated everyone – either choking them out or making them submit from an arm lock or leg lock. Paul had tried to attack using *irimi*, the entering technique used in aikido. Royce Gracie had slithered sideways and within a few minutes had choked Paul out. Did that make Gracie jujitsu superior to aikido?

Is kung fu better than boxing? Would Mike Tyson beat Bruce Lee? Despite the martial artist's protests that things don't work like that, people insist on making comparisons. It's rather like saying, 'In a short-story competition, who would win – Chekov or Hemingway?' There are too many variables to make sensible comparisons. But a top practitioner who is strong and fit, who practises a low-level art, such as boxing, will always beat someone who is neither strong nor fit and is not very competent at a high-level art, like White Crane style kung fu, which takes a reputed twelve years to learn the full range of moves. A streetfighter may steal a march on both with his broken rhythm, bluff and bravado.

A fight is usually won by making the other man play by your rules. The Gracies constructed the Ultimate Fighting Challenge in a ring against one opponent, who is unarmed. This undoubtedly favours the grappler. But in real life people are very often armed – with broken bottles, knives, razors, clubs or heavy oak chairs. The grappler is at a disadvantage here, and would certainly not win if he struck only to grappling. Paul was forced on to

Gracie territory – which meant finishing on a choke, a KO or an arm lock or leg lock. Gracie jujitsu is designed to deliver the victim up to this kind of end, so it was not surprising Paul was defeated. 'He was just so relaxed and quick,' he told us. But if they had both been armed with swords it would have been a different story, perhaps. Certainly for non-serious one-on-one street brawling, Gracie jujitsu is hard to beat, as long as the floor isn't covered with broken glass and your opponent's mates aren't kicking you in the head with their steel toe cap boots.

Will and I shared a room, with the unfortunate addition of Adam, who gibbered and cried out in his sleep, doing pretty much what he did when he was awake, in fact. We managed to get rid of him by putting him forward as sensei tea boy, his job being to keep the teachers, especially Mustard, in hot tea. That way we were spared more reminiscences about his dysfunctional family, particularly lengthy descriptions of skateboard crashes and being stopped by the highway patrol for dropping roaches out of the window, or driving stoned along the freeway, etc. Mad Dog took to dropping into our room. One evening he and Adam had an interminable conversation about whether they preferred a stickshift or an auto. I couldn't believe it when Will joined in too. I felt I was sitting in an archetypal North American male conversation. After a lot of discussion everyone came down in favour of the stickshift, though Mad Dog preferred an auto 'for heavy town driving'.

During one 'rest' period there was a desultory walk to a shrine, which turned into a hunt for a cigarette shop for Mustard. R'em pointed at Darren's t-shirt and said, 'What's that picture of a rabbi doing on your shirt?' Darren snorted derisively. The bearded image on his shirt was a late photograph of Ueshiba. R'em was still only hazily aware of his existence. When a Japanese martial artist is confused with a Jewish priest by an ultra-religious Israeli who is currently devoting his life to martial arts, you get a rare glance at the unholy confusion of our minds.

There had been talk about the last session of the training

camp being cancelled in favour of a long hike in the mountains. The senshusei were diplomatically in favour of the hike, but could not come out too openly in favour of it as this would be construed as disloyalty to the course and lacking correct spirit. I must have heard the following interchange a thousand times: 'What's the most important thing about Yoshinkan aikido?'

'Spirit!'

The teachers came down in favour of a lesson. We weren't badly bruised, but we'd had enough of the hard mats. As Paul was taking the lesson we expected a reasonable beating. With a murky dread I took up my spot in *kamae* and waited for the order to attack with full ferocity, again and again, which was the essence of what we mainly did at this point. It had a definite kinship with dog training, except dog trainers know that a setback in training can erase six weeks of careful skills acquisition. In aikido, teaching has not yet reached this level of subtlety.

Then Paul said something wonderful. He announced that this class would be devoted to teaching us what he had learnt at the Gracie jujitsu seminar. No *jiyu waza*! No endless breakfalls! It was a measure of our learning fatigue that the chance to learn a new art was greeted with such joy. Paul added, 'But don't tell anyone at the dojo we've done this.'

The Gracie system featured a series of basic exercises that built up certain important grappling muscles, in the same way our basic movements built up aikido muscles. One set of exercises involved lying on your back and flipping over and flipping back again, as a lot of grappling depends getting on top at the right moment.

I trained with Will. We were both extremely wimpy in our practice grappling, like two old grandads frightened of slipping on an icy pavement. Ben was more wholehearted, and in his enthusiasm strained his elbow. Another aikido survival rule: know when going 100 per cent is best, and when 30 per cent is best.

After the class there was a communal bath. The water came

from a hot spring and was scalding. After larking around with the others Will and I drank Japanese green tea in our room. I looked out over the wooded stream in the valley; mist had gathered and the air had chilled. Will poured out more tea and continued the conversation. I was perfectly contented, released into pure happiness, savouring the moment and not caring a jot for the future.

That year's Ultimate Fighting Challenge, which took place in Tokyo, ended in a fiasco. Royce Gracie, the undefeated champion, faced 'Kimo', a prison-reformed born-again Christian kickboxer, whose bald muscled torso was mutilated with homemade tattoos. Written across his back was: 'Jesus Saves'.

Kimo entered the stage carrying a huge wooden cross strapped to his back. This he took off in the ring, in a fumbling way that gave an indication of the weight of the crucifix. He then got down on his knees and bellowed out his 'prayer to God for victory', since Kimo's victory, in his own obscure theology, would mean a victory for Jesus in the modern world.

Royce Gracie stood and stared from his corner, appalled, as if he had witnessed the Antichrist popping round for a quick chat. No doubt his staunch Catholic upbringing had thrown him into confusion. His plastic mouthguard popped in and out with agitation.

Kimo was as tough as old boots, and he took a pounding in the kidneys and around the face, which usually persuaded opponents to change their grip – the opening Royce was always waiting for. The punches in Gracie jujitsu are rather like those in aikido: designed to hurt and tire as a form of distraction for the killer finishing blow, not a technique in themselves.

Kimo hung on and hung on but had obviously damaged Royce in some way. Eventually the Christian made a mistake and Royce choked him out.

But Royce was so badly beaten up that he couldn't fight in the final. He was easily the best fighter, but his injuries prevented him from winning. By some strange quirk the Gracies had designed a competition in which trying to win just didn't pay. The Ultimate Fighting Challenge was too much like life and not enough like sport to be successful. We all thought Royce deserved to win but, just as in life, it's the bastards who get ahead.

We got off the train, and unplanned and unasked for, Big Ben made a speech of thanks to the teachers, which we we all clapped and cheered. Away from the Japanese overlords Mustard had been able to be the giant silverback gorilla, his natural role.

As we started to walk along the platform Darren mentioned quietly to me that Mustard was carrying his own bag. I tried to grab it but Mustard wanted to carry it himself. But he gave me his sincere blue-eyed look and said he appreciated it and didn't forget such things. Maybe Darren had sealed my fate, bringing me at last back into the fold, ready to take the black-belt test.

Natural Nazis

'After reading books and the like it is best to burn them or throw them away. Reading is for the Imperial Court, whereas the Way of the Samurai is Death.'
From the seventeenth-century Samurai manual *Hagakure*

December

I put my order in for amino acids to Mark Swiley, a Texan weightlifter who trained as a regular student at the dojo. It seemed like a better idea than Aga's miracle sports drinks that dyed your mouth red, or his stamina chewy bars that cost more than a full meal. I felt I needed some extra assistance in preparing for the black-belt test, and the Texan's amino acids sounded perfect.

'I take um all the time. I can work out for two hours, run another one and still feel fresh,' Swiley claimed.

I also had toothache and had finally made an appointment with Sara's Japanese dentist to fix me up. She had arranged the appointment, irritated by my constant complaints about the pain. The problem had started when a mistimed punch from Adam cracked the top off a back tooth that was already decayed. I was so annoyed I did an exemplary session of *jiyu waza*, the most precise I'd ever been.

But the pain became slowly worse and I realized I would have to do something I'd never wanted to do: put myself in the hands of a Japanese dentist.

The Japanese attitude to teeth is coloured, literally, by their previous affectation for finding blacked-out teeth attractive. Incomprehensible to anyone born in the age of brushing regularly, it was considered demure to make the mouth of a woman a discreet hole, devoid of animal excrescences like teeth. Lead was used to make the teeth black, a practice that continued with geishas well into this century.

The blacking may have been to make the best of a bad job. Perhaps finding double, slightly bucked and wayward teeth in young girls 'cute', which most Japanese do, is also making the best of a hopeless situation. And just as the Japanese have the worst eyesight en masse – in one class of twenty high-school girls six wore glasses and eleven wore contact lenses; a figure inconceivable in the West but not uncommon in Japan – they also have the worst teeth.

On the subway to the dentist I checked out each mouth that came into range. It was horrifying: grey fangs, discoloured and prominent gums, incisors and canines double parked; fanciful bridgework that owed something in inspiration to the Pompidou centre; whole teeth encased in gold or stainless steel; mouths that flashed like Aladdin's cave when a person started to talk. Such random samples never serve their purpose, which is to reassure. I thought instead of Sara, with her small and perfect, unfilled teeth. Maybe her dentist was different.

A minor toothache marked me out as lucky. Virtually all the foreigners and several of the cops had recently suffered injuries. Danny had broken a finger. Ben had a chronic neck problem and most of the rest had received some wound or other from Craig.

Craig Morrison Tidswell. Even his name had a sinister, psychopathic ring to it. It confused Ando, who called him Tidswell rather than by his first name, which is how the rest of us were addressed. 'Tidswell! No! Tidswell kneecurve! Kneecurve!' Ando was the only Japanese teacher who ventured into English. He stood less on his dignity than the others, not caring if he made mistakes translating directly from the Japanese. 'Eyeline! Eyeline!' was his order to maintain a correct gaze, a direct translation of '*mesen*'. Mostly, Ando told us to get lower.

Being the shortest person in the room, about five foot two I guessed, he always had the lowest stance. Gaijin were always too tall, too high, Craig especially, who, because of his long absence and despite his heroic catching up, could still not do the basic movements as perfectly as the rest of us. Perhaps that was why he took out his aggression on his partner.

Craig did not look after his partner and he could not control his temper when he made a mistake. But he was tough and did not mind when revenge was enforced. In one game devised by Ando on a Saturday morning, everyone stood in a big circle and one guy was thrown by all. When it was Craig's turn there was a cry for blood by the cops, who disliked him most. I have a lasting memory of Craig being thrown again and again with great force by the police and shouting to them as he fell: 'Come on! Do your worst! I can take it from you pansies!'

I saw Oyamada give Craig a pasting and come pretty close to dumping him on his neck. I thought a broken neck was going too far, but the principle was correct. In the 1960s Kancho had broken his deputy teacher's elbow because the man was too hard on his students. Craig was a natural Nazi. If you were soft on him he interpreted it as weakness. He mentioned to me that when Little Nick weakened he threw him even harder. He told me he thought such behaviour 'natural'.

Maybe the foreigners were scared of Craig. When he injured Little Nick doing a poorly executed hip throw, there was not much sympathy for either of them. I remembered my own injury at the Armenian's hands.

With Little Nick unable to train, Craig was passed around. The cops obviously detested his harsh methods. So did Will. After one session of *jiyu waza* there was almost a breakdown in discipline in the line-up. They swore and called each other names and only stopped when we urged them to, fearful that the teacher would hear. A breakdown in discipline – the worst crime we could commit, for which we would be shown the door. At times like this the dojo showed its similarity to a seminary run by devout monks.

But Craig did not change. In the end most of us just hoped he'd become better at aikido, since the injuries always occurred on the techniques he couldn't do but was trying too hard to make work.

While Craig beat people up I was wrestling with a lack of confidence in *jiyu waza*, the ten- or twenty-throw continuous attack and defence. After twenty throws we were always out of breath. One day Ando made us go sixty throws as attacker and then swap to make sixty throws as defender. Those who managed it were exhausted. Several threw up.

In another lesson Mustard ordered me up to the front and I had to throw Mad Dog ten times. But instead of swapping he kept me up and ordered Craig up to take Mad Dog's place. I thought I was now in for the usual heavy-handed treatment that Craig handed out. But no, I had to throw him ten times. Then the next senshusei, and the next, and then Yoji, and Paul and Stumpy. I really tried to crank it on Paul and he enjoyed it. There is one move where you dive at the feet of your attacker and they have to roll over the top. If mistimed it can be dangerous as you may trap the feet of the attacker and cause him to break his knees with the momentum of his body. Some teachers frown on it altogether. I did two in succession on Paul – of course he had no problem, but by then I was so tired I feared no retribution for such actions.

I did one hundred and thirty throws, the last sixty in a weirdly concentrated but distanced state of mind. I had no strength left and yet by putting my body in the right position I was still able to throw people. When I finished everyone clapped. Will said, 'I actually watched you get better out there.'

It was another glimpse at the truth of Tesshu's words: 'The mind has no limits. Use such a mind.'

It was also the kind of action teaching that made Mustard extraordinary. But by now I was so into the programme he could really do no wrong. In order to survive I had gone along with the group deification of the man. Even R'em would say: 'Mustard is a good guy, a very good guy. We are all he has. He really cares for us.'

The dentist's surgery was empty when I arrived with my vague appointment for Wednesday or Thursday afternoon. The receptionist pointed out the gaily coloured slippers I should wear and I awaited with some nervousness the arrival of the dentist. The surgery had that same dental smell (fear and mouthwash) that I remembered from childhood. I peered at the chairs and angle-poised drill holders. Were they modern? I couldn't tell. This was Japan – surely they'd be the latest hi-tech? The spotlight was dusty and seventies looking. Was it too late to back out?

The dentist, an apologetic and tired-looking man, beckoned me over to one of the two chairs. The amiable female receptionist donned a white coat and became his assistant. Perhaps they were married. His Japanese was low and persuasive, but he did not tell me much. Without warning he produced a huge metallic syringe and gave me a gum injection. Then he set to work.

I'd like to say that all my disciplined training in a pain-filled environment had made me tough. I'd like to say I'd become like John Coffey, who stood under waterfalls and could laugh at excruciating anguish and call his body 'a piece of shit'. I'd like to say that but I can't, for the truth was that that dental experience was outstandingly painful and unpleasant – worse even than when I had my wisdom teeth out, and a lot, lot worse than a direct hit on the knobbies, a punch full square on the nose, or the rib cracker Little Nick served up.

The anaesthetic didn't work. The broken tooth had been painful even before the top had been knocked off and it didn't stop when the injection was made. With my mouth full of drill, on a relentless four-wheel-drive setting that ground on mercilessly, I tried to whimper in Japanese: 'Itai,' I called out feebly ('it hurts'). The dentist had lost his benign grin. In fact he was wearing a facemask and his tired eyes gave no hint of compassion, only a grim determination to finish the job. It was, in microcosm, a summation of my senshusei philosophy: 'Just when you think it can't get any worse, it does,' for, after the drilling, he produced a smoking piece of wire which he rammed deep into the cavity to extinguish all life in the nerve. *AAIIEE!*

In all I had to make five visits to get that tooth fixed, but none was as bad as the first. By the time I came to pay the bill it was just a dim throbbing memory. I handed over Will's insurance card (closer to my age than Ben) and he noted down the details, too polite to exclaim that I was American rather than the Englishman Sara had promised. He asked for no further payment. Japanese dental care is notoriously priccy and I was getting it for free. I smiled gamely and left. The whole thing was both horrible and mysterious, but it followed the second part of my 'survival' philosophy: 'Nothing lasts for ever.' The pain had gone. I could train again without chewing on a couple of aspirins first, and it had all been for free. I asked several Japanese about this afterwards and they were equally bemused about it. Perhaps Sara had made a secret gesture, but I never found out.

Chris was amused by my reversal of attitude towards Mustard, but he made few comments. On most subjects Chris was gossipy and highly opinionated, but on the subject of the course he increasingly restrained himself to stop Ben and me from being discouraged. Fat Frank had no such qualms. 'Paul thinks you're a spaz,' he confided. 'Thanks a lot. I really wanted to hear that,' I said. Two months before, in September, Fat Frank had felt Ben was getting a bit above himself. They went on an expedition to climb Mount Fuji and Frank reduced Ben to tears by not allowing the lanky Australian a rest on the way to the top. 'It's the Iranian way of climbing mountains,' said Fat Frank.

Chris and Frank were due to take their test the day before ours. They did *jiyu waza* in front of the senshusei, and though their throws were more complicated than ours their movements were not as flowing. I saw, then, that the course was about discovering the dynamism in human movement and liberating that dynamism to (ideally) devastating effect.

The miracle amino acids had been held up by customs and just to rev myself up each morning I was drinking two cans of hot sweet coffee before training. I could see why caffeine was banned by most sporting administrative bodies. It left my stomach sick and nervous, but the buzz was enough to kick-start me into serious exertion straightaway. Previously, the first lesson had always been a hard slog, but now the coffee gave me enough energy to cross a threshold, the exertion threshold, where fatigue and sluggishness don't operate. The price was a constantly upset stomach. It seemed a small price to pay.

I stuck with coffee rather than the more dubious caffeine pills or Jolt X3, the caffeine-enhanced cola that left you tired and edgy after six hours of heart palpitations. Coffee seemed the acceptable face of drug abuse.

A week before the test two disconcerting things happened. I separated my shoulder and I made the same mistake during a technique six or seven times running.

It was during a Chida class, where we were running through every technique both *tachi* (standing) and *suwari* (kneeling). The particular technique was a double-wrist-grab *kotegaeshi*, a technique where a lock on the wrist allows you to throw the attacker's whole body. We were doing it kneeling and I had a sudden mental block about what to do. Chida noticed, of course. The class of cops and foreigners remained motionless while he quietly told me to repeat it again. Same mental block. Someone, Aga I seem to remember, called out instructions while I fiddled with the final pin trying to get it right. Chida offered no help as he knew I already knew the technique. After the seventh repeat I got it right. To hold up the entire class for so long at such a late stage of the game was deeply humiliating. The rest of the foreigners edged away from me after that lesson, as if I was carrying some bad luck.

As I sat in the changing rooms alone and feeling deeply rattled, Maeda-san, the 'gorilla' cop, came in. I'd never really liked him, but he came up to me and was genuinely friendly and concerned. 'Are you OK?' he asked several times. 'I'm OK,' I said. 'Yoshinkan aikido – who cares!' he said, and I had to laugh at that. It was good to be speaking to someone who didn't take aikido very seriously. When I asked him if he would continue after the course, he snorted, 'You've got to be kidding!'

He'd noticed and sought me out to console me; no foreigner would think to do that, especially a 'top dog' in the group, as Maeda was. But being popular in a group in Japan entails responsibilities: you have to show consideration for the troops below you. It was similar to how Westerners misunderstood the *sempai–kohai* relationship, not realizing that it is closer to a mentor–aspirant relationship than the prefect–fag set-up we assume it to be.

The shoulder separation was less mentally taxing but had worse physical consequences than my mid-training brain seizure. I would have to stop training for several days at least. The tendon between the collarbone and the shoulder had pulled apart when I landed badly during an eighty-minute *jiyu waza* session in an Oyamada class. The sad thing was, I had willed it upon myself.

I had noticed when I played schoolboy rugby that some people always got injured and some people never did. Excluding the foolhardy, it was hard not to conclude that some people actually wanted to get injured – either for attention or to escape somehow.

It was the same in aikido. Eva, Paul's Swiss girlfriend, had been doing self-defence training with a hugely muscled Israeli girl. The Israeli beat the much smaller Eva up every day, but as they were training for an instructors' test Eva put up with it. Then one day she came in and she knew she didn't want to be there. When Chino, the instructor, went to throw her she stayed on the ground and didn't flip. Her collarbone snapped instantly. Later it had to be pinned, it was such a messy break. But Eva

267

had no grudge against Chino. She blamed herself. Her belief was: 'If you don't want to be there, leave, or you'll injure yourself just to get an excuse to leave.'

I couldn't believe that Oyamada would make us do continuous *jiyu waza* for an entire lesson. It was inhuman. Even Mad Dog, with all his experience, was getting seriously tired. And just as soon as I thought, I can't go on, I landed with an awkward thud on my shoulder. I lay on the floor like a footballer, which was against aikido etiquette but I wanted 'to show' I was hurt. When I got up I couldn't move my arm above chest height. Almost gratefully I slid to the sidelines in *seiza*. Mild pain, but nothing special, nothing compared to a root canal filling, for sure. But shoulder or no shoulder I had to take the test. The black belt wasn't the end of the course but I'd feel a lot happier when I was wearing it. Even assuming I passed the test I still had three months to go. I knew if I dropped out early, even with a black belt, I'd still feel I'd failed in some way. I knew then that the senshusei course was everything, if you finished it – or nothing, if you didn't. Chris was correct, it was a form of initiation rite.

The black-belt test for the cops was a few days after ours. Their test included self-defence and arrest techniques and an element of teaching. This is what we would be studying after the black-belt test; for us the present test would be several techniques: two kinds of *jiyu waza* (front-strike attack and wrist-grab attack) and the basic movements that were always part of any Yoshinkan test. I asked Sherlock if he felt ready. 'No,' he replied, laughing.

Ben and I watched Chris and Fat Frank's test. They were good, but not as good as us, we felt. No doubt they felt the opposite. We'd spent so long on our knees, our kneework was bound to be more dynamic than theirs. Chris and Frank passed. Now it was our turn.

The night before the test we went to the public baths to have a good soak. The Japanese discreetly cleared out of the bath when Ben and I both got in. I overheard two old men muttering about the size of Ben's penis. I found it funnier than he did.

268

After the bath Chris gave us a thorough massage. We shaved our heads and drank a beer, as Mustard had commanded.

The next morning I downed some fresh coffee and, cycling to the dojo, Ben and I practised murderous *kiais* (attacking shouts, warcries) as we hurtled along the empty streets.

The tea room was quiet for once and full of discernible tension. The cops came in and wished us luck. Sherlock pinched my backside, for additional well wishing, I guessed.

After an hour's practice we had a short break. I put on a clean dogi. I was holding to all superstitions in such matters. I selected my favourite dogi, a slightly baggy number, and regretted that I didn't have my original white belt, which had been filched some months earlier.

In the line-up we knelt along with the cops and the assistants and the teachers who were watching. Mad Dog and I would be on last, which meant we had forty minutes of kneeling before our test.

Each pair went up and performed, I thought, with admirable vigour. With all the militaristic training we'd been subjected to the senshusei did at least look like they meant business.

Adam and R'em went hell for leather during their *jiyu waza*. Adam attempted a fancy back breakfall during a throw when he should have made an ordinary flip. There was a sickening crunch as he hit the ground.

But the Adam who got up, and without a pause continued to attack R'em with the other arm, was a different Adam from the whining and whingeing Adam of before. He slid the bad arm into his dogi and did body breakfalls until the session was stopped. He ran back to the line and slumped forward in pain. Will told him to sit up straight and he did.

Mad Dog and I were on next. The techniques worked without a hitch. During the *jiyu waza* I braced myself for another bout of repeated dumpings over Mad Dog's hip and on to the mat. But he didn't do *one* hip throw. Between the last lesson and the test he must have made the connection that a rugbyish pounding did not look good. Because he had spared me I had enough energy to concentrate when it was my turn to throw him. I fixed my eyes on his and waited.

He came at me with a growling shout, his eyes agog with Mad Dog rage. Such a committed attack was easy to deal with. I deflected his forearm strike, and pulled him by the neck to the ground. His next strike I blocked and turned, twisting his arm back over his shoulder in a *shihonage* type throw. I used my arm like a bar to pressure his elbow against the joint for the next two attacks before I realized I was 'stuck'; my mind blank except for this same technique. Mad Dog knew it and summoning a last burst of strength attacked with greater vigour. It broke the pattern, as I ducked down and allowed him to go hurtling over my head. It was nowhere near perfect, but it felt . . . satisfactory. We ran back to the line and awaited the concluding speech by Chida.

Before speaking, Chida ordered Adam out of the line to go to the office and have his shoulder and arm seen to. By then I'd forgotten Adam, but Chida had not. (Adam said later that he'd never had so much attention in his life. Nakano strapped up his shoulder, which was fractured, and the other teachers and *uchideshi* ran around making him tea and generally treating him like a hero. By Yoshinkan standards he had passed the real test: he had taken the pain and carried on fighting and gone back to the line when he was ordered. This was real Spirit, more important than mere technique.)

Chida gathered us round after Fat Frank and Chris had congratulated us and the teachers had shaken our hands. Chida told us to stand up and relax our knees. Almost offhand he told us we had all passed. Craig, however, was not given a black belt because his basic movements were not good enough – he was promoted to one below, *shokyu*, and would still have to wear the white belt. Mad Dog, who was already a black belt, was not promoted to second-degree black belt – he still didn't have it in the knees, Chida said. Everyone shook everyone's hands again, but Craig, I noticed, was crying.

The following evening was the Christmas party, exactly a year since Shioda had questioned me on Japanese Spirit, John Coffey had told me about his Zen experiences and Roland had warned me that, 'Aikido can kill'.

We gathered in a beer hall, Japanese style, with plates of dried squid and other partially revolting knick-knacks to go with the foamy beer. Fat Frank and I sat opposite Chino, and for the first time I had a proper conversation with this teacher who had terrorized me. Frank joined in and said to Chino: 'People say you like to do techniques powerfully.'

'It depends on the student. But foreigners worship power, so I do techniques hard on them usually, until they are able to perceive something else,' he replied.

'Is it bad to want power more than anything else?'

'It's a good starting point!'

I knew Kancho only read sports papers, the Japanese equivalent of the *Sun*, and I'd only ever seen Chino flipping through porno comics in a 7-Eleven near the dojo, so I asked him what books he read. Chino told us he read sports biographies, mainly because they gave him insights into mental training. He considered progress in aikido to be mainly a mental thing for him, at this stage.

'Why did you start aikido?' asked Frank.

'I did judo as a boy, like many Japanese, and I believed I was very strong. But I saw that in judo the bigger man often wins – which is why they have weight divisions. I would never beat the heavyweight champion by using judo, so I looked around for something where technique was stronger than weight. This is why I studied aikido, because in aikido the smaller man has an advantage.'

I spoke to Ando Sensei about poetry.

'Do you teach poetry in your country?' he asked.

'Yes,' I lied, since in Japan to be any good at a subject is to teach it.

'You must show me your poetry,' he said, quite drunk and extremely affable.

Would Ando really want to see my poetry? The one about war criminals? And the poem I wrote about Changi Gaol? I didn't think so. I liked the man. He was good hearted without being hearty. You felt he cared about you. But he was still Japanese and the poems I'd written in Japan were not suitable for Japanese eyes.

I fell into step with Chida on the way back to the station. He looked at my highly polished shoes. 'Ah, the English Gentleman,' he said, laughing.

There was more revelry at the gaijin house where Little Nick lived. I went there with Will and Chris and drank a pint of *shochu*, a rough potato liquor, on the way.

The place was packed and people were dancing. Aga, I noticed, had his tongue in the ear of an Australian girl who habitually flashed her breasts at such gatherings. Mustard was there and he told me he had asked Chida to reconsider Craig and give him the black belt. Chida had refused. I felt Chida was right. Craig had missed three of the hardest months. No one would forget that.

Adam was wearing a plaster arm cast with pride, and Little Nick was being very rough with someone who thought they knew about the martial arts. I sidled up to Darren. 'At last, I think I've learnt the Yoshinkan way,' I said.

'Oh yes?'

'Yes. The Yoshinkan way is kissing ass,' I said.

'I don't think it has to be that way,' he said.

'I do,' I said, and staggered off.

'You have to be in the mood for this sort of thing,' said Will.

'We are! We've passed!' I said.

'You're right,' he said, with an equal lack of conviction.

I wandered outside, smoking. It was raining. Spots of rain

discoloured the white paper of the cigarette. I started to walk in the vague direction of home. Taxis roared past, illuminating the now slanting rain with their headlights. For a long while I followed a road which ran underneath an overhead railway. The tracks started to curve, leaving me disoriented. There were no more taxis in this part of town. A man on a bicycle rode by, angling his umbrella into the downpour as he pedalled along. There was a lit doorway up ahead and I stumbled towards it. A discreet neon sign announced it was some kind of late-night club or bar. A tough-looking Japanese stood in the door wearing a black suit. As I approached he made the all too familiar crossed wrists sign, which means *dame*, not allowed, forbidden, gaijin not welcome. I trod in several puddles and sat down on a shop step out of the main downpour. I struck several damp matches and lit another cigarette.

The Mount Fuji Test

After the test my immune system just gave up. I suffered the worst bout of flu I'd had in years. In bed for a week, I was too ill to train, and then the holidays started and training was no longer compulsory. I missed the police black-belt test but Ben reported that Sherlock and Sakuma had both passed.

The flu developed into a nasty wheeze, an intermittent asthma that kept me awake at night and made me fretful about restarting training. I visited a doctor, who showed me a coloured catalogue of drugs and invited me to pick the ones I thought suitable. The Japanese are very fond of antibiotics and drugs of all kinds, which are usually much weaker than their Western variants. He gave me some pills that stopped the wheezing but set my heart racing and my stomach churning.

Chris decided we should serve Christmas dinner for all the waifs and strays we knew who were still in Tokyo. We didn't have an oven so Sara agreed to cook the turkey at her parents' house and transport it in an insulated box across town by bus and taxi.

I got a call at 6.00 a.m. on Christmas morning: which way up should the turkey go? I had no idea. It was a completely unexpected question, but Sara and her mother had never cooked a turkey before. I hazarded a guess and when the turkey arrived it was perfect.

Ten people crammed into our tiny apartment and ate a traditional Christmas lunch. Outside it was cold but there was no snow on the ground. Chris put some Gregorian chant on the tape machine and we smoked big cigars. I remembered my first Christmas in Japan. I'd had to work all day at a language school and when I got home I ate a tiny Christmas pudding my mother had sent me in the post.

Sara had worked the night before at her new part-time job as a waitress in a Turkish restaurant and they had fittingly donated the turkey. She reported that the place had been full of young couples, out on the most romantic night of the year, talking in low whispers about which love hotel they would visit. Inexplicably Christmas Eve in Japan has become a sort of Valentine's Day, since Valentine's Day has been usurped by the necessity of giving *giri-chocs*, the obligatory chocolates you have to give to any male to maintain his fragile self esteem.

Now that Sara's parents at last knew of my existence she asked me to spend New Year's Day at her house, which has much the same significance as Christmas Day in the West. Visiting a girl's parents in Japan carries significant overtones. I wondered if I would pass whatever obscure tests would be set me.

At the New Year's Day dinner Sara's ninety-year-old grandmother interrogated me on a variety of subjects: my job, my university, the number of brothers and sisters I had. She was surprised I could use chopsticks, and was suspicious and disbelieving when I said I liked traditional bean soup. Then Sara's father said gently something I'd never before heard from a

Japanese: 'Why are you surprised that he likes our food – we are all human beings, after all!'

'I am surprised you do martial arts,' said Grandma. 'Your face does not look decisive enough – it is too kind.' She paused as she swigged back some of her 'medicinal' cherry brandy. 'Foreigners understand the things we Japanese are forgetting. It is good to be in the dojo, studying in the cold weather. Japanese people think too much about money. Here, show me your hand!'

Amidst a certain amount of embarrassment from the family, Grandma read my palm and pronounced that I had wasted many opportunities, but that the next fifteen years would be very productive for me. I laughed and she looked me gravely in the eye. 'Never buy a caged bird,' she said. 'It will be bad luck for you.' After this performance Grandma was hustled off to her room with the brandy 'to get some rest'. Sara's father gave me a small speech on the virtues of martial-arts training for foreigners. I assumed this was to make me feel better.

'Of course it is strange for the Japanese to see their traditional arts practised by foreigners – but equally it must be strange for you to see Japanese wearing suits and not kimono.' He guffawed at his example and continued. 'I myself studied judo at university; it was very healthful for training body and spirit. It was a useful practice. We can say that the Japanese have a better understanding of the way body and spirit must work together. Naturally the West has become interested in this. But things born in Japan do not flourish outside Japan. They must change. I believe it is mainly due to climate.'

We drove around to see relatives and I realized what a huge commitment it would be to be married into a Japanese family: the relatives one couldn't afford to offend, the hierarchies you have to observe, the bland conversation designed to avoid the possibility of confrontation, the impossibility of refusing certain forms of food. I could see that Sara's family were eccentric by Japanese standards, but I didn't want to have to wait until I was ninety before I could speak my mind.

In the end I think I made a poor impression. Each relative, from Grandma down to Sara's eight-year-old cousin, asked me the same set of questions. Eventually, I fear I got rather offhand. The questions were: 1) Do you like Japanese food? 2) Do you like Japan? 3) How long have you been in Japan? and 4) When are you going back? Sara's father was an economics professor and bore a striking physical resemblance to Chairman Mao. In the evening he sat me down round a huge ornate brass ashtray and quizzed me about 'The English Disease' – that seventies concept of English workers preferring tea breaks and shop-floor strikes to actually working. We then played *Shogi*, a Japanese form of chess, where captured pieces can be used against your opponent. He thrashed me.

When Sara told her father she was going to visit India (she was saving up her money from the restaurant for this purpose), he asked if she was going with me. Sara told him no, she wasn't, she was going with a female schoolfriend instead. Good, he said, I'm glad you're not going with him. Sara reported all this to me but offered no comment. I went back to the apartment and continued to wheeze.

Fuji Heights was at bursting-point. No one was working, no one was doing aikido and it was too chilly to go to the park. We sat around making plans for jungle trips and ocean voyages. Throughout the course I'd been plagued by a sudden desire to sail around the world. I assumed it was just displacement activity, a reaction to my self-imposed imprisonment.

Frank, too, was suffering from a variation of cabin fever. He became obsessed, now that he was going out with Rebecca, with the literature, history and cultural achievements of the Antipodeans. He took to testing Ben on arcane Australian trivia:

'Where was the first kerosene fridge made?'

'Don't know.'

'Really? I thought all Australians knew that. Koolgardie. It was called the "Koolgardie Kooler".'

'Who wrote "Waltzing Matilda"?'

'Don't know.'

'That is surprising. Don't tell me you've never heard of Banjo Paterson?'

Banjo Paterson was Australia's national poet and he quickly became Fat Frank's favourite too. He took to quoting lines from such revered Banjo classics as 'The Man from Snowy River', 'The Empty Tucker Bag' and 'A Stockman Remembers'.

Despite the onset of winter the microroaches had not disappeared; instead they had burrowed deeper into the warm circuitry of the printer, the television and the answering machine, causing, no doubt, the slow and irreversible tide of damage and dysfunction that these machines suffered.

As the nights got colder there was an escalating fight for the best quilts and blankets. For a long time I slept in a sleeping bag, but it began to feel constrictive, so I joined in the general bedding scramble at bedtime. Four grown men in a room ten feet by six feet, short of bed linen and money, that was the winter in Fuji Heights.

One fine day, one of those cold 100 per cent clear days you get in Tokyo in January, with the sun shining and the hint of frost gone by 9 a.m., Fat Frank and I decided to walk around the Yamanote Line. Halfway round we were joined by Sara.

In Mejiro we walked past the Sasakawa corporation headquarters. Outside the gleaming towerblock stands a bronze sculpture of Sasakawa carrying his mother on his back, emphasizing the traditional Japanese belief in filial duty. Sasakawa – notorious war criminal and financial backer of the LDP, Japan's major political party, founder of powerboat racing as a gambling moneyspinner, ultra-nationalist and friend of organized crime – certainly was one of the most influential Japanese of the century. For a long while the dojo had sent a teacher, one week on, one week off, to Sasakawa's powerboat school on a lake beneath Mount Fuji. The Yoshinkan teacher was there to teach Sasakawa's powerboat jockeys *Yamato Damashi* – Japanese Spirit. During his first stint in Japan Payet had been sent as one of the teachers. They had complained to Kancho that he was a foreigner, so how could he teach Japanese Spirit? Kancho replied that Payet knew just as much about Japanese Spirit as any Japanese teacher, so they had better accept him. The powerboat jockeys were all under five foot (men and women, though it was hard to tell the difference, their bodies white and their heads and hands burnt black from the sun). 'It was like teaching a class of little monkeys,' said Payet.

'What do you think of Sasakawa?' I asked Sara.

'Bad man,' she said, with scarcely a look back.

No doubt Sasakawa would parrot Tesshu's view on service: 'Forget about yourself, keep your countrymen in your heart, and you mouth closed. Never boast of serving your country this way or that way – then you will be truly serving the fatherland.' But in Sasakawa's mouth these words would ring hollow. The man had quite obviously feathered his own next at the expense of others. Tesshu had not. He died penniless, and when his wife asked if he had any words for posterity he had the wisdom to reply, 'No.'

Sasakawa would continue to erect phoney monuments to himself and his family, demonstrating in stone and bronze that his kind of gangster politics, so far from Tesshu's Samurai ideals, had triumphed in Japan. When the Japanese had been warmongers, Sasakawa rattled his sabre; now they were for world peace he shook his charity bucket. He was a powerbroker and rabble rouser, nothing more, but who in Japan felt righteous enough to criticize? After all, he had even been paymaster to the Yoshin-kan dojo.

Crossing the footbridge over the highway through Yoyogi park we could see quite clearly the looming cloudlike cone of Mount Fuji. Due to the pollution I had never seen this mountain from central Tokyo before, but the cessation of traffic over the New Year period gave a small window of clarity in the smog, allowing this view, once commonplace but now rare, of the fabled symbol of Japan.

What can account for the Japanese obsession with Fuji-san? ('San' is an alternative reading of *yama*, mountain, and does not mean Mr Fuji.) I have thought about this on a number of occasions. Even foreigners, I notice, pick up this compulsive relationship with the mountain. Partly, perhaps, it is because Fuji looms, like the moon, huger than anything else, ghostly and visible for miles. One looks out for Fuji as if for a full moon, confirming perhaps some distant order to the universe. Some commentators trace it back to the Ainu (Fuji is an Ainu word) who worshipped the mountain. Original inhabitants of Japan, the Ainu have now almost completely lost their indigenous characteristics through intermarriage. But ancients worshipping the mountain only pushes the modern obsession one stage further back.

In the end I am forced to conclude that Japanese obsessional behaviour cannot be explained with any accuracy. One can only note the phenomenon. One cannot explain, to any satisfaction, such diverse phenomena as: why white is the most popular car colour *by far* in Japan; why girls always sleep in their knickers; why people on Japanese trains move to the corner seat rather than the door seat as soon as it is free; why bus drivers wear white gloves; why Japanese people find wigs and baldness incredibly funny; why *ET* was a success and *Mutant Ninja Turtles* a big flop in Japan; why schoolchildren actually like to wear their uniforms (in polls I conducted 70 per cent of students said they preferred wearing their uniforms to school rather than their own clothes); why Japanese men slurp their noodles; why they read sicko-fantasy comics; why perfume is considered a cover-up for B.O.

Of course you can make a stab at answering these questions, and most journalists and commentators do. But all these succeed in producing is an interesting interpretation; one possible view amongst many equally plausible explanations. Japan is the structural anthropologist's dream – a country where every complex decryption is right, and therefore, by extension, wrong.

When Sara wanted to torment me she used to say: 'No Westerner can ever understand Japan.' And Mustard had never forgiven the Japanese teacher who commented: 'No foreigner can really understand aikido.' The problem is partly in the translation. To understand in Japan is to experience something in the same way as another person. Understanding betokens empathy. To Westerners, understanding means more the successful cracking of a code. A Japanese who says the West can never understand Japan is acknowledging the unique experience of being a member of the cult of Japan. He is saying, in effect, 'only a Japanese can be a Japanese'.

The Westerner who says he doesn't understand Japan may mean, too, that he will never be treated as a Japanese. He may also mean that his explanation for Japanese behaviour seems arbitrary and flimsy at best.

I believe this is because Japan is an assimilative culture – it picks and draws from China, Korea, England, France, Germany, the United States and Africa. The criteria it uses for deciding what it likes are not some basic homegrown Japanese set of tastes, but are themselves the product of importation.

Even a knowledge of all the sources of Japanified products and concepts only helps some way in explaining this, because of the novelty-seeking, ultimately faddish nature of the Japanese, noted by the earliest visitors to Japan.

How can you explain the startling popularity of Hunting World bags? The standard explanation is that the suave-looking and finally convicted salaryman murderer, who was filmed day after day going to court, was carrying a Hunting World bag every time he entered the court house. After this sensational trial (the salaryman was initially a witness) sales of Hunting World bags soared, rivalling even Louis Vuitton.

But why would that seed nationwide popularity? In the end any explanation comes to an end, runs into the sand, evaporates. Ultimately, one can only hope to observe and describe, leaving explanation to those who prefer comfort to truth.

The Japanese believe it's good luck to dream of Mount Fuji on New Year's Eve. Freudians might be surprised to learn that dreaming of a white snake is also considered lucky – it means wealth will come your way. I could not imagine dreaming of a mountain, but on my way back through Ikebukuro station I stopped in Seibu bookstore for a browse. I picked up a travel book about Japan, which started with the author saying how he longed to return to Japan, to sip warm *sake* and see Mount Fuji. Phoney rubbish, I thought, but then again, it is like no other mountain you've ever seen.

Breaking the Mirror

'Ordinarily, looking into the mirror and grooming oneself is sufficient for upkeep of one's personal appearance. This is important. Most people's appearance is poor because they do not look into the mirror well enough.'

From the seventeenth-century Samurai manual *Hagakure*

January

Mirrors. Mirrors are everywhere in Japan. Boys as well as girls carry around pocket mirrors to check that they aren't growing an unsightly pimple. Shopping centres are mirrored enclaves for checking yourself and others out as they hurry by. One wall of the dojo was completely mirrored over, like a ballet school, and Little Nick never broke the habit of glancing at himself during techniques to see how he looked. Even the bald and ascetic Sato kept one eye on the mirror during training, revealing an unsuspected narcissism. Naoko, my troublesome student, always carried a mirror – once, I had to confiscate it as she flashed sunlight into my eyes.

Nonaka Sensei took me on one side in the teachers' room. She whispered, conspiratorially, that she had some news. I followed her up to the place where the green tea was kept. Under cover of making me a cup of tea she told me the following story.

'The "black sheep" has been disgraced,' she said. She called Naoko "the black sheep" in English. Nonaka Sensei had a huge stock of English idioms and she liked to use them on me.

'How?' I asked.

Nonaka checked around the room to make sure no one would overhear.

'The nurse has told me. The girl has been disgraced. She went to the nurse because she was too frightened to go to her family doctor.'

'Why?' I said, though I was beginning to get the picture.

'She has been promiscuous. The "black sheep" has fallen.'

'She's caught a veneral disease?' I said. Though I used the word for syphilis, *baidoku*, which was the only appropriate vocabulary I could muster.

'How do you know that word?' asked Nonaka Sensei, with genuine interest and not a little outrage.

'The dictionary,' I said. 'But I meant not syphilis, but like syphilis.'

'So, so, so,' she nodded vigorously.

'Poor girl,' I said.

Nonaka Sensei smiled grimly.

'The black sheep has disgraced herself. But this is a secret.'

I tried to be considerate towards Naoko after hearing this news. She was quieter than before and I noticed she no longer had the ubiquitous mirror lying on her desk each lesson.

Kagami Biraki, breaking the mirror, is a traditional ceremony held at the beginning of each year when training resumes in the dojo. Traditional New Year food is eaten – sweet bean soup with a floating glutinous rice cake – and the teachers give a demonstration. This year, because of the death of Kancho Sensei, the demonstration would be of more than usual importance. The old sponsors, tied by personal connection to Kancho, now had a legitimate excuse to stop giving money to the dojo. They would all be present at the opening ceremony and it was felt that a good show had to be put on to convince them that their money would be well spent.

In previous years Japanese teachers had sometimes chosen foreign partners for the demonstration, but this year only Japanese aikidoka were taking part. Some of the sponsors had right-wing connections and it paid to humour them.

There is a traditional explanation as to why the ceremony is known as 'breaking the mirror', but I prefer an esoteric one advanced by Christophe, a lone Frenchman who had lived for years in a Zen monastery. When he trained at the dojo he did six or seven regular classes a day. He would mysteriously disappear for a few weeks and then he would be there again. This time he had been gone for nearly six months. I thought he had left for good, but in the New Year he suddenly popped up again – smiling and cheerful and sticking his chest out with glee.

The mirror, he said, contains the old image, for we look with old eyes on its necessary similarity to remembered images of ourselves. Our mind forces us to connect the picture we see with past pictures, creating a false continuity. But we are new every moment. Every moment we have the possibility of breaking the old pattern, which is just a mental construct, and creating something new. Every cell in your body, said Christophe, is different from the cells you had six months ago. This is an analogy. In reality we are trapped by wanting to be the same as our false self, the self we use for living, what we call 'me'. But this is false. Do you know who you are? Break the mirror and find out. Detach from the past, continuous self and feel the eternal present. That is the meaning of *Kagami Biraki*, a chance to glimpse the reality we veil with the mundaneness of day-to-day living.

The dojo mirror was huge and cost over $15,000. To touch it during training constituted another serious breach of etiquette. Every day it was polished spotless by six senshusei, Little Nick taking longer than anyone over his section. In the ceremony, of course, no actual mirror was broken.

We had watched the Japanese teachers training for the demonstration. The youngest *uchi-deshi*, Yoji, rubber man, was paired with Shioda junior. No one envied him, but if anyone could escape injury from the brutal speed of Shioda it was Yoji.

The night before the demonstration I left the dojo late. From inside the training hall I heard the repeated slap of someone breakfalling. I peeked through the door and saw Yoji in the unlit gloom, flipping and flipping, hitting the mat and bouncing up with measured grace and then flipping again. I shut the door quietly on this dedicated practice. Breakfall noises continued to filter down from the dojo windows as I unlocked my bike and fixed my light for the cycle home.

Before the ceremony the senshusei were detailed to produce three hundred bowls of the sweet bean soup. The dojo kitchen was packed with Japanese and foreigners tearing open plastic packs of rice cakes and dumping them in bubbling tureens of boiling water. Even Chino lent a hand, snipping open a couple of packets with delicate precise motions using a pair of scissors. A break was called so that we could witness the demonstration, which would happen before the meal.

The dojo was full of people: students of all ages, well-wishers, the families of students and the mothers of kids who trained in the afternoon children's class. The sponsors, grave and elderly Japanese males in uniformly dark suits, sat on a line of reserved seats. The rest sat in seats further back or stood when the seats were all taken.

After speeches and much bowing the demonstration began. Right from the start it was obvious the teachers were making a big effort. Even Ando smashed Sato, usually so calm and composed, into a breathless stumbling mess by the end of his lightning-fast *jiyu waza*. As each teacher performed, the show became harder and tougher. There was no doubt they were trying desperately to impress the old men, who sat impassively in their suits and said nothing. Shioda junior chopped and slashed and hurled Yoji in a way that looked sure to end in an accident. But Yoji, always smiling and as quick as Ando, was up to attack him again and again, despite the severity of the throws. Shioda was considered the benchmark of brutality. His demonstration had passed without injury. Surely now things would level off with only Nakano and Chida to perform.

Kikuchi attached Nakano with a committed punch and was

thrown and then pinned to the ground. At this point Kikuchi could do nothing. He was face-down to the ground with one arm in the air. Nakano crouched at Kikuchi's head and grasped hold of that arm. With shocking swiftness he heaved on the arm with his whole body to tighten the lock. There was a loud 'pop' audible throughout the dojo. Kikuchi's arm had been broken.

Chida winced at the pointless brutality of it, letting everyone see that he was displeased.

Kikuchi had been defenceless. He had given his arm to a top teacher so that the teacher could demonstrate how to immobilize a man in a safe manner. The teacher, the fancy coiffed Nakano, had betrayed his trust by snapping his arm like a piece of dry wood. Kikuchi was roughly hauled to his feet and only then did he cry out with pain. Nakano and an *uchi-deshi* frogmarched Kikuchi to the sidelines. There was some debate about whether the display should go on. A voice from the sombre-faced sponsors asked that the show continue.

Chida performed several effortless moves with Ito, his double, without a trace of excessive violence. The demonstration was over.

I felt a sick revulsion for what I'd seen. It was one thing to injure someone during the free-for-all of *jiyu waza*. It was quite another to crank a lock on so hard, on someone who could not possibly resist, to the point of breaking a limb in three places. The following day it was confirmed that the limb had a multiple fracture and required pinning.

Nakano was an expert. He had trained with Kikuchi many times before. There were two explanations for his behaviour. The charitable explanation was that everyone was so hyped up for the demo that Nakano, trying to show Yoshinkan to be a tough art, had just gone too far. The uncharitable explanation was that he had a grudge against Kikuchi and wanted to teach him a lesson he wouldn't forget in a hurry. I had witnessed Kikuchi being pulverized by Shioda, and this, together with the previous knockout by Nakano, added up, perhaps, to an attempt to force

287

Kikuchi to leave the dojo. Yoji was better at aikido and younger; perhaps it was felt that Kikuchi should give up his live-in status for the younger man. But Chida's disgust was not faked. And he was the head of the dojo. There is no way he would have countenanced such brutality just to make someone leave.

As we senshusei ran round filling beer glasses for the guests seated on the dojo floor, I watched Nakano, who was seated next to his dishy wife. Will said: 'One look at the hairstyle and the wife tells you that Nakano is in love with himself.' The brute was swilling back beer and laughing merrily, having seen that Kikuchi was taken to hospital. One visitor had videoed the whole incident. Nakano went and checked himself out on film. Chino, too, showed great interest in the incident and kept asking for it to be rewound.

Paul was an apologist for the teacher: 'These things happen. The problem is that Japanese bones are thinner than ours and break so much more easily.' Everyone else was against Nakano. Even Mustard commented, 'It was a pity, a real pity. And not necessary. Not necessary at all.'

We had our black belts – stiff, unyielding cotton, or silk, if you were suckered into Aga's 'special' deal (which ended up thirty dollars more than he'd said at the beginning) – so why on earth was I still there? It seemed madness to come back for two more months of hell, but everyone did. It wasn't enough to just get the black belt, you had to have the full course certificate too. And ours would be the last ever signed by Kancho, rumoured Little Nick. 'How'd he manage that?' asked Will. 'From the grave?'

Little Nick intimated that Kancho had signed masses of certificates before dying, rather like Salvador Dali autographing blank canvases.

A few days later life became tough again with *kangeiko*, early morning winter hardship training. We were up at five to be at the dojo for six-thirty. Training started at seven o'clock, with the windows open for the coldest ten days of the year. In those ten days of continuous training the entire basic curriculum of Yoshinkan aikido was practised. This involved the teacher demonstrating a technique twice, and everyone doing it for several minutes before moving on to the next technique.

Nakano was distinctly absent from the teachers' roster. He was obviously in disgrace. Too many people, including the parents of children studying aikido, had seen his excessive force. Not surprisingly only two or three kids showed up for the hour of early morning training each day, whereas the previous year there had been ten or twelve youngsters.

The senshusei were expected to provide *uke* for the demonstrating teachers. We were supposed to run up and offer ourselves for the honour of being thrown.

The Nakano incident had shaken me up. I wasn't going to sacrifice myself so that some bullyboy could show off his skills. On the other hand, I calculated, as a reaction everyone would probably be going soft on their *ukes*. And, hateful consideration though it was, being a demonstration partner was definitely a useful way to curry favour.

My dilemma was solved by Oyamada choosing me for a technique. I was still nervous at performing with a teacher, and so anxious not to let him down that I stiffened up and moved with a more than usual lack of grace. Ben referred to it as 'attack of the iguanodon'. But I'd been a top teacher's *uke* (though Oyamada was bottom of the list of top teachers) and felt as proud as a schoolboy selected to captain a school sports team.

We were now back to regular training, preparing for the final test and the ultimate prize, a course completion certificate. Stephan Otto had said, 'The last six weeks, man, were the hardest for me, psychologically the hardest.'

The day after *kangeiko* finished Mustard forced us to do a *hajime*. Mustard's *hajime* sessions were always ill timed. He made us do one before our black-belt test that just resulted in general fatigue rather than the 'fight-on' attitude he anticipated. This New Year *hajime*, the last we would do with our old partners, prompted a dismissive, 'You're still too weak. You must be stronger.'

I had suffered an attack of asthma during the exercise. Unable to catch a decent breath I was close to passing out by the end. The veins in my temples were throbbing madly as I felt the iron grip tighten each moment on my protesting lungs. After the lesson I swallowed one of the heart palpitants and found I could breathe again. After a few weeks the wheezing, flu-like symptoms had disappeared, but the brief appearance of asthma had frightened me greatly; it seemed of another order to a muscular or bone injury. I realized now why English Nick had been so scared when he hyperventilated. The training environment meant that you could not stop until you died or fainted, and not being able to breathe felt closer to death than simply blacking out.

Mad Dog, too, was unhappy. 'I just can't seem to get that "Mad Dog feeling" back,' he complained in the tea room.

The new partners were announced. I had half hoped for Will or Ben, and I got Ben. Will ended up with the crazed Armenian, Little Nick. Mad Dog got Craig and seemed perfectly happy.

Ben, at six foot five, with huge swinging arms, reminiscent of a child's leg rather than a man's arm, required a whole different approach from previous partners.

Not only were we living in the same tiny room, we were now training together five hours a day, wrestling and deliberately hurting each other from time to time. I told Mustard about these sudden urges to punish Ben with a viciously hard lock. 'Don't worry,' he said, 'everyone goes through that phase.' Ben's reaction to bullying was to alternate fighting back, which pleased me, as it gave further reason to give pain, and being doggedly pious and cheek-turning at every opportunity, which was infuriating.

Ben increasingly spent time away from the flat with his new girlfriend, a descendant of Japan's first polar explorer, a plain-faced girl who also did aikido and, rumour had it, had already had her virgin snows trampled by the pillaging Aga. This didn't stop Ben, who was young and romantic enough not to be put off by a girl who was quite clearly out to get a foreign boyfriend, whoever it might be. My own vague grudge against her was strengthened when she sat carelessly on the precarious toilet bowl in Fuji Heights, broke it away from its fastenings and caused a festering flood from the loo into the kitchen.

Fat Frank fixed the loo and pronounced it good for another year. But we all knew the days of Fuji Heights were numbered. When the course ended Ben had to get back to Melbourne and university after his year off in Japan and Frank was planning to leave soon for Australia with his new girlfriend. Chris was undecided, but he was talking about Australia too. I wouldn't be sad to leave the place, it was a grotty hole at the best of times, but I'd miss the company, I'd definitely miss the company.

Ben and Chris visited Kikuchi in hospital. He was cheerful and sitting up in bed and happy to see them. He told them that Nakano came every day to visit him and pointed out a slim vase of white flowers. 'Those are from Nakano Sensei.' An ironic grimace was the only clue he gave that he found such visits by his persecutor intolerable. No doubt part of Nakano's public penance was to visit his victim each day, irrespective of how the victim felt about such treatment.

Later, when I told Christophe about the incident, he rolled his eyes and made those curiously French noises of sympathy that cannot be translated without moving your whole body in a shrug. 'Nakano is a macho, a frightened man. When he looks in the mirror it is dirty, he does not see himself clearly. Perhaps the mirror is there to be polished, not broken in anger.'

After his arm was pinned Kikuchi returned to the dojo wearing a white sling with his white dogi. He was as cheerful as ever, but the white sling was especially huge, as if he was deliberately warning us. I took it as a sign to take care of myself in the final few weeks of the course

An Honourable Exit

*'Long ago, abdominal pains were called "cowardice grass".
This is because they come suddenly and render a person
immobile.'*
From the seventeenth-century Samurai manual *Hagakure*

'Self defence is a joke,' said Darren, standing in the locker room
and towelling himself off before rushing to his evening job.

'How do you mean?' I asked.

'It's all staged, those set routines just don't happen in real
fights. It's like in that fight before Kancho's funeral – I just kind
of relaxed down on the guy and choked him out. That was
aikido, just being able to transfer my weight down like that. But
this *"san kajo* defence against bearhug" or *"irime nage* defence
against front kick" – pretty academic if you ask me.'

Because we were practising we couldn't headbutt or gouge or
elbow the attacker in the temples – all likely moves in a real
encounter. Because we had to look after each other we had to
devise defences that looked real and fast and effective, but where
the attacker didn't get hurt – just like in the movies, in fact.

This playacting aspect appealed to Ben and me. Off in our
corner of the dojo we worked out endless permutations for
defending against a front kick, side punch or double-belt grab
attack. We worked in slow motion and only speeded up when
we had it planned perfectly. If someone swung a punch at the
head you could duck under the punch and twist the arm back
on itself. If the punch was too fast you could block it and palm
smash the attacker's jaw. Or, in a third variation, grab the
moving arm and use it as a lever to throw the guy over your
shoulder.

We had a list of about twenty possible attacks and we had to have three or four defences against each. If you kept doing the same defence for each attack during the test the examining teacher kept you up there with your partner, who had to repeatedly attack you until you came up with something different.

Some of the attacks were curiously Japanese: the double-belt grab from the front, for example, which dated from the pre-war years when the *obi* (belt) was a prominent part of your dress, since it held your kimono together. There are no belt loops on a kimono, so it is tempting to grab, but as an attack there is no Western equivalent of this.

Chida, like most of the top sensei, thought self defence a little ridiculous. They were interested in principles, abstract secrets of the human body that could only be studied and learnt through 'pure' aikido training. Of course in any 'self-defence' type situation these same sensei would be lethal – precisely because they could adapt their principles to any surroundings, using an ashtray instead of a fist, or a hard plastic chopstick instead of a knife. Like Kancho in Shanghai they preferred to develop an intuitive response to a violent situation and not a series of set moves. As Chida said: 'You cannot plan a fight.' Paradoxically, the sometimes false-looking exercises and techniques for developing principles were more useful in the long run than more realistic counters to staged attacks. Aikido exercises allow for the use of full force in a controlled scenario. A staged attack must use much less than full force because things become too dangerous otherwise.

But Chida liked to see inventiveness. If he saw a repeated defence he would tell us about his methods with the cops – if a cop kept doing the same defence they replaced his partner with an *uchi-deshi*, who was ordered to 'attack sincerely'. This meant all punches connected and all kicks landed. Chida imitated a cop holding his bleeding nose and bruised testicles in anguish. Then he would straighten up. '*Omoshiroi ne?*' ('Amusing, isn't it?')

Chino, being, I now saw, a kind of deadly schoolboy, liked us to practise self-defence in a circle – 'the circle jerk', as Will called it. One man was in the middle and he was surrounded by five others. They would each attack him in turn using either the same attack, an attack Chino called out or, most amusingly for Chino, a completely improvised attack.

Certain rules of engagement were quickly agreed upon – a soft elbow to the ribs meant the attacker should let go, because if he didn't, when it was his turn in the middle he would get a hard elbow as a reminder. As usual, Craig played by his own rules, giving a breathy commentary as he attacked: 'I'm coming in. I've got you here. What d'yo do? Attack one point! Attack one point! Now you've got me. Then I do this. Attack another point!'

Adam got annoyed by this. During one session when Craig had him firmly pinned down and shouldn't have, and was giving his usual advice about attacking one point, Adam shouted out: 'There aren't any fucking points left to attack!' Luckily for Adam, Chino, who was teaching, chose not to understand English obscenities, or missed them altogether. When he scanned through a pile of porn videos imported from the US for the cops, he failed to notice one entitled *Chino Sucks Cock*.

The other component of this part of the course was being taught how to teach. We were each given 'the blue book', which was a direct translation from a Japanese manual of basic Yoshinkan techniques. We were told to memorize the book.

The teaching test consisted of explaining, as if to a class of beginners, a complete technique in exactly five minutes. At first it seemed like a very hard thing to do, just as the synchronized display had seemed very hard. But we practised repeatedly and sure enough we all learnt to perfectly estimate giving a five-minute demonstration with accompanying explanatory speech.

Bizarrely, the teaching was done in a mix of Japanese and English. As we were destined to be instructors abroad the language of actual instruction was English. R'em wanted to do his in Hebrew but it wasn't allowed, so this turned out to be one of the hardest parts of the course for him. But the introduction and conclusion of the teaching set-piece had to be done in Japanese.

Practising teaching was done in a typically Japanese way. You paired off with your partner and took it in turns to 'teach' a set technique. As everyone was teaching the same technique there was a babel of rising voices as each 'teacher' sought not to be distracted by his neighbour. It was completely mechanical and as far away from most modern ideas of 'good teaching' as you could get.

In fact, what the dojo wanted was competent instructors who would all teach the basics identically. This was the bottom line. If, as a bonus, you could actually teach, then this would come out when you started to run classes yourself.

The real teachers had all developed a style that was far removed from basic instruction. This was to be expected. Chida's style was gnomic. His role, it seemed, was to make everyone humble. He would demonstrate stuff that no one could ever do except him, and when we tried to do it he would laugh gently at our efforts. Ando, on the other hand, was completely explicit. He had a genius for breaking moves down so that anyone could conceptualize and learn them. Oyamada chose to use repetition – the same technique for hour after hour – doing it through and past boredom so that eventually you learnt something new. Mustard was an inspirer – he was never very technical in his explanation, but he had the rare skill of forcing you to force yourself to greater efforts. Shioda got you working at speed – his style was the opposite of Chida's relaxed, ultra-flexible approach. Chino's speciality was the one-shot lesson that you would never forget.

Chino had become increasingly friendly as the course end approached. Apart from Chida, who was always the same, most of the Japanese sensei started to ease up at this time. The foreign teachers, bar Darren, did not. Sometimes it felt as if the foreign teachers were determined we should take away bad memories of the course, which would mean it had been really serious. The Japanese were more light hearted. For them aikido was a lifetime occupation; if you were too intense you wouldn't last it out.

Just when everyone was developing a huge boredom with teaching into thin air, and an active dislike of having to weather continuous assault from each other, Chino announced a lesson on punching and striking. We would all get to punch him ten times, as hard as possible, in his unprotected stomach.

We formed a giggling and unbelieving line, as Chino stood at the front. The first few men pulled their punches out of courtesy. But this was not what he wanted. He was training himself as much as us. He wanted absolutely full-force punches. For every punch that came he would move in fractionally and send the force back up the puncher's arm, or move back and let the person over-extend. The cocky ones (R'em and Little Nick) also got a rapid slap round the chops or palm to the nose.

After the punches he took front and side strikes, which he blocked with his iron forearm. We could not believe our good fortune. After a year of being beaten up by our teachers we could give some of it back. And he let us have two rounds – so it was twenty of the hardest punches from each man. At the end I saw he was out of breath. It was the first time I had ever seen Chino lose his icy demeanour. Even during an earthquake he carried on teaching as if nothing unusual was happening. He was standing at the head of the class and we were kneeling and listening. He was talking at length about some technique when the dojo started to shake. Stacked chairs fell down and I started to think about running for the exit. People glanced nervously around but Chino did not miss a beat, nor did he make any reference to the quake then or after it happened.

One day, leaving the dojo, I met Sherlock, who had come to say goodbye. He was being posted to diplomatic duties at the Finnish Embassy. I was pleased to see him and we went for a drink at a bar near the station.

I noticed his teeth still looked pretty bad. He brought the subject up himself.

'I'm going to get them fixed,' he said, 'then I can get a girl.'

We got on to the subject of foreigners dating Japanese girls. Sherlock was adamant: 'It's not right! There aren't enough girls left for Japanese men!'

I thought he was joking, as usual, but he was entirely serious. He had also heard from his friends about Adam's recent run in with the cops whilst drunk in charge of the Mobile Cancer Unit. He had been stopped whilst speeding without a helmet, and if they had tested him he was over the alcohol limit as well. We had been told not to use our Yoshinkan credentials as an excuse with the police, but Adam had been desperate. He started to chat gaily with the increasingly friendly cop about his other friends in the police force. He dropped every name he could think of: Hanzai, Maeda 'the gorilla' (that got a laugh), Saito, Murayama, Fujie. Eventually they hit on a common acquaintance. The road cop had been at police school with Shimoda, otherwise known as Dopey. His attitude to Adam now completely changed. He wished Adam well, but told him to go carefully – out of concern and not bossiness. 'Good luck,' he called in English, as the Cancer Unit wobbled off in its usual cloud of black smoke.

Sherlock thought it was hilarious. Japanese cops are not like English ones. To the English police everyone is guilty. (As Mustard said in his cups, 'I have to tell Paul from time to time: "Stop interrogating me, I'm not a suspect."') The Japanese police are more like the army. They do not see themselves as moral guardians; but simply maintainers of the appearance of peace. Certainly they are better integrated into society than Western police. And they don't seem burdened by that hateful desire to tell everyone what to do.

I asked Sherlock if he'd used any of his aikido yet. He looked at me as if I was mad and imitated getting his gun out of its holster and shooting the bar girl. He was joking, but underneath it lay the modern reality of self defence. The modern Samurai packs a 17-shot Glock automatic, not a devilishly cunning knowledge of the body's pressure points.

Aikido isn't about self protection, not really; it is a way of self perfection, however imperfect its methods; and the pain is necessary because the pain makes it real. As Tesshu explained: 'First you learn to take pain. Then you learn to give it. Finally you are friends with pain. Death frightens you no longer because without considerations of pain life and death have no power over you.' He painted on a skull:

Cut off death
And you will have only bliss
Imitate a dead man
And you will be worse off
Than a corpse.

The morning of the final test Will performed with Little Nick the most accomplished *jiyu waza* I had yet seen by any of the current senshusei. In a way it was a pity because he could not possibly match it in his test later that day. 'I'm gonna smoke that little bastard,' he told me, and he had.

I, too, had my own minor triumph. I did aikido for the second time in my life. Everything else had been just training. I'd had my insights and my breakthroughs but apart from these two occasions, I hadn't performed magic, I hadn't done anything spectacular, amazing, a move that convinces people you have the 'real power'. Aikido in this sense means the ideal, when the force applied is way out of proportion to the effect it has, because, through perfect timing and technique, the force is magnified beyond belief.

The first time had been when I was practising a free form of *tenchinage*, a throw which depends on first overbalancing your partner. I was training with Fat Frank and he gripped my wrists with all of his ex-champion wrestler's strength. Almost distract-edly I did the technique and he slammed to the floor like a sack of potatoes. He was as shocked as I was and suspected some foul play, some secret gimmick I'd learnt to knock him down. 'I just did it right,' I said.

The second time was just before the test. Mustard had instructed us to do the technique standing on one leg. R'em attacked and I was thinking so much about keeping my balance I didn't stick out my arm to enter and throw him until I was sure it was too late. It was almost like an afterthought. But the timing was perfect and he slammed to the mat shocked and gleeful.

I had done aikido twice and I was facing the final test.

This test – and I was heartily sick of them by now, the stomach-churning anxiety, the looming fear of failure, the fear that you might actually do worse than the last test – would consist of basic movements, three basic techniques (just three out of one hundred and fifty, surely no problem), one session of *jiyu waza*, self defence and the teaching of a five-minute technique.

The examining teachers included Inoue Sensei, who was chief instructor of the police, older than Chida and ninth-dan to Chida's eighth. At their level, dan grades were more honour than ability based.

Because the tests took so long we were allowed to leave the line during the preceding partners' test in order to warm up and stretch legs that had been kneeling for an hour. Ben and I loitered in the corridor outside the main dojo with Adam and Danny, who were on at the same time as us. We could hear Aga 'teaching' a technique to the assembled teachers. His voice rose higher and higher as the explanation went on. By the end of the technique he was gabbling in a helium squeak at breakneck speed.

Suddenly it is all happening. Ito calls us up. We run to our spots and it starts. Nerves bad. Basic movements jerky and not smooth, but at least I can do them, unlike poor Craig who still stumbles changing his weight from one foot to another. Then the techniques. I do one. Ben does one. Then I do another. Then he does another. One more to go. I can't forget now. I've done every technique a hundred, a thousand times. They call a technique and I'm convinced I've never heard of this technique before. The bastards, I think. They're doing this to test me. By the form of the words I cobble together a mental picture of the technique. Then I start to do it. Ben resists and makes some movement with his eyes. A kind of warning. But we can't talk. To talk in the test is to fail. It means you've lost control. So I force him into doing something weird, which works. But as soon as I do it I realize I've made a mistake. It's wrong. I've failed. That's it. The end. And it was the same technique – kneeling *kotegaeshi* from a double-wrist grip – that I'd had a mental block about before in a Chida lesson. The end. I'd failed.

The test continued and since I had nothing to lose I went all out with a doomed sense of defeat but less worry. During the self defence I was instructed to repeatedly attack Ben from behind with an arm lock around the neck. I was so hyped up I took a run at him, and since he was six foot five I actually had to leap off the ground to make it realistic. We'd never practised this before but he coped admirably – flinging me to the floor while I made plenty of theatrical noises.

Then it was my turn. An easy call – single grab to the wrist. I snapped down on Ben with what felt like instant speed and he splattered straight to the floor. The second time I nobbled him with less finesse, slightly hurting him in the process (I knew by now when I'd gone too far with Ben), but he gamely powered ahead. Then it was *jiyu waza*. We both tried to be smooth – attack, throw, fall, attack again. I was running out of breath, but when I noticed this it was over. Failure, but honourable failure.

After the test Paul came up, grinning, to congratulate us. I did not have the good manners to meet his grin. 'I fucked up,' I said, grimly. He didn't give me sympathy. Instead he just shrugged. I know how tedious it is to congratulate someone who hasn't the good grace to accept congratulation, but that was what I was like. We waited for Chida's verdict.

He knelt on the ground and looked around smiling. He

consulted his clipboard and scratched the palm of his hand. Then he gave the results. Craig had his black belt but must work on his basics. Will had passed. Aga should slow down his teaching voice. Mad Dog had gained his second-degree black belt. He broke into a big grin and looked into the video camera which his wife, Anna Marie, was pointing at us from the sidelines. Chida made no comment on my mistake, he said that I should project my voice more when teaching, that was all.

Apparently, amazingly, I had passed.

I looked at Will. 'We did it. We showed them. We did it.'

Danny came up, grinning and shaking my hand. 'The way you decked Ben, I thought, Way to go, Rob. Way to go!'

Chris relaxed his critical air. 'I think I'd think twice about attacking you guys after watching that,' he said.

It was all over, bar the drinking. I thought again about the possibility of enlightenment, the blinding flash of the big one, or the odd spark of the mini variety. I thought about what the Zen priest told me when I first came to Japan: 'Some people have one big enlightenment and others have lots of mini-enlightenments.' Tesshu, of course, had a big enlightenment, on March 30th 1880. He drank eighteen bottles of beer with his Zen master and wrote a poem to celebrate:

'For years I forged my spirit
Through the study of the sword
Confronting every challenge
As steadfast as could be
Then the walls around me
Suddenly crumbled to the ground
Like pure dew reflecting
The world in crystal clarity
Total awakening has now come.'

Though I was more a mini-enlightenment type, I knew now, I'd had my glimpse of what the old Samurai was talking about.

I wanted to sit next to Mustard at the celebratory party, and I did, at both venues. He was next to Nakano, and whenever Nakano brought out a cigarette Mustard whipped out his lighter to light it. I tried to do the same for him but he didn't wait as if it was his due in the way Nakano did, so I missed 50 per cent of the time. I tried to tell Mustard how grateful I was for him inspiring me to do the course. He made the apple-polishing sign they make in Japan when you want to show you're being over-flattered.

Chida sat a few places up. Suddenly he turned to me and for the first time ever addressed me in a serious voice.

'Inoue Sensei looked at you and said that he believed you had done aikido a long time. He said your style was like old-style Yoshinkan. He has a father-in-law who did aikido for sixty years and he is the same physical type as you. This is what Inoue Sensei said. He said that it proves that human types are common to all races, there is no specifically Japanese style.'

He paused and lit a cigarette. He smoked, like most Japanese men. But not heavily, nothing like Kancho's hundred-a-day habit. He gestured towards Ben. 'If Ben gives up aikido after three or four years I won't be so surprised. He is still of that age to give up. But you will continue for thirty years. I am sure of that.'

Then he waved his cigarette at Little Nick, who looked proud and aloof in his well-cut suit. 'Just like the young Chino. The same. Just the same.'

'Chida likes to take the piss,' said Mustard. But this time I knew he was wrong; Chida was being dead serious. This was Japan, where I had learnt that teachers were closer to gurus than anything else.

The time came to make speeches. Darren chose me to kick off. I made a speech and the cry came up for a poem. I improvised a rude limerick about the size of Darren's penis that was all but lost in the mêlée of drunken shouting. Mad Dog stood up and told the assembled crowd that he had an announcement to make: he and his wife would soon be hearing the pitter patter of tiny feet. She was pregnant! His wife looked shocked and squawked in protest. There was confused shouting and congratulation. Then Anna Marie stormed off. It was simply not true – Mad Dog had been playing a joke on her.

I went up to Roland 'the Terminator'. 'You're a hard bastard, aren't you?' I said. He smiled, his potato face benign and inscrutable. He said: 'But you finished the course. You did it. I didn't think you would, but you did.'

Outside in the street Mad Dog started banging his head repeatedly against a fragile metal sign that looked about to give way. He was overcome with remorse about joking at his wife's expense.

'Nick,' called Chida softly, 'Nick.'

Big Nick turned and saw his teacher grinning and shaking his head. Immediately the flustered Mad Dog broke into a torrent of apology.

The party broke up amidst plans to go on to a nightclub. The teachers had to get home to their wives and families. I saw Chida quietly take his leave. The worlds greatest practitioner of aikido was soon disappearing into a crowd at the station, becoming indistinguishable in his dark suit amongst the late-night revellers and office workers running for trains. For a moment I followed the movement of his close-cropped head and then he was gone, swallowed up by the mass of hurrying people.

Unlikely Bodyguard

'The curse it continue.'
Letter with unintentional spelling mistake from R'em

'Until one reaches the age of forty it is better to put off wisdom and discrimination and concentrate on vitality. Even though a person passes the age of forty, if he has no vitality he will get no respect from others.'
From the seventeenth-century Samurai manual *Hagakure*

After the course Will and Craig were asked to be *sewanin* for the next year's intake. Will turned the offer down but Craig took it up. Quite against prediction he became an exemplary assistant to the teachers: tough, but not a bully. Craig, it seemed, really did care. Mad Dog took a job teaching English to small children and was asked to act as a part-time *sewanin*. R'em continued riding his 'Ninja' superbike and selling jewellery. Robert Mustard married Carol and returned to Canada to set up his own dojo. Ben, Danny and Aga returned to Australia, Danny taking his seventeen-year-old Japanese girlfriend with him. Little Nick returned home to his mother's cooking in Toronto. Will still lives in Japan with his wife and child. Adam is back in Seattle, I hear, probably still skateboarding. Fat Frank got married to his Australian girl and now lives in the outback on a camel farm. Chris resumed his wandering existence, as if searching for something always beyond his reach. Sara made plans to visit India.

After finishing the course I wandered around Tokyo at a loose end. I had so much time, I took to just riding the subways aimlessly, sometimes going to the end of the line far out in the countryside before riding the line back again. I wanted to get a grip on myself, put into practice all the discipline I'd learnt over the preceding year. But it was hard and I convinced myself I needed time to come down from the whole experience.

I took a job in a Tokyo bookstore, but the tedium after the intensity of the course was deadening. One day on the way to work I was stopped by some fully equipped Riot Police at a subway entrance. I tried to see through the smoked plastic visors if there was anyone I recognized. I felt I knew these guys, but to them I was just another foreigner. I was politely pushed back. I asked what was going on: 'Gas attack!' they said. I took a bus and at the bookstore everyone was listening to the radio – it was the day five thousand people were injured and eleven killed by the Aum cult sarin gas attack.

Stacking shelves in the bookstore my heart would suddenly start pounding for no reason. I'd look at my watch: ten o'clock, the start of the second lesson. My body was still gearing up for something that was no longer happening. I went to the dojo once a week and met Will, whose elbow had swollen like an egg from repeated bruising. Finishing the course had caused his body to go on strike: 'No more abuse – I want rest,' his body was saying. But rather than stop completely he dropped his training to only twice a week.

I became used to weird adrenalin surges, caused by going from so much activity to almost zero, hormonal rushes that caused me to start running down a street for no other reason than to try to make myself feel tired. At other times I'd get bursts of aggression, which found harmless but antisocial release in staring down anyone who caught my eye.

The power struggle for control of Kancho's empire smouldered behind the scenes in the dojo for months. Chida Sensei, because he was in his late forties, was seen as lacking sufficient gravitas to become the new Kancho. Shioda junior was too unpopular to take over from his father, and was also felt to be too young. Eventually Inoue Sensei, grey haired and now in his sixties, was drafted in from the police to become the new head of Yoshinkan Aikido. Even though Inoue had compared my aikido to that of his aging father in law, he had at least compared me to a Japanese, and not seen me as just another gaijin making a fool of himself in a pair of white pyjamas. I was grateful to him for that and glad that he was the new boss.

The symbolic importance of hair should never be underestimated in Japan. Inoue's grey hair had been a useful qualification for the job, but once in control he needed to assert his vitality. A few months after taking over, Inoue Sensei dyed his grey hair jet black.

I knew I couldn't return to the old drifting days of Fuji Heights. I had to get out of Japan. Nonaka Sensei, who had now retired as a high-school teacher, provided the escape route. She had saved up a lot of money and she also had her husband's pension. She and a friend had decided to travel. They wanted to go to Mexico, the United States and Europe.

Nonaka, like most Japanese, was frightened about travelling without a group. Especially in Mexico and the US, which are considered in Japan to be about as safe as wartorn Bosnia. She arranged to meet me in the Mitsukoshi coffee shop to outline her plan.

Mitsukoshi, which is like a Japanese Harrods, has a coffee shop that specializes in English teas. Over scones and Earl Grey, Nonaka Sensei gave me an appraising look.

'Now you are *Kidotai* you must have duties,' she said.

'Umm?'

'I am making a trip. I told you so. The fortune teller said that Mexico is . . . propitious.'

Her vocabulary never ceased to amaze me. But I thought it prudent not to mention the recent uprising in Chiapas. Nonaka Sensei, I could tell, had made up her mind.

'I shall be the "minister of finance" . . .' she continued, looking down at her napkin.

It takes two to be direct in Japan – one helping the other towards a hinted-at conclusion.

'I could be the bodyguard,' I said.

'So, so, so,' she clapped her hands with glee.

Now I'd grasped the point she elaborated her plans in detail. An English-speaking, Japanese police-trained 'bodyguard' was the perfect solution for people like Nonaka and her friend, who disliked groups but wanted to see 'dangerous' countries such as Mexico. She would pay for everything and give me a reasonable salary too. It conjured up ludicrous images but it beat standing around selling books from nine to five. It was probably a safer option than Tokyo too, now that Aum were running around with gas bombs.

I took Sara out for a farewell meal before she flew off to India. We went, appropriately, to an Indian restaurant. 'But the rice in India will be much better than this,' I said. 'Japanese rice is no good for Indian curry.' She showed me her new knapsack and I said what a good deal she'd got.

There was an air of finality about the meal despite all the reassurances of meeting up again, writing letters and staying in touch. I knew I'd meet Fat Frank and Chris and Will and Ben again, that not seeing them for a year or even two would make no difference to our relationship. With Sara it would be different, it had to be, and despite the animated chatter over the popadoms and mango chutney, the bottles of Kingfisher beer and the entertainment of milky tea poured from a great height to make it frothy, there was a spreading sadness about the occasion. I tried talking more to cover it up, but we both knew it was there. By the end of the meal I'd succeeded in making myself quite depressed.

Outside in the cold night air Sara put her hand into my overcoat pocket to hold mine. It was unbearably touching. At the bus stop I kissed her and the bus came too soon. She swung her new knapsack on to her back and climbed up the steps. It was now or never.

'Why not come with me to Mexico? We'll have a great time.'

Sara looked me in the eye and said, with quiet seriousness, 'That is your plan. It's a good plan. But it is not my plan. You have to follow your own plan, don't you?'

'Yes,' I said, miserably. 'You have to follow your own plan.'

Then she smiled and kissed me again and waved madly with her free hand as the doors vacuumed shut; the little girl's wave of all Japanese women saying goodbye.

Nonaka Sensei's fortune teller set a date for departure. It happened to be the day before the new Riot Police course started. I bought a pair of tinted glasses and a dark suit for the trip. The haircut remained, regular senshusei, no. 1 buzzcut all over. I looked in the mirror back at Fuji Heights: not bad, not bad. Ridiculous, of course, but not bad.

> Do not think that
> This is all that exists
> There is much more to learn –
> The sword is unfathomable.

> The world is wide
> Full of happenings.
> Keep that in mind
> And never believe
> 'I'm the only one who knows.'

> Yamaoka Tesshu

Fighting Talk – A Glossary of Useful Words

aikido – martial art derived from jujitsu and reputed to utilize 'secret' powers such as *ki* and *kokyu* power. In the Yoshinkan format secrets were only muttered about, in other styles they are more openly discussed but more rarely demonstrated.

aikidoka – practioner of aikido.

atemi – a strike or hit of any kind. Includes punches, kicks and even body checks. Kancho concluded that any real fight is 70 per cent *atemi*.

black belt – having mastered the first seven *kyu* grades, the white-belt student receives a brown belt. When all ten *kyu* grades are passed the student receives a black belt. Subsequent ranks, *dan* grades, are recorded, but no new belt is worn. On the senshusei course all students wore white belts despite their achievements before the course. Only after passing the senshusei black-belt test were they allowed to wear black belts.

bokken – a hard-wood sword, lethal in trained hands. Sometimes used by Japanese sword masters to beat opponents armed with a real sword.

bosozoku – youth motorcycle gang, a common recruiting ground for the *yakuza*.

budo – literally 'war arts', but now means modern martial arts of Japan.

dai-jokki – pronounced dai-jockey, a large litre-sized glass of beer with too much head.

dan – a level of achievement in a martial art, signified by a black belt. *Shodan* is the first level, *nidan* the second, *sandan* the third.

dogi – training suit or white pyjamas.

dojo – a martial arts training hall. Also the name for the building complex which contains the training hall.

faito – corruption of 'fight on', shouted as encouragement at baseball and other games.

gaijin – foreigner. Politer form, *gaikokujin*. Has sufficiently negative connotations to polite Japanese ears for them to refrain from using the word if they think you understand.

gambatte – 'persevere', shouted as encouragement.

gasshoku – training camp.

goshin waza – self-defence techniques.

Gracie jujitsu – a judo style of wrestling with punches and streetwise reputation. Currently the most hyped martial art.

hajime – literally 'begin', but to senshusei it meant perform the technique over and over as fast as possible, not stopping until the teacher gave the command to do so. Exhausting.

hayaku ukemi – literally, fast breakfall, in other words, 'the flip', going from standing, up into the air and over, to land on the shoulder and arm.

hijiate kokyu nage – throwing someone by using their extended arm as a lever. Can be an elbow snapper.

hijishime – locking out the elbow against the joint.

hiriki no yosei – basic movement involving sliding forward and raising the hands as if holding a ball out in front of you. Builds whole body power.

irime nage – an entering throw. *Irime* is entering, getting in close to your attacker in order to take his balance.

jiyu waza – freestyle attack. One person is attacked repeatedly by one or more *ukes*. The attackers are thrown using standard throws and moves. Helps build speed, timing and a sense of distance.

jo – four-foot three-inches-long wooden poke stick. Also good for swinging around and hitting someone in the chops.

Kagami Biraki – the January festival of 'breaking the mirror', it commemorates the re-opening of the dojo for a new year.

kamae – stance or basic posture. In Yoshikan aikido *kamae* was held to indicate your inner abilities. The Yoshinkan *kamae* was weight forward over one foot which was also forward, one arm outstretched and another below it, as if holding a sword in front of you. The hands are open, fingers splayed.

Kancho – the word means 'head of school', but it came to be used in Yoshinkan to mean Gozo Shioda, the school's founder.

kangeiko – winter hardship, early morning training.

kata – form of mixed techniques or movements.

katate mochi – wrist grab.

kendo – Japanese fencing with bamboo swords.

kenshu – special study classes. More intensive than regular training, but much less intense than senshusei.

ki – mysterious essence of the universe, life force, vital energy. In Yoshinkan *ki* was relegated by Kancho to being 'mastery of balance', but perhaps this is the most useful manifestation of *ki*.

kiai – a war cry or battleshout supposedly indicative of your inner state and commitment. A strong *kiai* is essential.

Kidotai – Riot Police.

kihon dosa – basic movements or training exercises designed to teach correct movement of the body. There are three and they can be performed solo or with partners – *tai no henko*, *hiriki no yosei* and *shumatsu dosa*.

kihon waza – standardized techniques designed for practising principles of movement rather than using in a self-defence-type situation.

kohai – junior, measured from date of joining dojo.

koho ukemi – back breakfall. Falling back on to the backside and breaking the fall with a slap of the hands.

kokyu ho – breath exercises which involve sitting on the floor and taking your partner's balance by harmonizing with his breathing and moving under his centre. In reality only the higher adepts know this as anything more than just another aikido exercise.

kokyu power – 'breath power'. The explosive power that comes when the whole body works as one and discharges its force through one point.

konjo – literally 'guts', or not giving up.

kotegaeshi – twisting the wrist in its natural direction to make someone lose balance. Ultimately a bone breaker.

kuro-obikai – literally, black-belt class. Held by Kancho before he died, these classes became synonymous with receiving instruction whilst kneeling for a long time in *seiza*. Also used for a long *seiza* class.

kyu – the first level of achievement is tenth *kyu*, the next: ninth *kyu*. The stage before the black belt is first *kyu*, or *ikkyu*.

maai – crucial distance, an innate knowledge of just how far you should be from an attacker.

mitori geiko – watching practice. When injured, senshusei had to watch all lessons either kneeling down, or seated, if the injury was to the lower body.

nage – a throw.

nikajo – a key aikido wrist lock. It involves holding the opponent's wrist and hand out in front of you with their palm facing outwards. Applying very little downward strength the opponent's knees buckle and give way.

ogi – secret techniques known only to the master.

osae – a final pin, usually using an arm, in order to immobilize an opponent on the ground.

ryote mochi – two-handed grab.

san kajo – a lock which involves twisting the wrist and arm while they are held away from the body.

seiza – kneeling down, Samurai style.

sempai – senior, measured from date of joining dojo.

sensei – teacher. Also a term of respect, a bit like a cross between 'sir' and 'doctor'.

senshusei – literally, a 'specialist'. Used to describe anyone doing the Riot Police course, also referred to as the senshusei course.

sewanin – Riot Police course assistants. There were two, acting like NCOs, their job was to interpret the desires of the teacher using brute force and discipline.

shidoin – an assistant teacher. Paul, Stephan and Darren were *shidoin*, as was Ito. Like junior officers, they were there to provide the teacher with usable troops.

shihonage – a key aikido move. It means 'four-directional throw' and involves twisting your opponent's arm back over their shoulder, taking their balance and either throwing them or taking them down to the ground.

shikko ho – knee walking.

shinkoku – daily roll call. Involved the week's '*shinkoku* person', a senshusei monitor chosen on rotation, lining up the senshusei and shouting a formulaic greeting and begging the teacher to provide a lesson that day. Another roll call at the end of the day provided elaborate thanks to the teacher.

Shinto – Japanese state religion until 1945, involving ancestor worship and verneration of nature spirits.

shite – unfortunate word pronounced 'shtay', instead of the more obvious reading, which in some cases is a better description of what is being done. The person who does the technique on *uke*.

sho-dojo – mini dojo.

shomen – front strike.

shumatsu dosa – the exercise usually performed at the end of the class, it involves sliding along the mat using *suriashi*, designed to train you to lower your centre of gravity.

suriashi – sliding across mats without raising the feet. Harder than it looks.

suwari – kneeling.

suwari-waza – aikido techniques performed while kneeling down. Developed as a way of fighting in Samurai times when it was forbidden to rise without permission in the presence of your lord.

tachi – standing.

tai no henko – basic movement involving turning to the side and then extending outwards and forwards, weight very much over the front leg.

tanto – a wooden training knife. Still hurts if poked in the wrong place.

tatami – traditional woven rice straw mat on a wooden frame. The size of a door, they are laid out to cover an entire floor. Sometimes covered in rubber to stop them from being soiled. Slightly springy.

tenchi-nage – literally, heaven and earth throw (or heaven and hell throw, as Ben called it). Your opponent grabs your wrists and you surge under him to steal his balance and throw him to the ground with a resounding thud.

tsuki – a punch.

uchi-deshi – dojo disciple. Some *uchi-deshi* live in the dojo, others simply come every day as if to a job. Paid a measly allowance, or sometimes just given food and board. There have been a few live-in foreign *uchi-deshi*, such as Jacques Payet.

Ueshiba, Morihei – founding father of modern aikido. Fused the then, almost secret, daito-ryu aikijujitsu with insights gained from sword fighting to come up with the modern projection of aikido. Kancho's teacher and a reputed miracle man, though all Japanese martial artists are subject to mythomaniacal reporting.

uke – the person on whom a technique is performed. Uke (pronounced 'oo-kay') has to attack with vigour and then take whatever punishment is handed out. It is an honour to be a teacher's *uke*, as feeling a technique done by a master is considered the only way to really learn.

ukemi – a breakfall of any kind.

usagi tobi – bunny hops, bad for backs, knees and spirits.

ushiro waza – techniques done where the attack comes from behind. Designed to build awareness.

waza – a technique or techniques.

yakuza – member of Japanese organized crime. Originally involved with just illegal gambling rackets, *yakuza* has now come to apply to the whole gamut of organized crime. Of the different branches of criminality, the *yakuza* have the most colourful traditions, including the celebrated finger chopping to appease the boss for misdemeanours committed.

yame – pronounced ya-may, the order to stop, finish everything, freeze.

yokomen – side strike.

yon kajo – a move which involves applying direct pressure to the pulse line in the attacker's wrist. Painful.

yoshi – Japanese word of encouragement.

Yoshinkan – style of aikido practised by the author. Originated by Kancho Sensei. Means the place of cultivating the spirit.

zanshin – lingering spirit of domination after concluding some move. Also broadened to mean awareness of any danger.

zazen – basic Zen meditation posture, legs crossed, hands joined together in front on the lap.

zenpo kaiten ukemi – diving forward rolls, but taken on one arm rather than both.